Fighting Nazi
Occupation

'... we shall defend our island, whatever the cost may be. We shall fight on the beaches, we shall fight on the landing grounds, we shall fight in the fields and in the streets, we shall fight in the hills; we shall never surrender'

Winston S. Churchill
4 June 1940

Fighting Nazi Occupation

British Resistance 1939–1945

Malcolm Atkin

Pen & Sword
MILITARY

First published in Great Britain in 2015 by
PEN & SWORD MILITARY
An imprint of
Pen & Sword Books Ltd
47 Church Street
Barnsley
South Yorkshire
S70 2AS

ISBN 978-1-47383-377-7

Typeset by Concept, Huddersfield, West Yorkshire, HD4 5JL.
Printed and bound in England by CPI Group (UK) Ltd, Croydon CR0 4YY.

Pen & Sword Books Ltd incorporates the imprints of Pen & Sword Archaeology, Atlas, Aviation, Battleground, Discovery, Family History, History, Maritime, Military, Naval, Politics, Railways, Select, Social History, Transport, True Crime, and Claymore Press, Frontline Books, Leo Cooper, Praetorian Press, Remember When, Seaforth Publishing and Wharncliffe.

For a complete list of Pen & Sword titles please contact
PEN & SWORD BOOKS LIMITED
47 Church Street, Barnsley, South Yorkshire, S70 2AS, England
E-mail: enquiries@pen-and-sword.co.uk
Website: www.pen-and-sword.co.uk

Contents

List of Illustrations

Acknowledgements

Any student of this topic must start by acknowledging the pioneering contribution of John Warwicker, for his seminal publications and his persistent efforts in breaking down the barriers of secrecy around the subject and in making sources publicly available. His book *Churchill's Underground Army* rewards constant re-reading. Thanks are also due to Stephen Sutton for permission to quote from his unpublished undergraduate thesis of 1995 and for making available documents provided by the Foreign Office SOE Advisor in the late 1990s. The important series of audio interviews that Stephen conducted with Auxiliary Unit veterans is now available through the Imperial War Museum audio collection. A personal thanks to Mick Wilks who pioneered the study of the topic locally, originally as part of the Defence of Britain project in the mid-1990s and latterly as the Defence of Worcestershire project. With Bernard Lowry he recorded the reminiscences of a large number of Auxiliary Units veterans at a time when they were still reluctant to discuss their secret wartime experiences. Peter Kindred and the volunteers at the British Resistance Museum at Parham, Suffolk were unfailingly friendly and helpful in opening up their unique archive. A special thanks is owed to Peter Attwater for his reminiscences of his time as a resistance wireless operator and for opening up new lines of enquiry.

Many other people have patiently answered queries. They include Stewart Angell, A.F. Judge (Military Intelligence Museum, Chicksands), Sallie Mogford and Will Ward. Thanks to the sources of the illustrations: East Sussex County Council Library & Information Service, Imperial War Museum, National Armouries, The National Archives, National Portrait Gallery, Geoffrey Pidgeon, Piers Pottinger, David Sampson, Troendelag Folk Museum (Norway), Getty Images and Corbis. Particular thanks to Susanne and Kate Atkin for their additional photography and to Discover History for modelling the front cover illustration. Every effort has been made to contact the correct copyright owner for illustrations but apologies are made for any errors.

This book would not have been possible without the assistance of Lee Richards at ARCRE Document Copying Service (www.arcre.com). The service has allowed cost-effective remote access to the documents held at The National Archives, which transforms the possibilities for research for those living outside London. Thanks also to Rupert Harding, Susan Last and the staff of Pen & Sword for their patience in seeing the book through the publication process.

As ever, my final thanks go to my wife, Susanne, for her unfailing support and patience during the research and production of this book and for compiling the index.

Any responsibility for speculation and conclusions remains my own.

Abbreviations and Acronyms

ADGB – Air Defence of Great Britain Command, which coordinated the air defence of Britain (fighter aircraft and AA guns) until the formation of Fighter Command in 1936.

Abwehr – German army intelligence organisation.

ATS – Auxiliary Territorial Service. Women's army organisation.

BEF – British Expeditionary Force (France 1939–40).

CSS – Chief of the Secret Service (SIS). Commonly abbreviated as 'C'.

CIGS – Chief of the Imperial General Staff.

DCO – Director of Combined Operations.

DMI – Directorate of Military Intelligence.

DNI – Directorate of Naval Intelligence.

Electra House – Secret government organisation responsible for conducting psychological warfare. In July 1940 it was merged into the newly formed Special Operations Executive (SOE).

FSS – Field Security Sections of Military Intelligence Corps. Until July 1940 part of D Division, MI5.

G-2 – Irish Intelligence Service.

GSO – General Staff Officer (graded 1–3).

GS(R) – General Service (Research). Original name for what became MIR.

GHQ – General Headquarters, Home Forces.

HDB – Home Defence Battalions. Unsuccessful attempt in November 1939 to attract retired soldiers for guarding vulnerable points etc within the UK.

HDE – Home Defence Executive. Created on 10 May 1940 under chairmanship of General Ironside, C in C Home Forces, to coordinate anti-invasion planning.

HD(S)E – Home Defence (Security) Executive. Created on 28 May 1940 to consider matters of internal security and defence against the 5th Column.

HDM – Home Defence Movement. Small cover organisation of the British Union of Fascists.

HDO – Home Defence Organisation. Popular name in modern publications for the Home Defence Scheme (HDS).

HDS – Home Defence Scheme. Intelligence and sabotage organisation created in 1940 by Section D of SIS. Otherwise known in 1940 as the Regional D Scheme.

HDU – Home Defence Units. RAF/RN coastal wireless monitoring stations as part of the Y Intercept Service.

IRA – Irish Republican Army.

ISIS – Irish Supplementary Intelligence Service.

ISPB – Inter-Services Project Board. Created in April 1940 to coordinate proposals between War Office, Naval and Air Force Intelligence services and SIS for the development of British irregular warfare. Chaired by Col. Jo Holland of MIR.

LDV – Local Defence Volunteers. Name changed to Home Guard on 22 July 1940.

MEW – Ministry of Economic Warfare.

MI5 – Secret Security Service, responsible for counter-espionage operations in the UK. Ceased to be a section of the War Office in 1931 and henceforth its official title became the Security Service, as an interdepartmental intelligence agency. The name MI5 was retained as a popular abbreviation and it took some time for the War Office to realise that the change had been made.

MI6 – Popular alternative name of Secret Intelligence Service (SIS). Although it frequently used a War Office address, it was controlled by the Foreign Office rather than Military Intelligence.

MIR – Military Intelligence (Research). War Office counterpart of Section D, SIS.

OB – Operational Base (underground hides of the Operational Patrols, Auxiliary Units).

OP – Observation Post.

RDS – Regional D Scheme for Home Defence. Alternative name for the Home Defence Scheme (HDS) of Section D, SIS.

RSLO – Regional Security Liaison Officer (MI5).

SAS – Special Air Service.

SCU – Special Communications Unit of SIS. This is the wireless unit that passed on intelligence to the SLU for onward transmission to the military.

SDB – Special Duties Branch, Auxiliary Units (*aka* Special Duties Organisation or Special Duties Section).

Section B.26 – Joint MI5/SIS section that allowed SIS to legally operate in the UK. Created in August 1940 under the cover of Section B, MI5.

Section D – Sabotage section of SIS, 1938–40 (*aka* Section IX of SIS or Statistical Research Department of the War Office).

Section V – Counter-espionage section of SIS.

SIS – Secret Intelligence Service (*aka* MI6). It is controlled by Foreign Office but existence was not officially acknowledged until 1994.

SLU – Special Liaison Unit of SIS. Responsible for deciphering the intelligence received by the SCU and passing it on to the military.

SOE – Special Operations Executive. Sabotage organisation formed in 1940 on the basis of the amalgamation of Electra House, Section D and MIR.

TAA – Territorial Army Association.

TNA – The National Archives.

TRD – Duplex wireless set developed for the SDB.

Y-Service – Signals Interception Service, with stations run by all three armed services together with SIS and the Post Office.

Introduction

... a closely coordinated sabotage and intelligence network among the civilian population who would be left behind in any territory which the German armies might temporarily be able to occupy.

Lawrence Grand, August 1940[1]

When Prime Minister Winston Churchill made his famous speech including the words 'we shall fight in the fields and in the streets, we shall fight in the hills; we shall never surrender' on 4 June 1940, he was speaking with the knowledge that Britain's Secret Intelligence Service (SIS, *aka* MI6) was in the process of mobilising not one, but two, civilian British resistance organisations to become operational after the country had been partially or fully occupied. They were ready to undertake both long-term intelligence-gathering as well as military and economic sabotage and, where necessary, assassination. This ruthless piece of pre-invasion planning made many in the military and government feel very uncomfortable in its lack of British 'fair play'. The organisations remain largely unknown, wrapped in continued secrecy.

Such organisations of last resort were accompanied by a range of other bodies which could be termed loosely as 'resistance' organisations, only in so far as they helped deny the Nazis an ability to sweep unopposed through territory beyond the formal 'front line' and to efficiently maintain its supply lines (whether back to the invasion beaches or via captured airfields). These were commando or guerrilla forces designed to operate in a short-term military campaign, attacking the supply lines of the enemy forces in the rear or on its flanks. Some were official and would fight in uniform and some would be *ad hoc* civilian guerrillas. Some were part of civilian intelligence networks passing on information to the regular forces during an active military campaign. They were important because the British defence plan accepted the possibility that a considerable slice of the country would fall under at least temporary German occupation for up to a month whilst a counter-attack was organised. Into this mix should be added the regular army intelligence gathering of the Phantom Units. Resistance after a settled occupation was a different matter. Together, the British plans for irregular warfare provided a unique multi-layered response to the threat of what had been the highly successful German tactic of *blitzkrieg*. Like the mythical Hydra, if one of these hidden bodies was overcome, the Nazis would find that another was already in place to spring up and continue the struggle. There is no doubt that if Britain had been invaded then these irregular warriors would have fought a bitter and brutal campaign. There is little place for romance in guerrilla warfare and the sobering fact is that a number of the proposed tactics would now be considered war crimes.

This is a complex story involving layers of secret organisations that were originally designed to confuse the Nazis and have done an equally excellent job of confusing later historians. It is still not possible to unravel the full story of the clandestine activities in Britain during the war and it may never be possible to do so. One can do no better than repeat the broad conclusion about the organisation of British Intelligence reached by the Gestapo in 1940:

> Nobody can truthfully say the service is organised in such and such a way, is located here or there, or employs this or that person who does this or that task. If any details about the British Intelligence Service are ever made known or published by the English, one can be sure that only those authorities and offices whose existence cannot be hidden in the long term will be high-lighted.[2]

The best known of these secret bodies is the GHQ Auxiliary Units organisation (see Chapters Six to Ten). An amalgamation of the plans by SIS and XII Corps Observation Unit, the Auxiliary Units included both the Operational Patrols and the intelligence network of the Special Duties Branch (*aka* Special Duties Organisation or Special Duties Section). Although this is now popularly labelled as the 'Resistance' organisation of Britain during the Second World War there is here a fundamental misunderstanding of its function. The Operational Patrols were a uniformed military organisation and were intended as an anti-invasion commando force, with limited purpose and lifespan. Under no accepted definition could they be described as a 'resistance' organisation. This is clear from all the contemporary documentation of 1940 and was the firm view of the first Commanding Officer, Lieutenant Colonel Colin Gubbins, and his second-in-command Major Peter Wilkinson. It is, however, a distinction that has been resolutely ignored in modern publications and by the media looking for an attractive headline. The history of the Auxiliary Units now risks being driven by its own mythology and is in need of a rather more detached approach. Contrary to popular belief, patrol members carried formal identity, were entered on the rolls of their local Home Guard and would fight in uniform during the period of invasion. This was all designed to avoid them being labelled as *francs-tireurs*, or terrorists, and to emphasise that they were a military formation. It was coldly calculated by their superiors that their life expectancy was only twelve to fifteen days. As the pioneer national historian in this field, John Warwicker has written:

> It was never intended that the Auxiliers were to compare with the men and women of the European resistance movements ... [they] were seen only as a short-term, expendable, harassing force intended – with the blessing of the British High Command – to be of some useful influence in local battles.[3]

The origin, role and command of the more secret Special Duties Branch of the Auxiliary Units (Chapters Nine and Ten) is more complicated, although it will also be argued that its organisation meant that it was dangerously flawed if intended as a resistance organisation. Initially it was cobbled together by the War Office from an origin in SIS and, like the Operational Patrols, was primarily intended to operate on a short-term basis during an invasion, as an intelligence-reporting organisation. The War Office do, however, appear to have been unsure what to do with their acquisition from the Secret Intelligence Service and this is reflected in the structure that subsequently developed.

The present essay is not in any way intended to disparage the role and bravery of the men and women who served in the Auxiliary Units. It is, however, important to set their role within the broader, quite remarkable, pattern of secret guerrilla organisations that would have been activated if Britain had been invaded in 1940, and to understand the conflicts between the competing visions of secret civilian resistance and military guerrilla organisation. Without such analysis the story of the Auxiliary Units is in danger of becoming a romantic myth, with received wisdom repeated from one publication to the next.

The history of the Auxiliary Units is also confused by issues of perception. As early as 1957, Peter Fleming (a pioneer of the XII Corps Observation Unit) wrote a warning on the use of the oral history of the Second World War in the Foreword to *Invasion 1940*:

> Yet legend plays a large part in their memories of that tense and strangely exhilarating summer, and their experiences, like those of early childhood, are sharply rather than accurately etched upon their minds. The stories they tell of the period have become better, but not more veracious, with the passage of time. Rumours are remembered as facts, and – particularly since anti-invasion precautions continued in force for several years after the Germans had renounced their project – the sequence of events is blurred.[4]

If true in 1957, the risks were even greater in the 1990s when researchers, in the absence of official documents, were obliged to rely heavily on the memories of those veterans who were prepared to break the wall of silence over their secret activities. The story was told from the 'bottom up', but what the Auxiliers or SDB wireless operators had been told, or what they remembered, was not necessarily the whole truth. The relative ease of contacting local veterans of the Operational Patrols also meant that there was disproportionate attention paid to them rather than the more strategic Scout Patrols. Sadly, many older members of the Special Duties Branch or indeed the Home Defence Scheme had already passed away and survivors kept their silence for longer. Most obviously, in an era in which visions of the Home Guard were distorted by the popular TV series *Dad's Army*, there was a natural inclination to over-emphasise the distinction between Auxiliers and the regular Home Guard. As men who were effectively to be left to their own devices and wits once invasion occurred, the veterans presented their own vision of their purpose, which might differ from the official view. This gap was widened by the natural tendency of their Intelligence Officers who, although it is clear they did tell the Auxiliers that their life expectancy was no more than one to two weeks, would not have been human if they had not sometimes given broad encouragement that they may have survived and operated for longer. The Auxiliers on the ground also tended to rigorously protect their secrecy from friends and family, not realising that the walls of secrecy within the War Office and Home Guard were being steadily eroded and under increasing threat from the army accountants (see Chapter Twelve).

Thus the idea of long-term 'resistance', as opposed to short-term anti-invasion warfare, became enshrined in print and film and became self-perpetuating. Auxiliary Units history has not been helped by TV producers and 'experts' with only a hazy idea of what they were documenting, or who tried to dumb-down the story into a convenient soundbite. BBC's *Countryfile* once implied that the Auxiliary Units were somehow a branch of the Boy Scouts! There are now many excellent county-based books that record the memories of individual Auxiliers and their patrols to create local studies of the Auxiliary Units. The present book does not attempt to compete with them, but rather has tried to take a more strategic 'top down' approach to the subject, taking advantage of recent releases of documents from The National Archives.

The popular focus on the Auxiliary Units of 1940–44, with their secret bases, special weaponry and strong community basis, together with the limitations of the surviving sources, has obscured their origins in the even more secret and shadowy civilian organisations founded by the Secret Intelligence Service (SIS, *aka* MI6). These were both the precursor of the Auxiliary Units/Special Duties system and, in part, continued alongside the latter well into the war in at least an intelligence-gathering capacity. It may even be argued that the War Office organisations provided a convenient cover and diversion for longer-term SIS operations. Even the name of these organisations is shrouded in mystery. In the true spirit of a secret organisation, at the time reference to them was deliberately vague and not committed to paper. They did not deal in 'sabotage' but in the more innocuous-sounding 'obstruction'. One of these secret organisations has become known as the Home Defence Organisation (HDO), but it is not clear if that was a contemporary nomenclature (see Chapter Four). It was organised by Section D of SIS and in their surviving records it is usually described merely as an organisation for 'Home Defence' or sometimes the 'Regional D Scheme', Project D/Y or the 'Home Defence Scheme' (the preferred name used in the present study). The HDS became usefully lost within a welter of bodies dealing with Home Defence, including the government Home Defence Executive, the army Home Defence Battalions or the RAF/RN Home Defence Units! It was hurriedly, and somewhat chaotically, created in May 1940 during the retreat to Dunkirk as a rushed attempt to provide a civilian guerrilla organisation. Some members of Section D wanted to use this to build a more populist guerrilla force, building upon the enthusiasm evident in the rush to join the new Local Defence Volunteers (forerunner of the Home Guard), but others saw this as a longer-term resistance organisation ready to replace the Auxiliary Units once the latter were wiped out.

Fortunately, these organisations never had to go into action against the enemy. Their story is, however, as much a story of conflict within the corridors of power in Whitehall, between some very forceful characters, as it was a battle against the Nazis. The story involves a fascinating convergence of the interests of men steeped in the old Etonian traditions of the British secret service (see the educational background of some of the key characters in Appendix 2), and the communist Tom Wintringham and his comrades at the Home Guard Training School at Osterley Park. If Eton was regarded as the chief nurse of English statesmen, then it also appears to have done an excellent job in preparing a large percentage of Britain's wartime spies and spymasters for some very ungentle-manly arts! It remains an open question as to how far Tom Wintringham had been brought into the official secret. The activities of the new Intelligence Corps should also not be forgotten, complicated by the fact that this was used, literally, as a badge of convenience to conceal the identities of the other security services. The critical months of 1940 also saw the start of the development of what would become a particularly British feature of the Second World War – the Special Forces. The new Commandos and Phantom regiment would closely interact with plans for irregular warfare upon invasion.

To date, John Warwicker's seminal *Churchill's Underground Army* (2008) is the most extensive discussion of the HDS (there called the HDO). What was not realised at the time was that a second organisation, known only as Section VII or 'DB's organisation', had already been put in place by senior officers of SIS as a more traditional intelligence network, although with a shadowy sabotage and assassination element (see Chapter Eleven). It is this that would have formed the basis of the 'real' British resistance, hidden behind the cover of the efforts of their colleagues in Section D and those of the War Office. This organisation could be regarded as one of SIS's greatest triumphs of secrecy during the Second World War. The organisation continued in operation until at least 1943.

Many of the records of the SIS operations were destroyed in a wholesale purge during the invasion scares of 1940 or post-war in an era of long-running official paranoia over the existence of the war-time secret services. The surviving files of Section D first passed to SOE, but here again there were purges towards the end of the war. They passed back to SIS in 1946 and almost immediately afterwards a disastrous fire in the former Baker Street HQ of SOE destroyed an unknown number of records. Later, in 1949, another weeding of documents reputedly resulted in the destruction of 100 tons of material![5] Thereafter, the history of both the Auxiliary Units and their friends in SIS was caught up in the same Cold War blanket of official security that covered all British clandestine operations of the Second World War. The wall of silence was not immediate or complete. There was a rash official press release in 1945 on the work of the Auxiliary Units, which was quickly stifled after reports appeared in a number of newspapers at home and abroad. Reuters circulated the story internationally that 'Britain had secret army'. A brief account was even published in the service newspaper *Sunday SEAC* on 15 April 1945, describing 'an elaborately organized maquis'.[6] Officially or not, *The Times* obtained a copy of the stand-down letter to the SDB and an account was published on 12 April 1945 under the heading 'Britain's Secret "Underground" – Invasion Spy Force Stood Down'. It went on to explain that the 'home underground' force had wireless sets, messengers, code clerks, and 'about 300 specially picked officers of the Army Special Duties Branch to guide their work'. A month later, on 14 June, the *Western Morning News* ran a story on the 'British Maquis', describing the work of both the Operational Patrols and the SDB. This was followed on 10 July by an interview with an unnamed Cornish patrol leader. Such leaks were soon quashed, but this provided a basis for later myth and terminology. Remarkably, an article in *The Spectator* by Peter Fleming on the XII Corps Observation Unit did manage to slip through the net in 1952, to be followed by a broader discussion of the Auxiliary Units in his 1957 *Invasion 1940*.[7]

Suppression of the Auxiliary Units' history was not unique. There were long battles to get memoirs of SOE veterans published during the Cold War, but what happened abroad was perhaps considered less sensitive than secret plans on the home front. Security gradually broke down around the Auxiliary Units Operational Patrols, encouraged by David Lampe's pioneering publication of *The Last Ditch* in 1968. The SDB remained a more mysterious quantity, by its very nature more isolated and perhaps more imbued with secrecy through its links to SIS. The SIS operations themselves were even more tightly controlled, assisted by the older age range of the participants, which meant that its members had largely passed away before it was seen as acceptable to tell one's story. From the perspective of the intelligence services there was also an evident concern that a good idea, used once, might be useful again in the future and so best to keep it a secret! Nonetheless, the amount of documentation that has survived, particularly of the Auxiliary Units, is much larger than previously thought and has now trickled into The National Archives, helping dispel some of the myths that have grown up around the subject since the 1960s and the publication of *The Last Ditch*.

Many problems of interpretation remain, no doubt to the gratification of those machiavellian intelligence planners of 1940. Not all of the stories of the secret agents can be neatly pigeon-holed into known organisations. The story has also become entwined in the story of SOE and its now well-known deeds of daring-do to fulfil Churchill's wish to 'Set Europe Ablaze'. Thus, accounts of the work of SIS have normally been published only as part of the founding of SOE and, indeed, as part of the apologia of the latter. SIS have rigorously protected their traditional values of secrecy – even at the cost of promoting their historic successes.

Modern historians of SOE, hampered by the slow release of official documents, have tended to be dismissive and even scathing of the efforts of SIS in creating a UK resistance network. Mackenzie mentioned this role only briefly in his otherwise comprehensive summary of the work of Section D in the first official history of SOE.[8] Later historians Foot and Stafford were seemingly content to use the contemporary antipathy towards the maverick Head of Section D, Lawrence Grand, and to uncritically repeat David Lampe's 1968 collection of their disaster stories. Lampe himself relied largely on SIS/SOE agent Sweet-Escott's whimsical account of events as his source on Section D's role in creating a UK resistance movement. Foot wrote-off Section D's attempts to create stay-behind units during the fraught months of 1940 as incompetent.[9] David

Stafford's opinion is that the work 'became a fiasco: too many of its organisers were arrested as German agents while preparing ammunition dumps and expanding badger sets as underground HQs.'[10] Lacking more detailed information, Stafford seems to have conflated HDS experience with early SDB disasters in which underground hides and buried radio sets were discovered.

As further sources have been made public or have been rediscovered in obscure government files within The National Archives, more recent historians have been more charitable about the work of Section D overall. In 2004 Davies suggested that there had been a 'systematic undervaluation' of the achievements of Section D, particularly in regard to clandestine political warfare.[11] This assessment was followed by Mark Seaman in 2006, who commented on 'the remarkable contribution of Section D and MIR to SOE's eventual success.'[12] Such a contribution can be seen in the number of Section D staff who retained key positions in the new SOE and in the fundamental contribution of the scientific section of Section D to the new body. Certainly the breadth of activity, as documented in SOE's unpublished wartime *History of Section D* and elsewhere, must be considered remarkable during its period of active operation in 1939–40.[13] Any chaos in their work is perhaps to be judged within the fraught context of those times and particularly within the wider state of British intelligence. A greater degree of bungling, laughable but for the loss of life that resulted, was to be seen in the first years of SOE.[14] Crucially for historians, the post-war dismissal of the SIS attempts to create a resistance movement through Section D has obscured both the fact that this was not their only initiative, and that there was a significant shift in strategic thinking in 1940 that sought a more military, if short-term, option away from the long-term civilian resistance model as originally proposed. At the time, there were many vested interests within government and the military that wanted the efforts of Section D to fail.

The first clue that there was more to the story of the British resistance movement organised by SIS than previously imagined came in 2010 when Keith Jeffery, in his official history of SIS, revealed in a single paragraph that there was a mobilisation of a secret wireless network in 1940, organised by senior SIS officers and not involving Section D. Jeffery identified this network as Section VII (usually thought to be merely the SIS accounting department).[15] Despite the propensity of Colonel Grand to claim any initiative that could possibly be linked to Section D as his own, it is notable that there is no mention of this wireless network in any publicly-accessible document relating to Section D. It will be argued here that the responsibility for SIS resistance operations was actually much wider than that of Section D. The sometimes chaotic contribution of the latter has provided a useful distraction from those other elements of SIS that were content to remain in the shadows. Documents from The National Archives have also demonstrated that the Section VII operation of SIS continued in existence well beyond the formal dissolution of Section D and the HDS in 1940, operating under the authority of a liaison section created with MI5 (Section B.26).

The following study focusses on the philosophy behind the various initiatives and their place within the wider context of the defence of Britain. Developments were greatly affected by the personalities of those involved and, as a consequence, thumbnail biographies of the key figures have been provided (see Appendix 2). The story is, by necessity, highly speculative in places, based as it is on surviving snippets of evidence. It is not, by any means, the complete story. There remain significant gaps, confusions and conflicts of evidence, as one might expect in trying to reconstruct the narrative of a successful secret intelligence operation. Some pieces of evidence simply do not fit the jigsaw and it is only possible to broadly suggest who might be responsible for their activities and to try to 'join up the dots' along the path of least resistance. The book has been written to stimulate a reassessment of existing information and the testing of any future evidence that might be released into the public domain by the intelligence agencies. Sadly, the opportunity to ask questions of those directly involved in this secret war has now almost completely passed.

Chapter One

Ungentlemanly Warfare

The preparations which are being made all over England to arm the civilian population for guerrilla warfare are contrary to the rules of international law. German official quarters warn the misled British public and remind them of the fate of the Polish *francs-tireurs* and gangs of murderers. Civilians who take up arms against German soldiers are, under international law, no better than murderers, whether they be priests or bank clerks. British people you will do well to heed our warning![1]

German radio broadcast, 16 May 1940

Today we are used to seeing wars waged by paramilitaries without formal uniform or identifiable badges of rank, but this was *not* the case in 1940, although the battle landscape was to quickly change during the course of the war. Before looking at the detail of the various schemes for irregular warfare that were proposed to operate in Britain, it is necessary to consider the wider context of what was considered acceptable behaviour in warfare and particularly the controversy over the role of civilians in combat that took place in Britain in 1939–40.

For centuries the armies of Europe marched into battle in ordered lines, announcing their presence by the beat of the drum and wearing brightly-coloured uniforms so that all would know for whom they fought, but in the early 19th century the French had to face the irregular Spanish *guerrilleros* who fought their 'little war' against Napoleon. Later the French had their own irregulars in the form of the *francs-tireurs* ('free-shooters') who took on the might of the Prussian army during the war of 1870–71 and had a lasting effect on the psyche of the German soldiers in both the First and Second World Wars. The term became widely used in the Second World War when defining the legal status of guerrilla fighters. Towards the end of the century the British were finally obliged to abandon their red coats for khaki just in time to face the Boers, who had the unsporting habit of shooting them from long range whilst sheltering behind rocks and trees in drab grey and brown civilian clothing.

The rights of citizens to defend their country and the legality of *francs-tireurs* had been hotly debated during the discussions leading to the 1907 Hague Convention. Whilst large states contended that lawful combatant status should only be given to members of recognised armed forces, smaller countries wanted to protect the right of a general population to defend itself against an invader. Article 1 of the Hague Convention eventually provided four criteria for lawful combatant status:

1. To be commanded by a person responsible for their subordinates.
2. To have a recognised emblem that was recognisable at a distance.
3. To carry arms openly.
4. To conduct their operations according to the laws and customs of war.

In a concession to the smaller states, Article 2 allowed the concept of the *levée en masse* for populations who spontaneously took up arms but carried them openly and obeyed the laws of war – but this was open to wide interpretation.

The consequences were to be seen at the start of the First World War. The atrocities committed by the German army in Belgium were excused as being a consequence of the activities of *francs-tireurs*. In actuality, the threat was more imaginary than real, but it showed the impact that such forces had caused to the morale of the army in 1870–71. Vivid accounts of mass executions of civilians, and rape and arson used as reprisals, became burned into the consciousness of the allies. The British government was determined to maintain the concept of lawful combatants and persistently resisted the efforts of the First World War Volunteer Training Corps – the Home Guard of its day – to be seen as a combat force. Only reluctantly were they allowed to bear arms, but great stress was placed on the need to wear a clearly distinctive armband, which was seen as having the status of a legal document, worn even when uniforms were allowed. Officially they were regarded as an organisation that merely *trained* men for possible active service, but they would not be recognised as a combative force under martial law until Britain was actually invaded. Ironically, much of the syllabus of the VTC was in training for guerrilla warfare – at the same time as the British army was walking upright in ordered lines across no man's land into hails of machine-gun fire and officers faced derision for replacing their distinctive cuff ranks for more discrete 'windy' epaulettes. In language that the Auxiliary Units or students at the Home Guard Training School at Osterley would have immediately recognised in 1940, the VTC Regulations of 1916 called upon its units to 'to constantly harass, annoy, and tire out the enemy, and to impede his progress, till a sufficient force can be assembled to smash him'.[2]

After the First World War, British troops served alongside White Russian partisans in 1919–20 and had to face the unseen threat of the IRA in Ireland during 1919–21. In Ireland the British government experienced at first hand the tactics of sabotage and terror and in doing so, army officers such as Colin Gubbins and Jo Holland developed a grudging respect for the IRA leader, Michael Collins. War in the 20th century was becoming less 'civilised' and 'gentlemanly'. Within the horror of a civil war, the Spanish conflict of 1936–39 brought new threats to the accepted conventions of war. Both sides committed atrocities on civilian populations and the summary execution of officer prisoners was well known. For the International Brigades, the chances of any man being taken prisoner by the Nationalists was slim and the experience of the British Battalion was to have a profound impact on the development of the Home Guard in 1940. The veterans of the Spanish war who taught at the Osterley Training School would provide an introduction in Britain to a new ruthlessness in warfare, but already, during 1938, Orde Wingate was putting the principles of irregular warfare into practice. As an Intelligence Officer in Palestine, Wingate created the 'Special Night Squads' of British and Haganah volunteers. They ambushed Arab saboteurs and raided border villages, criticised by friend and foe alike for their sometimes brutal tactics.

During the Second World War, Winston Churchill (Plate 6 and Appendix 2) famously exhorted the para-military SOE to 'set Europe ablaze' and encouraged foreign civilian resistance. Nonetheless, the British government still maintained the legal definition of the *franc-tireur* as a terrorist and strenuously resisted various schemes to officially arm its own civilians. Thus it was that the victorious allied nations at the Nuremburg War Trials took a conservative line about what constituted being a 'lawful combatant', and the partisans of Yugoslavia and Greece, despite being allies and supported by British military missions, were declared *francs-tireurs*. The court agreed that the Nazis were legally entitled to have executed them – which they had done in their thousands – but they were, however, found guilty of doing so in a summary fashion without any form of judicial process.

> We are obliged to hold that such guerrillas were *francs-tireurs* who, upon capture, could be subjected to the death penalty. Consequently, no criminal responsibility attaches to the defendant List because of the execution of captured partisans ...[3]

Such legal concerns were to have a great impact upon the government's plans for guerrilla warfare in Britain. Nonetheless, although the War Office might have been unwilling to be associated with the creation of civilian *francs-tireurs*, they were not so squeamish in the matter of summary executions. As will be seen, the Auxiliary Units patrols carried death lists of suspected collaborators, or simply people that might have known of their existence, whom they were ordered to execute after invasion. Both SIS and Auxiliary Units Intelligence Officers promoted the use of mutilation of their victims to act as a warning to others. Were there memories here of the tactics used by the IRA against British intelligence operations in Ireland during 1920?[4]

A large section of the general public had no such legalistic qualms about taking up arms in an era of total war. For them, Ernest Hemingway's book, *For Whom The Bell Tolls*, which was first published in 1940 and focussed on the fate of a guerrilla band in the Spanish Civil War, became a romantic inspiration, following on from T.E. Lawrence's classic First World War *Seven Pillars of Wisdom*. The concept of guerrilla warfare became attractive to many sections of the Home Guard and books on guerrilla tactics and the manufacture of improvised explosive devices (in modern parlance) became instant bestsellers to the general public in 1940 and 1941. Tom Wintringham's *New Ways of War* and Yank Levy's *Guerrilla Warfare* both included explicit details of how to make improvised explosives and booby-trap devices that would cause outrage in modern society. Captain Cronk's pamphlet, *Explosives for the Home Guard* (1943) even explained how to dismantle service grenades in order to make alternative weapons. The preface stated somewhat optimistically, if not irresponsibly, 'I hope it will assist to dispel the prevalent idea that the handling of explosives is a dangerous business'. In June of the previous year, Charles Pearce, a corporal in Halesowen Home Guard, had been killed in an explosion in his garden shed. He had been attempting to remove explosives from a shell case, probably to make improvised grenades. *The Manual of Guerrilla Tactics* was published by Bernards in a convenient size suitable for one's back pocket and sold for just one shilling. It included a special section on the 'preparation and use of explosives' in a style highly reminiscent of the official manuals issued to the Auxiliary Units. The War Office, determined to control the intrusion of civilians onto the battlefield, must have looked upon such publications with horror, but their patience was finally tested beyond the limit by Tom Wintringham's enthusiastic 'We make a mortar for 38/6d' published in *Picture Post*, July 1941. This article described how to make what amounted to a medieval cannon, firing a jam-tin bomb, and demanded careful coordination between the length of fuse on the mortar and that on the bomb. The promised second part of the article on how to fire the mortar was never published and one suspects that the War Office desperately tried to persuade the magazine to withdraw it on grounds of public safety!

The War Office faced a particular problem of how to deal with the women who wanted to become involved in the fighting. These calls were led in Parliament by Edith Summerskill, who eventually founded the Women's Home Defence Corps as what amounted to an illegal private army. In popular culture, films such as *Mrs Grant Goes To The Door* (MOI, August 1940) and *Went the Day Well* (Ealing, December 1942) also showed women taking up arms alongside the men. John Langdon-Davies, another left-wing champion of the Home Guard, called for a Women's Home Guard Auxiliary and for them to be given a clear part in the defence strategy. He did, however, draw the line at them being involved in the fighting and could not escape a patronising tone:

> I think the average Home Guard has joined it because he wants to protect his hearth and home; and would feel a bit annoyed if the hearth and home insisted upon coming along with him and doing some of the protecting.[5]

Individual Home Guard units soon began to unofficially recruit women into first aid and communications roles. Eventually the War Office had to give way and in 1943 gave official recognition to what were officially called 'Nominated Women' in the Home Guard – more commonly (and confusingly) called the 'Home Guard Auxiliaries'. They were only supposed to take on a non-combative role, although the Commanding Officer of the Air Transport Auxiliary at White Waltham, Kent, in 1943–44 told his Home Guard Women's Shooting Team that their role, if attacked by a parachute raid, was to climb onto the roof of the aircraft hangars and shoot the paratroopers as they descended.[6] Within the guerrilla groups under discussion in the present study, the SIS and SDB openly acknowledged the role of women serving as agents, couriers and wireless operators; the ATS operators at the IN stations and the Section VII wireless operators were armed with revolvers for personal protection. There is, however, no specific mention of female saboteurs. The issue continued to be fruitlessly raised by individuals in Parliament. In November 1941, MP Sir Eric Errington commented:

> I am surprised to read that the War Office has decided that women are not to be trained as Home Guards. To say one is surprised is perhaps an exaggeration, but it seems to me that whatever may be the attitude of the War Office, the Ministry of Home Security ought to take an entirely different view of the situation. I have had an opportunity of speaking to a number of women of different classes, and they all ask what they can do if the invader comes. They are told by the Prime Minister and by other Ministers that invasion is likely to take place, and they complain that they are not told what they can do. They are asking what they should do if a German came to their door. [An Hon. Member: 'Shoot him'.] But they have nothing to shoot him with, and the women are not to be trained and given information to enable them to protect themselves ... Why should not our women be taught the use of hand-grenades and revolvers with which they could protect themselves?[7]

Despite the worsening situation during 1940, great suspicion remained regarding the moral and practical consequences of embarking on a programme of civilian guerrilla warfare. Few in authority agreed with the rousing devil-may-care attitude of Colonel J.C. Wedgwood, MP for Newcastle-under-Lyme, who on 7 May 1940 had cheerfully expressed the view in Parliament that civilians should be armed.

> They ought to be taught that they should not leave it to the regular forces to do the fighting but that they must fight themselves ... We should use them like *francs-tireurs*. They would no doubt be shot if they were taken, but they would be able to harass any small invading forces and not wait until some regular troops came to help.

Wedgwood, who had a distinguished war record from the First World War, was roundly criticised for being irresponsible in openly endorsing a suicidal terrorism.[8] How would the House have reacted had they known that this was exactly what Section D of SIS had been trying to engineer across Europe since 1939 as the 'D Scheme' and which it would shortly introduce into Britain in 1940 as the 'Regional D Scheme' or 'Home Defence Scheme'? (See Chapter Four.)

Following Wedgwood's speech, the Home Office felt obliged to issue a press release, published in *The Times* on 11 May, to advise civilians what they should, or should not, do in the event of invasion: not to take pot-shots at the enemy, and to leave the fighting to the army. Parliament, from the very start of the war in September 1939, had repeatedly expressed concern about the definition of the *francs-tireur*. By July 1940 this debate had focussed upon the status of the Home Guard armband as denoting a legitimate military body and the difficulty of legally arming the ARP. On 30 July 1940, as part of the debate on the Emergency Powers (Defence) Bill, Lord Atkin stated that it would be a mistake:

if members of the public were encouraged to believe that, without belonging to the Home Guard, they could seize their shotguns and shoot down the first parachutist that they saw. They would then be *francs-tireurs*, and would be so treated, I have no doubt, by the enemy, and would bring themselves and their families into danger.[9]

A contorted legalistic argument in favour of civilian resistance was made by Edward Chichester, 6th Marquess of Donegall, during 1943 in his regular column 'Almost in Confidence' in the *Sunday Dispatch*.[10] He took the optimistic line that a *franc-tireur* could not formally exist until after a surrender: 'Before that happens any civilian is in duty bound to assist in repelling the invader'. It seems doubtful that the SS or Gestapo would have appreciated this legal subtlety and in any case this would not have protected civilian spies.

Such parliamentary concern over the definition of *franc-tireur* had, no doubt, been spurred by the furious Nazi reaction to the foundation of the Local Defence Volunteers (LDV), later to become the Home Guard.

The British Government is committing the worst crime of all. Evidently it permits open preparation for the formation of murder bands.[11]

Such concern over the formation of the LDV was shared within the British government. Brigadier W. Carden Roe, then a Staff Officer in IV Corps, was summoned to a meeting at the War Office where the senior civil servant Sir Frederick Bovenschen (Permanent Under-Secretary of State for War) complained that the whole idea of the LDV was most irregular and slap-dash. He questioned the legality of the new force, asking 'Why all this precipitancy?' At this, Brigadier Roe lost his temper and snapped 'In order to try and avoid losing the war'.[12] The British government moved quickly to legalise the formation of the new defence force by passing, on 17 May, The Defence (Local Defence Volunteers) Regulations, 1940, making it clear that the Local Defence Volunteers were members of the armed forces of the Crown and subject to military law as soldiers.[13] Nonetheless, some lord lieutenants who had continuing doubts as to the legal status of the LDV/Home Guard were still later described as 'obstructionist' in failing to provide support for their mobilisation.[14] If they reacted in this way to the Home Guard, how would such men react to the idea of a civilian resistance movement being created within their counties? It was not surprising that Section D of SIS faced direct opposition from some Regional Commissioners as they proceeded with the mobilisation of the Home Defence Scheme. SIS Regional Officers were nominally responsible to the Regional Civil Commissioners and were supposed to consult them before recruiting their civilian guerrilla army, but objections came from the most senior level in the War Cabinet. Grand wrote on 14 June:

The formation of an underground army was obviously important, both for the purpose of obtaining information for our own forces and later for carrying out resistance projects of all sorts. I therefore asked permission in principle and for facilities to contact the Regional Commissioners. This was refused by the Chief Commissioner [Neville Chamberlain] on the grounds that the distribution of arms and explosives would be dangerous. The danger of invasion, however, seemed to me so great that I appealed to the P.M. (as Minister of Defence) and he gave permission to go ahead.[15]

Individual Regional Commissioners did complain. On 21 June 1940 William Spens, the Commissioner for East Anglia, expressed concern to General Ironside over the people 'staying put' in case of an invasion. He had it on his conscience that 'we were arranging sabotage behind the lines if the Germans succeeded in landing.'[16] As the War Cabinet had only agreed to create the Auxiliary Units on 17 June and initial recruiting in East Anglia did not begin until the very end of June, Spens must, therefore, be referring to a contact with an SIS Regional Officer from Section D. Major Peter Wilkinson had a similarly awkward meeting with Spens when the latter threatened to arrest any member of the Auxiliary Units acting 'illegally', whether before or after German occupation.[17] The whole matter remained of concern to Spens, who returned to the subject in 1941 when he raised with General Alan Brooke (Viscount Alanbrooke) the 'undesirability of non-combatants joining in the shooting'.[18]

Such concerns extended to the then Commander in Chief, Home Forces (General Ironside, Plate 7) and the Secretary of War, Anthony Eden. Eden wrote a memorandum to the War Cabinet on 8 July 1940:

It is the view of the Commander-in-Chief, Home Forces, with which I am in agreement, that actual fighting should be restricted to the military and Local Defence Volunteers, and that no civilian who is not a member of these forces should be authorised to use lethal weapons. Only if this principle is accepted would it be possible to ensure control of military activities by the military authorities.

I therefore ask the War Cabinet to decide that active defence plans are to be based solely on the military and Local Defence Volunteers; that no civilian who is not a member of these forces should be authorised to use lethal weapons; and that the organisation of the defence of factories, etc., described in Rule 6 should be carried out by the enrolment of personnel concerned in the Local Defence Volunteers.[19]

This statement was, not least, a fierce rebuttal of the support that General Ismay and Colonel Hollis of the Chiefs of Staff Committee had expressed for an unofficial proposal of 19 June from Captain Davies of MIR to create a new civilian resistance organisation. Davies was not, apparently, aware that such an organisation was already being mobilised by Section D of SIS (see pp. 53–4).

In the Cabinet meeting, Churchill supported Ironside and Eden in their objections to civilian warfare, despite, if Grand is to be believed, Churchill already having recently confirmed approval in mid-June to recruit civilian saboteurs for the HDS of Section D. Churchill later sought to back-track on this official stance by claiming (23 August) that his previous statements in the War Cabinet had not meant to prevent civilians from taking up arms or to punish them for doing so as 'the citizen retained his natural right to fight in defence of his family and his home. This might well result in civilians joining in the fight in support of the military'.[20] Meanwhile, the role of the HDS was refined over the course of June/ July 1940 to make clear that it was not to become involved in fighting during the anti-invasion campaign and thereby compete with the plans of the War Office. Instead it would operate after enemy occupation; in any case, SIS might have considered themselves beyond the scope of the July stricture. The whole basis of their existence was that their work could, if necessary, be disowned by government. Such debates were, however, to have a fundamental impact on the organisation of the Operational Patrols of the Auxiliary Units as more than just a nominal part of the Home Guard.

One particular aspect of warfare that appears particularly disturbing today in the 21st century but which did not raise so much concern in the 1930s and 1940s, was the role of children in combat. Teenagers could be found fighting in the guerrilla organisations of many countries. During the Spanish Civil War George Orwell reported that the POUM militia contained children as young as 11. He complained about their stamina as much as anything else:

> At the beginning it was almost impossible to keep our position properly guarded at night. The wretched children of my section could only be roused by dragging them out of their dug-outs feet foremost, and as soon as your back was turned they left their posts and slipped into shelter; or they would even, in spite of the frightful cold, lean up against the wall of the trench and fall fast asleep.[21]

In the Second World War, military service for some teenagers was simply a matter of survival. Many members of the Jewish youth movement *Hashomer Hatzair* fought in the Warsaw Ghetto Uprising of 1943. Young boys similarly served with the partisans of the Soviet Union, Poland and Yugoslavia. In Germany, there was a Hitler Youth Panzer Division and boys as young as 12 were eventually drafted into military service. In Britain, Boy Scouts regularly served as non-combatant ARP or Home Guard messengers, but in 1942 the age of enlistment into the Home Guard was lowered to 16 years. In the context of the present study there are instances of boys and girls as young as 14 being used behind enemy lines as couriers by SIS and the Auxiliary Units. Perhaps most disturbing of all, 14-year-old Worcester Grammar School boys were reportedly being trained in guerrilla warfare, including tactics that approach the idea of suicide bombing (see Chapter Eleven). Guerrilla warfare and 'resistance' were indeed the most brutal and uncompromising form of warfare.

Chapter Two

Ungentlemanly Ideas:
the Fourth Arm

Everything you do [Lawrence Grand] is going to be disliked by a lot of
people in Whitehall – some in this building. The more you succeed, the
more they will dislike you and what you are trying to do.[1]

Admiral Hugh Sinclair, Chief of the SIS, 1938

If society was divided as to the propriety of civilian guerrilla warfare, this did not
stop the Secret Intelligence Service (SIS) and the War Office from exploring
the options. The present chapter explores the creation of the 'sabotage service'
(Section D) of SIS and the War Office research section, MIR.

Secret Intelligence Service: Section D

The Fourth Arm was a term adopted by Lawrence Grand (Plate 3 and Appendix 2)
in 1940 to describe an organised programme of sabotage and subversion under
independent direction away from the three regular armed services – army, navy
and air force.[2] This inspired the Minister of Economic Warfare, Hugh Dalton,
who went on to write a paper 'The Fourth Arm', explaining his vision for the new
Special Operations Executive (SOE) as an independent service; it became one of
the most famous innovations of the Second World War.[3] The concept of a new
and distinct arm of warfare is important in signifying how far the idea of irregular
combat had come since a brief discussion within the SIS in 1937.

In 1937 Claude Dansey (Plate 2 and Appendix 2), thought by some to be the
best intelligence officer of his era – and by others to be the most evil man they
had ever met – was running the SIS Z Organisation (a shadow intelligence network designed to provide a backup for normal SIS operations in case the latter
were compromised by an enemy).[4] He suggested to the then Chief of the Secret
Intelligence Service (CSS), Admiral Hugh Sinclair, that SIS should form a small
unit for the study of sabotage materials so as to be ready for what was already seen
to be the likelihood of war. The intention was that SIS would direct suitable
sabotage agents as and when required, but that these would be distinct from their
intelligence-gathering networks (the traditional priority for SIS). The saboteurs
would be, according to Dansey, 'agents we have employed from time to time
[who] were more fitted for this kind of action than they were for obtaining
information'. Sinclair was attracted to the idea but, to Dansey's horror, then
broadened its scope far beyond what he had envisaged as a series of *ad hoc*
arrangements.

In April 1938, Sinclair seconded 40-year-old Major Lawrence Grand of the Royal Engineers to SIS in order to follow up Dansey's suggestion and to explore the potential for sabotage against Nazi Germany. It was a radical departure for SIS. They were preparing to go on the offensive by extending out of their traditional remit of the quiet gathering of intelligence into the noisier world of guerrilla warfare. Formerly of the Royal Military Academy Woolwich and Imperial Chemicals War Research department, Grand's main existing claim to fame, or infamy, was that whilst on the North-West Frontier he had doctored ammunition that he knew would be stolen by the Pathans so that their rifles would blow up in their faces. His fellow officers regarded this as ungentlemanly behaviour, but it brought him to the attention of the Chief of the Secret Intelligence Service, Admiral Sinclair and his then deputy, Stewart Menzies (Plate 1).

Grand's first question to Sinclair, was 'Is anything banned?' to which Sinclair replied: 'Nothing at all'. Grand later claimed that Sinclair also made it clear that the task would not be popular: 'Don't have any illusions. Everything you do is going to be disliked by a lot of people in Whitehall – some in this building. The more you succeed, the more they will dislike you and what you are trying to do.' In what became almost a mantra for Grand, Sinclair added 'There are a lot of jealous people about so don't tell anyone more than you have to'.[5] Sinclair was dead by the time Grand wrote his account of this meeting and so it is not possible to say whether this was a very perceptive prophesy of what became a poisoned chalice, or merely Grand providing a historical justification for subsequent events. Nonetheless, it accurately summarises the situation as it developed from 1938–40 and Sinclair may well have had Dansey in mind when giving the warning.

Grand was originally appointed for only two months and had no staff, so his priority was to write a report showing the possibilities of a new type of warfare that was viewed at the time with enormous suspicion and distaste.[6] Grand's report was approved and in June 1938 he became Head of the new Section IX, *aka* Section D, *aka* the 'Sabotage Service', *aka* the 'Statistical Research Department of the War Office' (henceforth referred to as Section D), reporting directly to the Chief of SIS. The twin aims of the new Section D were:

1. Undertake sabotage and create anti-German political unrest in neutral and occupied countries.
2. Provide lines of communication from neutral countries into enemy countries for the purpose of introduction of propaganda. The latter might be partly produced by Section D or from other departments.

It should be immediately obvious that this was work with which HM Government, in a time of peace, might not wish to be officially associated and would therefore pass to an organisation that did not officially exist until 1994! Dansey visited Grand and was annoyed to find that the brief of the Section had been extended by Sinclair, although he blamed Grand personally for the change.

> I immediately realized that, far from confining his activities and thoughts to the original purpose, he had got tied up with propaganda interests and

'whispers' and such like ideas, which he was pleased to term 'The 4th Arm' – an unfortunate phrase which has lived, although Major Grand has disappeared.[7]

The task of Section D at this stage was merely to explore the *potential* for undertaking sabotage and propaganda in enemy and neutral countries in the expectation of war against the Nazis. They were 'To investigate every possibility of attacking potential enemies by means other than the operations of military forces'.[8] Their 'charter', such as it was, therefore excluded the traditional role of SIS in collecting intelligence.

There were originally only a small number of full-time staff in Section D. Grand's first two appointments were significant: Commander Langley was an explosives expert (inventor of the time pencil) who was to command the research and supply base at Aston House, Stevenage (later known, under SOE, as Station XII); Edward 'Dead-eye Dick' Schröter was a civilian expert in telecommunications recruited from Philips. He built wireless sets for the first insertion of agents into occupied Norway and France and, after inventing a duplex transceiver, he would go on to oversee the development of clandestine wireless sets for SOE.[9]

Other men and women were recruited to Section D on a 'Territorial' basis to be trained in peacetime and then co-opted as full-time intelligence officers in time of war (when they would be given an army commission). Such recruits included a number of important industrialists who could give specialist advice and assistance, including the Director of Royal Dutch Shell, Viscount Bearsted (Plate 4 and Appendix 2). By September 1939 Section D had expanded into a self-sufficient department of SIS, where staffing levels were rivalling the rest of SIS put together and which excited equally large amounts of suspicion and even enmity.[10] Most of what has been written about the work of Section D has focussed on their plans for foreign sabotage because this later became the basis of the organisation and work of SOE. Grand used this experience in what became known as the 'D Scheme', to devise a novel plan for a network of civilian stay-behind cells in Britain, to be activated prior to any threat of invasion, known as the 'Regional D Scheme' or the 'Home Defence Scheme' (HDS). The operatives were to be civilian and their work outside the normal conventions of war. The organisation was to be unavowable by any British government and was given the highest possible levels of security, despite some well-publicised (at least within government and the War Office) disasters. Much of this secrecy survives to this day.

Section D was very much under Grand's personal direction but he was not a natural organiser. He was more of a free thinker, not something that sat easily within the corridors of power in either the War Office or SIS HQ at Broadway in central London. Kim Philby, one-time Section D officer, described him thus: 'his mind was certainly not clipped. It ranged free and handsome over the whole field of his awesome responsibilities, never shrinking from an idea, however big or wild'.[11] Such men tend to inspire and infuriate in equal measure. They would undoubtedly have created a nightmare for pre-war senior civil servants and the government establishment. Eventually Section D was divided into a number of more formal sections, including the central organising sections of planning, research, supply, communications and geographical sections for each country in which D operated. Each section was indicated by initials as D/M, D/Q etc., although many cannot now be identified. The organisation remained opaque, deliberately designed to compartmentalise projects and confuse outsiders – including both the head of SIS and government scrutinisers! The code for the Home Defence Scheme (HDS) has been identified as Project D/Y, which may simply refer to one of these internal sections, but given the sensitivity of the operation, 'Y' might also indicate a top-level link to the HQ of SIS, which had its own distinct plans for resistance.[12] In pre-war SIS, the code 'Y' was used to identify staff at headquarters.

The whole concept of a section to directly organise and undertake disruption and sabotage caused great unease within SIS and the Foreign Office to which Section D reported. The task was fundamentally at odds with the primary role of SIS in quietly collecting and assessing intelligence. Bickham Sweet-Escott, an officer in Section D and later SOE, put it thus:

> The man who is interested in obtaining intelligence must have peace and quiet, and the agents he employs must never, if possible, be found out. But the man who has to carry out operations will produce loud noises if he is successful, and it is only too likely that some of the men he uses will not escape.[13]

The grim reality of this is seen in the casualty figures for SOE operations: of the 393 officers sent into France, 119 were killed or arrested. Such concerns were even shared within Section D. Philby claimed that long-time SIS officer Major Monty Chidson believed that the attempts to foment resistance groups in Europe would lead to anarchy.[14]

The running of domestic agents in Britain would have been particularly sensitive following disputes with MI5 and Special Branch in the late 1920s to 1931 over the operation of the SIS 'Casuals' within the UK. At one point their chief agent, Maxwell Knight, was placed under Special Branch surveillance and was quietly told that the latter would make his life, and that of his agents, a complete misery unless he stopped operations![15] This network was finally transferred to MI5 as M Section in October 1931.[16] Thereafter, SIS theoretically had no responsibility for domestic operations within three miles of British territory. The justification for the creation of the two wartime SIS resistance organisations, HDS and Section VII, was that they were designed to operate after the British government and army had ceased to have any control in the UK, which would then have the status of an occupied country. It is no coincidence that one of the strongest supporters of Section D in 1940 was Desmond Morton, at the time Churchill's personal assistant and intelligence advisor, but formerly the head of the SIS 'Casuals' in the late 1920s.

The military establishment was particularly suspicious about the activities of Section D, based as it was on the very unmilitary principle of warfare undertaken by civilians. It was rather too close for comfort to the tactics recently used against them by the IRA and now being practised in Palestine by the maverick Orde Wingate (arousing protests from all sides). It seemed to them that Britain was planning to unleash its own brand of international terrorism before any war was declared. One of the early detractors was the then Director of Military Intelligence, General Pownall. In Pownall's opinion, Grand was 'gifted, enthusiastic and persuasive, but I do not regard him as being well-balanced or reliable'.[17] In 1940 Pownall was Inspector General of the Home Guard and was similarly opposed to the efforts of Tom Wintringham to promote Home Guard guerrilla activity. The view of the establishment may be summarised in the conclusion by Lord Hankey in his March 1940 report on SIS. 'At first sight the natural instinct of any humane person is to recoil from this undesirable business as something he would rather know nothing about'.[18] Even organisations in the same sphere of work as Section D could sometimes be shocked by their ruthlessness. Of its operations in the Balkans and Middle East during 1939/40 the Deputy Director of Military Intelligence, Brigadier Shearer, commented that Section D had 'no scruples, few morals and was without shame'. He went on ruefully 'It was therefore an ideal tool in the hands of the C-in-C [Commander-in-Chief, Middle East].'[19]

In the rarefied atmosphere of the Section D research base at Aston House, Commander Langley also recognised unease within official circles.

> And so we did our utmost to maintain our secret cover. The people who received our weapons knew neither where they came from nor who had made them. None of the Defence Ministries knew of our existence; with the exception of my chief [Grand], the only high-ups in London who were aware of our activities were the Chief of the SIS and a couple of Cabinet ministers. Even so rumours must have started to circulate. A Cabinet minister might ask himself what business the Secret Service had in running some sort of secret war. The SIS were supposed to concentrate on getting useful information, not be mixed up with a lot of piratical ruffians who might well blow up something which would sully the allied name.[20]

The history of Section D, written by SOE in 1941, also concluded with some sympathy and feeling (being then under similar pressures from the War Office and SIS):

> D Section was not only unwelcome, but considered unnecessary by all the older established Government agencies. Therefore, in order to prove its own worth the Section was forced to produce results at the expense of sound organisation. It was not sufficiently firmly established to allow time to form a solid system in the field as the necessary preliminary to the achievements of result.[21]

Although written with particular regard to operations in the Balkans, the statement applies equally to the efforts of Section D to create a British resistance movement via the HDS. Unfortunately, Grand became a liability in winning widespread acceptance of his revolutionary and unpalatable ideas. He was not a professional intelligence agent and did not fit easily within the SIS establishment; he was a visionary who inspired great loyalty amongst his staff but who could be carried away by his own enthusiasm, prone to rashness and theatrics. He made too many dangerous enemies across the government and military – notably Campbell Stewart (who was in charge of the propaganda unit known as Electra House and saw Grand as a direct competitor) and the peevish politician Hugh Dalton who schemed to make himself head of the new SOE and referred to Grand as 'King Bomba'.[22] Gladwyn Jebb, soon to be Chief Executive Officer of SOE, but then the Private Secretary to Sir Alexander Cadogan, Permanent Under-Secretary at the Foreign Office, wrote to Cadogan on 13 June that Section D was 'in many respects a laughing stock' and 'to pit such a man against the German General staff and the German Military Intelligence Service is like arranging an attack on a Panzer division by an actor mounted on a donkey'.

Jebb was feeling the strain of his existing liaison role between the Foreign Office and Section D and did not relish the suggestion that he should now act as a Coordinator of Section D operations, vetting their projects in neutral countries and effectively acting as Grand's supervisor. Ironically given his subsequent role with SOE, he said one reason for not accepting the post was that it would include responsibility for semi-military schemes, for which he did not have the temperament or training.[23] Jebb's post-war conclusion was somewhat more charitable and suggests his earlier opinion may have been based on Foreign Office frustration with dealing with the notoriously ultra-secretive Grand. He now said that the 'great criticism of the old D Organisation had been that nobody knew what it was up to and that none of those departments which should have been consulted was consulted'.[24] In April 1940 there was an attempt to bring Grand under control by introducing a better system of section management 'to relieve Grand of the burden of departmental detail', but it clearly did not work and in July an 'advisor' was appointed to improve liaison with the rest of SIS.[25] This also proved unsuccessful.

Lord Hankey, Minister without Portfolio in Chamberlain's cabinet and a key security advisor, in 1940 launched a special investigation into the operations of Section D as part of his wider review of SIS. Opinions were mixed and largely focused on the personal reputation of Grand. Desmond Morton, then a senior civil servant at the Ministry of Economic Warfare and soon to become personal security advisor to Churchill, was more charitable than most. With careful wording Morton explained in his evidence to Hankey in January that the sabotage plans of Grand abroad 'were put into effect by agreement with the Ministry, the Service departments and the Foreign Office', thus countering the claims that Grand was a complete maverick. The evidence continued: 'This system, in Mr Morton's opinion, worked well and he had no complaints to make, though the dynamic personality of Major Grand was in some respects a difficulty.'[26] The Press Attaché in Belgrade, S.L. Childs, concluded a glowing appreciation of the work of Section D in Hungary by saying:

> As for XXXX [Grand] himself I think his qualities more than outweigh his defects and that he has been over-criticised by people in secure positions.

He has perhaps too great a sense of his own cleverness and should be told not to gird at the powers that be but I think he is already more cautious and as I say I know of no one who could have taken his place and done what he has done. He has broken some eggs but the omelettes were produced.[27]

As well as preparing to undertake sabotage abroad and making links with foreign opposition groups, Section D was also distributing propaganda, and it was perhaps this that caused the greatest tension with other departments. In February Professor Edward Carr, Head of Foreign Publicity at the Ministry of Information, pointed out to Jebb for forwarding to the Hankey Inquiry:

The principal function of this organisation [D] is entirely unconnected with propaganda and the association of propaganda with its other work seems wholly undesirable. Moreover the fact that this organisation is engaged on other important work of which this Ministry is quite rightly kept in ignorance, makes it particularly easy to conceal from the Ministry things which we ought to know.[28]

Carr was accusing Section D of carrying out work without consulting the Ministry of Information and not providing frank information. Nonetheless, the Ministry was one of Section D's main customers and on the whole seemed pleased with their performance. In Turkey, the MOI acknowledged that they could do little to counter the German 'whispering campaign' without the covert mechanism provided by Section D.[29]

Gladwyn Jebb, Private Secretary to the Permanent Under-Secretary of State at the Foreign Office (the formal link between SIS and the Foreign Office), had the difficult task of acting as the conduit between the evasive Grand and the Treasury, providing official authorisation from the Foreign Office to pay for Section D's operations. He also criticised Section D's role in propaganda warfare, believing that it was over-stretching the section and would jeopardise the security of the rest of D's work. He therefore sought Hankey's support in removing all responsibility for propaganda from Grand and placing it in a separate section of SIS.[30] In the end, Hankey recommended that the Ministry of Economic Warfare should be responsible for producing the actual propaganda material, whilst Section D would be responsible for getting it into enemy countries and distributing it, but this proposed division of labour was only partly successful. Jebb's task as a buffer between the secret world of Section D and the ordered world of the rest of government inevitably caused infuriation with Grand and had far-reaching consequences when Jebb eventually became Chief Executive of SOE.

An example of the task faced by Jebb and the inventiveness of Grand occurred in March 1940. Grand asked for a cheque for £50,000 to relocate fifty-four Danube river pilots and their families so as to deny their services to the Germans and bring the Danube river trade to a halt. Not surprisingly the Treasury were unwilling to pay without asking for further details. After Grand had briefed Lord Hankey, there was a private meeting between the Prime Minister (Chamberlain), Lord Hankey and the Foreign Secretary (Halifax), and as a result, on 9 March Hankey reported that 'we had a slight feeling that the sum involved was rather large' but supported the payment. Despite this high-level decision, on 12 March the Treasury still complained about the 'rather vague' information they had been given. Problems over this scheme and others rumbled on. In June there was a suggestion that Jebb was blocking payments agreed between Grand and the Ministry of Information over the 'whispering campaign' conducted by Section D on behalf of the Ministry.

Grand's mind was wide-ranging, coming up with ideas that were beyond his remit and no doubt irritating to his colleagues. On 6 July 1940 he was writing to Desmond Morton suggesting the establishment of a fake 'Panama Corporation' to buy luxury goods for importation into the UK (to demonstrate economic value of alliance with Britain, free UK production for the war effort and provide a profit for the Treasury). He also proposed 'Detection Lines' to provide outer perimeter defences around key points to deter fifth column surprise attacks.[31] In June 1940 he again stepped on the toes of GHQ Home Forces by suggesting a reorganisation of UK defence into small all-arms 'Brigade group' areas. At the same time he proposed a new 'Ministry of Progress' to improve efficiency of the implementation of government decisions.[32] There were few sections of government that he had not antagonised.

Working until 1940 with small resources, in an atmosphere of great suspicion and a rising sense of urgency as Europe drifted towards world war, Grand felt under extreme pressure: 'Examining such an enormous task one felt as if one had been told to move the pyramids'.[33] To have been able to force an acceptance of this form of irregular warfare by 1940 was in itself a major triumph, especially in the face of such intense personal animosity. The conflict also had a major impact on the nature of the development of SOE and other special forces. William Mackenzie, the official SOE historian appointed after the war by the then Major-General Gubbins, concluded:

> D Section and all its works were a nuisance to the Foreign Office, the Secret Intelligence Service, and the War Office alike ... There were therefore many people who were anxious to make a case against D Section for not achieving what no one could have achieved in the conditions of the time ... on the whole there are few departments which did much better in 1939–40.[34]

Section D: from Theory to Practice

Following the Nazi occupation of the still-independent remainder of Czechoslovakia on 16 March 1939, Section D was able to persuade the SIS, Foreign Office and General Staff that it should extend its remit from theoretical planning into cautiously preparing specific operational activity in countries that Germany had occupied or might do so in the future.[35] With characteristic speed, Grand presented the 'D Scheme' on 20 March to the army in the shape of the CIGS (Lord Gort), DDMI (General Frederick Beaumont-Nesbitt) and DMO (General Henry Pownall). In view of the sensitivity of the proposals, another meeting was held on 23 March with the Foreign Secretary (Lord Halifax) and Colonial Secretary (Lord Cadogan), as well as the CIGS and Admiral Sinclair (CSS). The idea was to foment a European-wide revolt against the Nazis and to create centres of resistance in presently neutral countries liable to be over-run. The nervousness of government over this new form of irregular warfare was clear. Grand had not spared them details of the brutal methodology that would be employed under the D Scheme: 'Where possible they would endeavour to execute members of the Gestapo with as much show as possible, in order to produce in the minds of the local inhabitants that the guerrillas were more to be feared than the occupying secret police'.[36] It was said that this technique was learned from the IRA in 1920. This would also become part of the tactics taught to the Auxiliary Units in 1940 (see Chapter Seven). The government approved the scheme – but wanted to know as little as possible about it; they would certainly not want such an approach to be discussed in Parliament. Unavowable action was, after all, the *raison d'être* for the existence of SIS. Thus, Lord Halifax 'said that he agreed in principle with the scheme, which he now intended to forget'.[37] The Foreign Office, however, dithered considerably over this 'arms length' policy. Here was the conundrum for Grand. He had outlined his plans at the highest level of Government and the War Office but it was politic for them not to wish to know further details. When he did present time-limited plans for sabotage the Foreign Office had a habit of being unwilling to commit to a decision or changing their minds thereafter. Many of the accusations of Grand acting in a maverick or incompetent manner were therefore unfair – but politically useful. A frustrated Grand wrote, 'although our existence was accepted, our activities at times met with obstruction when official assistance was required or could at least have helped'.[38] Blame for some of the problems in the foreign operations of Section D must at least be shared with the government who repeatedly delayed or countermanded instructions as they got cold feet about this new form of warfare. This had a knock-on effect when schemes for UK operations were planned.

The numbers of staff in Section D began to grow rapidly and it became a semi-autonomous secret organisation within another secret organisation; by July 1940 Grand claimed to have 140 staff.[39] The arch-enemy of Section D, Claude Dansey, demanded instant results to prove the worth of the new body – or rather to fail enough for him to say to Sinclair 'I told you so'. He later wrote one of his famously caustic memos on the subject.

In the spring of 1939, Admiral Sinclair sent for me and said he was not entirely happy about the activities of his Section D. and he wished me to spend a day in the offices at St Ermyns finding out what was actually going on. Then Major Grand gave me an exposé of his activities. I was not impressed. There were many ideas, but it did not seem to me that practical possibilities had been examined ... I further said that the original idea had long been lost sight of. The number of appliances or aids to sabotage that I could be shown was very small.

I heard little more about this Organisation until I returned to England at the end of 1939, when it had grown beyond all knowledge, and, as far I could determine, nothing was ever accomplished.[40]

In November 1939 Dansey also declared the D Section to be 'mafia-like'.[41] At the time under discussion by Dansey (spring 1939), Section D had only just been authorised to commence operations and so the accusation is unfair. The subsequent contribution of the Section D research facility at Aston House in developing clandestine devices cannot be doubted. Dansey found Grand infuriating, believing that Grand should 'conform and co-operate' rather than 'galloping about the world at his own gait'.[42] It is no coincidence that Dansey disliked the new SOE (in much the same terms as he had attacked Grand) because its sabotage role interfered with the quiet gathering of intelligence.

With the utmost irony, Dansey also complained that Grand maintained secret finances, which meant that his work could not be properly monitored; exactly the same complaint was made about Dansey's operations in Europe. The most strident views on Dansey have come from Lord Dacre (Hugh Trevor Roper) who described him as 'an utter sh*t, corrupt, incompetent, but with a certain low cunning'. Edward Crankshaw, former intelligence officer in Moscow, described him as 'the sort of man who gives spying a bad name'.[43] Such exceptions aside, most of his contemporaries felt obliged to acknowledge Dansey's skills as a devious spymaster. His comments on Grand must, however, be judged in the knowledge that he was perfectly prepared to destroy anyone whose views differed from his own, and in the summer of 1940 the destruction of Lawrence Grand may well have been seen as being in the interests of the traditional intelligence-gathering role of SIS, and in the more considered plans for the British resistance being implemented by SIS HQ.

The new CSS from November 1939, Stewart Menzies (Plate 1 and Appendix 2), had to admit that Grand had become uncontrollable. Having taken the advice of the previous CSS (Admiral Sinclair), Grand was reluctant to elaborate on his organisation, even to his new boss.[44] This is as much an indictment of Menzies as it is of Grand. Menzies had allowed much of the day-to-day running of SIS, and especially its agent networks, to fall under the control of his *de facto* deputy, Claude Dansey – now officially Assistant Chief of the Secret Service (although nominally subordinate to Valentine Vivian, the Deputy Chief). Dansey was the *éminence grise* of Menzies; he regarded Menzies as his apprentice rather than his superior officer and increasingly controlled access to him.

As was common at the time, the intelligence staff of Section D tended to be drawn from men who had a private income from business and the law rather than coming from the services. They included Chester Beatty, an American-born mining tycoon, who provided unaccountable private funding to Section D and thereby added even more to government confusion as to the scale of Section D expenditure. Viscount Bearsted put his contacts within Royal Dutch Shell in Scandinavia at the disposal of Section D and instructed them to provide funding to the agents building spy networks in Sweden and Norway. In order to give SIS officers some official status and legal protection during wartime, in 1940 such men were given formal army rank, with a choice of appearing either on the General List or the new Intelligence Corps. Thus 41-year-old John Todd, wealthy stockbroker, future Auxiliary Units Intelligence Officer and likely SIS regional officer

(Plate 15 and Appendix 2), received his commission onto the General List in May 1940, keeping this badging throughout his Auxiliary Units service; only in October 1941 is he listed as being a member of the Intelligence Corps, reflecting his move from SIS to SOE. The attitude of SIS to both badging and rank was cavalier. Walter Samuel, 2nd Viscount Bearsted, had won a Military Cross in the First World War as a captain in the West Kent Yeomanry and was re-commissioned as a lieutenant in September 1939 on the 'Special List' of the Territorial Army Reserve. By March 1940 he was an Acting Colonel. Bearsted had been recruited to SIS in 1938 by his friend Stewart Menzies and then was co-opted to Section D in 1939, originally to organise possible work in China. He was involved in Section D's efforts to establish intelligence networks in Scandinavia and was also involved in the propaganda section, Section D/Q. In the summer of 1940 Bearsted was the officer charged with the task of transferring elements of the HDS to the Special Duties Branch of the Auxiliary Units (see Chapter Nine).

Section D was originally based at SIS HQ at 54 Broadway, under its cover of the 'Minimax Fire Extinguisher Company', an address known to London taxi drivers and German agents alike as the home of Britain's secret intelligence service. Section D soon outgrew the cramped accommodation and in April 1939 it moved its administration to the sixth floor of nearby 2 Caxton Street, linked to the St Ermins Hotel; further expansion meant it took over the fifth floor as well. With the outbreak of war imminent, Squadron Leader Rowe was sent out to look for countryside war stations. An out-of-London base was established in September 1939 under Major Chidson at the Frythe Hotel, Welwyn (later SOE Station IX), where short courses in sabotage were held. After a brief stay at Bletchley Park (where the cryptographers complained of the noise from testing explosives), from October 1939 a research and supply base was established under Commander Langley RN, close to The Frythe at Aston House, Stevenage (later SOE Station XII). The propaganda section established itself in The Old Rectory, Hertingfordbury, in mid-September under Leslie Sheridan. In July 1940 a short-lived training centre for foreign agents was created at Brickendonbury Hall (Hertfordshire) under Commander Peters RN. An emergency command centre for Grand and his staff was also established from May 1940 at an unnamed country house somewhere in the West Country.

The security blanket around the UK operations by SIS is all the more remarkable given the fact that information on other Section D activities had been leaked to both the Nazis and Soviets. Two members of Section D proved to be Soviet spies: Guy Burgess (from January 1939) and Kim Philby (from July 1940). Philby provides no information on UK activities in his autobiography.[45] Neither is there any mention of the SIS plans to organise British resistance in the collection of reports provided by other agents in SIS to Soviet intelligence.[46] There was a fear at the time that any intelligence gained by the Soviets would be passed to the Germans. The strict compartmentalisation of the HDS and the strictures of Sinclair appear to have worked. From the outbreak of war the effective counter-espionage operations of MI5 prevented the Nazis from updating their information. The Liddell Diary for 4 December 1944 refers to documents recovered from a German Intelligence conference in June 1942, at which the Abwehr assessment of the organisation of British Intelligence still relied heavily on the information extracted from SIS agents Best and Stevens, kidnapped by the Nazis in September 1939 at Venlo. Liddell's caustic comment on the fact that Dansey and Grand were both named in the Abwehr document was 'So much for the super underground organisation of Colonel Dansey on the one hand and Major Grand on the other.'[47] Both men had been included in Schellenberg's 1940 assessment of British intelligence. Nevertheless, there is no evidence that the Nazis became aware of plans for a British resistance movement until a curious incident in 1943 (see below, Chapter Eleven).

The Venlo Incident in September 1939 would undoubtedly have reinforced Grand's existing paranoia over security, even within his own organisation – and he was not alone in this. In his official review of SIS in 1940, Hankey was completely frustrated in his attempt to tie down the operations and finances of Section D. Grand had learnt well from his new master at SIS HQ, Claude Dansey. When General Marshall-Cornwall was appointed to review the poor relations between SOE and SIS in 1942 by spending six months in each organisation, he was frustrated that in his time in SOE he felt he had learned everything about the organisation, but during his time with Dansey he had learned absolutely nothing about SIS! Nonetheless, Marshall-Cornwall had to admire how Dansey kept everything compartmentalised, to the point that only Dansey 'knew anything about his agents, who remained very much his own'.[48] This then is the context for the contemporary, and subsequent, secrecy surrounding SIS operations in Britain.

Dansey was a machiavellian spymaster whose method of operation provides clues as to the workings of the HDS and their relation to the later Auxiliary Units. Although not mentioned directly in any document relating to the UK operations of SIS, his influence runs like a fine thread through the story. From the early 1930s, Dansey had run a totally unofficial network of agents in Europe known as 'Claude's private ventures'.[49] In 1936 he set up the Z Organisation, which in wartime was designed to take over from the normal SIS network based upon passport control officers which, it was assumed, would be quickly destroyed after war broke out. To aid the deception, Dansey and Sinclair concocted a story that the former had been dismissed in disgrace from the service for embezzlement, intended to lead to the assumption that the Z Organisation had also been wound up. Instead, Dansey was actually installed in a suite of offices on the eighth floor of Bush House, where he managed what was, in effect, a shadow SIS, and he maintained this top-secret office throughout the war. A parallel may be made with the later dismissal of Grand and official disbanding of Section D to obscure the presence of Section VII as a deep-cover organisation shielded by the existence of the vulnerable Special Duties Branch of the Auxiliary Units. Dansey also managed one of the most successful spy operations in the Second World War – the 'Lucy Network' in Switzerland, which consisted of a complex system of spy rings, each unknown to the other but together passing on convincing intelligence to Russia and acting as a conduit to and from the head of German intelligence,

Admiral Canaris.[50] Again, a comparison may be made with the complex layering of intelligence organisations that would emerge to operate in Britain following invasion.

The War Office: MIR

In December 1938 the War Office established a working group, GS(R), under Lieutenant Colonel Jo Holland (Plate 5 and Appendix 2), a near contemporary of Grand and also from the Royal Engineers, to research more military-based irregular warfare than the civilian, agent-led, work being simultaneously developed by Section D.[51] Confusion over nomenclature appears to have been a prerequisite of intelligence organisations of this period. GS(R) reported to the Deputy Chief of the Imperial General Staff but also became known as D/M Branch as it was housed with, and part-funded by, Section D of SIS (see below). D/M was given a more formal establishment from April 1939, was chartered as MI1(R) in June, then became known as D/MIR and finally simply as MIR, under the Directorate of Military Intelligence (DMI). By October 1940 the establishment was one lieutenant colonel, four majors, nine captains and six clerks.

Its wide mandate included general research and preparation of projects involving the employment of special or irregular forces to assist normal operations, directly or indirectly; technical research and production of appliances was required for such projects. It was also responsible for the implementation of such projects as were agreed by DMI and where such operations were not the responsibility of any other body, although this was a function of last resort. Apart from its technical section, it was seen essentially as a think-tank rather than a body that ran operations. Holland later complained that they had been drawn into an operational role, through the Independent Companies, because the creation of the structures needed to properly implement their initiatives lagged behind the urgent need for action in 1940. The Independent Companies were founded in April 1940 on the initiative of MIR. Each Independent Company consisted of 21 officers and 268 other ranks and was designed to operate as a self-contained unit, specialising in harassing enemy flanks and raiding operations. They were to provide a significant model for MIR's views on the development of guerrilla warfare in Britain. The organisation of the Independent Companies was only resolved when the Independent Companies and the new Commandos were eventually combined in October under HQ Combined Operations.[52]

Holland, an unsmiling visionary with a fiery temper, according to his secretary, Joan Bright Astley, was a more calculating organiser than Grand. He had experienced guerrilla warfare in Ireland and India and had contributed to an early paper by GS(R) on 'An Investigation of the Possibilities of Guerrilla Activities'. There were obvious points of common interest between MIR and Section D and SIS were keen to make sure they were kept informed. To exercise an element of control, initially SIS provided accommodation within the Section D offices in Caxton Street and they part-funded the work, which had some advantages to the War Office as it avoided the need to present public accounts for these activities to

Parliament. Thus GS(R) was given a designation within Section D, originally as D/M and later as D/MIR; its staff were also given SIS identifier codes. Initial relations were harmonious. Indeed, in March 1939 Grand and Holland wrote a joint paper on the possibilities of guerrilla action against Germany if the latter overran the oilfields of Eastern Europe.

Control of D/MIR was, however, a touchy matter. The War Office resented any suggestion that it might be subservient to the Foreign Office and firmly maintained that D/MIR reported to the Deputy Director of Military Intelligence rather than to SIS. This is clear in the Charter of June 1939.[53] The only mention of any link to, or work with, SIS in the MIR War Diary is the simple note that 'MIR funds are allocated by C'.[54] Nonetheless, Grand later maintained that he had been responsible for the creation of MIR and had directed its overall work, a claim which came from more than just the provision of funds and accommodation.[55] On 20 March 1939, Grand proposed his 'Scheme D' for Europe-wide sabotage and subversive operations. Scheme D was intended to encourage large-scale risings in occupied countries and also prepare centres of guerrilla warfare in countries that might be over-run in the future, and when presented to the War Office (in the form of the CIGS, DMO and DDMI) it won agreement in principle. In typical Grand fashion he proposed working towards a general uprising in German-occupied territory in three months' time; such optimism seriously damaged his credibility. At a follow-up meeting on 23 March with the Foreign Secretary, Colonial Secretary, Chief of the Imperial General Staff and the then Acting CSS (Menzies), Grand specifically asked for the attachment of Jo Holland to Scheme D, as well as for a number of other staff. In Grand's mind, this was the birth of D/M Branch, under Section D control.[56]

Bombastic exaggeration or not, Grand convinced some members of D/MIR of the accuracy of his version of events in regard to who had overall control of their organisation. In her autobiography, Joan Bright Astley, who had originally been recruited by Section D but was assigned to work for D/MIR, simply stated: 'We became part of Section D'.[57] Joan did actually undertake some tasks for Section D and was the emergency contact for the pre-war 1939 'Cruising Club' of Section D under Frank Carr, which used yachtsmen to surreptitiously survey coastal waters from Scandinavia into France, for possible landing sites.[58] The fact that Holland was the more senior officer (being promoted to Brevet Lieutenant Colonel in January 1938 as opposed to Grand's then rank of Major) would not necessarily dissuade Grand from this point of view.[59] Seniority within the intelligence services did not necessarily relate to military rank.

Perhaps as a means of reinforcing his authority, but certainly adding to the confusion, Holland was appointed Chairman of the Inter-Services Project Board of which Grand was also a member. Whatever the truth of Grand's claims, they added to the irritation of the War Office towards him. At the outbreak of war, Holland was able to physically break away from Section D and, promoted to substantive Lieutenant Colonel, he moved D/MIR to the War Office where it lost the D prefix to become MIR.[60] Whatever personal rivalries there may have been between Section D and MIR, they masked a much more fundamental difference in approach by Grand and Holland to the whole topic of guerrilla warfare. In his evidence to the Hankey report on SIS in March 1940, the Director of Military Intelligence explained:

> There was one side of SIS work which up till recently had given rise to particular difficulties and to a certain amount of friction. This was sabotage; and the friction was perhaps, to a certain extent, due to the dynamic personality of Major Grand. It had however now been arranged in principle that MIR, which consisted of ten officers, should devote itself primarily to plans and research and that actual sabotage in enemy countries should be undertaken by the SIS. If, however, there was a possibility of our own troops acting in conjunction with the local Government, then the actual work of sabotage should more properly be entrusted to MIR.[61]

This conclusion was accepted in the Hankey report: the division of responsibility was for MIR to organise sabotage in arenas where regular British forces were directly involved whilst Section D undertook operations in areas under enemy occupation or in neutral countries.[62] This distinction is of fundamental significance in the later development of the British resistance movement. The Operational Patrols and Special Duties Branch of the Auxiliary Units were designed to operate under the control of GHQ whilst there was still military resistance to an invader. If, however, Britain had been occupied, then responsibility for civilian intelligence and sabotage would pass back to SIS.

For a moment, think the unthinkable – although it was a scenario that was taken seriously in the summer of 1940. Ministers such as Halifax and Chamberlain argued for a negotiated peace until outmanoeuvred by Churchill in late May. If Germany had then won the air and sea battle for Britain Hitler expected Britain to surrender under the pressure of the peace lobby; to be able to make landings unopposed and then perhaps to establish an occupied and an unoccupied zone as in France. The regular troops would have been obliged to lay down their arms under such an agreement, and the Auxiliary Units of GHQ would have been included in this order. The very purpose of SIS was, however, to be able to carry out tasks that a government could disown and could therefore continue to provide a core of civilian-based intelligence gathering, and if necessary sabotage, to support a government in exile.

Joan Bright Astley, who witnessed the mutual bewilderment of the Section D spies and military men of MIR working alongside each other, summed it up thus:

> Grand's Section D deeds would be done by undercover men, spies and saboteurs, who, if caught, would be neither acknowledged nor defended by their government. Holland's MIR plans would be subject to proper strategic and tactical requirements and carried out by men in the uniform of the established Armed Services for whom the normal conventions of war would operate.[63]

Here is the essential difference between SIS operations and the work of the later Auxiliary Units. Holland put it thus:

> As regards the division between our work and what is known as the D Section of the SIS, Grand and I have always been in very close touch, and, broadly, the division which we have adopted is that wherever something has to be done by agents, it is for his organisation, and wherever something is semi-military in character or involves a military mission – perhaps of an irregular kind – the work is for us.[64]

In 1940, Holland seemed to win the debate over the use of civilians or military in guerrilla warfare and his vision ultimately saw success in the development of elite units such as the commandos and SAS. In August 1940 he was even proposing the development of helicopter-borne special forces.[65] Arguably, the targeted contribution of such military special forces far outweighed the result achieved by civilian resistance networks, especially when the massive reprisals against their activities are taken into consideration. Holland soon recruited Lieutenant Colonel Colin Gubbins (only a few months junior in rank to Holland) to the staff of MIR (Plate 11 and Appendix 2). His task, as approved by the CIGS on 13 April 1939, was to develop Holland's theory of guerrilla warfare in a military context. He had personal experience of partisan warfare as employed by the White Russians in 1919 and like Holland had served in Ireland against the IRA. His ideas soon crystallised into the Independent Companies.

Section D and MIR provided mutual inspiration during this period of joint working. Gubbins published two seminal pamphlets *The Art of Guerrilla Warfare* (written with Holland) and *The Partisan Leader's Handbook*; both were ready by June 1939. These, together with his subsequent success in creating the new commando units (Independent Companies) for the Norwegian campaign, were to establish his credentials to set up the new Auxiliary Units organisation. In August 1939, Holland also recruited Peter Fleming, the well-known author and adventurer, then a reserve officer in the Grenadier Guards, to research the potential of assisting and developing Chinese guerrilla warfare against the Japanese. Fleming would also later play a key role in pioneering the Auxiliary Units.

Along with Section D, MIR was supposed to be absorbed by the new Special Operations Executive over the summer of 1940 and on 16 October MIR was formally abolished. In a last act of cunning, the War Office had, however, already reallocated a number of its duties to MI1 and MO9 in order to avoid a wholesale loss of its functions and staff. Jo Holland, however, returned to the Royal Engineers and a more conventional army career.

Chapter Three

The Impact of Dunkirk: Rethinking the Options (May–June 1940)

we shall defend our island, whatever the cost may be. We shall fight on the beaches, we shall fight on the landing grounds, we shall fight in the fields and in the streets, we shall fight in the hills; we shall never surrender ...[1]

Winston S. Churchill, 4 June 1940

Planning for a new generation of irregular warfare had begun in 1938 with the establishment of Section D of SIS and MIR of the War Office. Nonetheless, until April 1940 and the successful invasion of Norway, the British defence planners (or indeed most people in the country) had not regarded invasion as a serious possibility. Aerial bombing had been seen as the major threat with invasion as 'an unlikely contingency', and as a consequence, there is no evidence of advance planning for UK guerrilla operations from either Section D or MIR.[2] Their focus was firmly abroad, primarily Scandinavia and the Balkans, but also gazing further afield into China and Asia.

This chapter looks at the impact that the shock of the fall of France had on plans for irregular warfare in Britain and the secret war against the 'fifth column'. It concludes with a discussion on the critical meeting of the Inter-Services Project Board (ISPB) held on 27 May that attempted to set out a strategy for the operations of Section D of SIS and MIR following any invasion. Few were aware that, as Chapter Eleven will show, more traditional elements within SIS had already quietly made their own preparations for enemy occupation.

In May 1940 Britain reached its lowest point in the European theatre of war. The Chiefs of Staff held a meeting on 7 May to discuss the new dangers but remained confident in the knowledge that the Low Countries and France still provided a secure buffer to the narrow Straits of Dover. The main threat from any possible invasion was seen as being on the east coast, but in just a few days Holland had been over-run and airborne assault was the new threat. The Local Defence Volunteers (LDV) were formed on 14 May by the new Prime Minister, Winston Churchill (Plate 6 and Appendix 2), to provide some form of response to the realisation that parachute landings could occur anywhere in the country; their role was initially not to engage the enemy but to report such landings to the authorities.

The speed with which France was next over-run shocked British and German generals alike. The campaign was supposed to take six months, but on 20 May the first Panzer units reached the English Channel and on 22 May the Chiefs of Staff recognised that invasion on the south coast had now become a very real threat. Their prognosis was pessimistic; a report to the War Cabinet on 25 May concluded 'should the enemy succeed in establishing a force, with its vehicles, firmly ashore – the army in the United Kingdom, which is very short of equipment, has not got the offensive power to drive it out'. They made it clear that if France fell and Britain was obliged to fight on alone, then it could only win with the full economic and financial support of the USA.[3] It is probably no coincidence that this was the day that Captain Peter Fleming (Plate 8 and Appendix 2) of MIR was instructed by the Directorate of Military Intelligence (DMI) to begin thinking of ways to use the LDV in guerrilla operations behind enemy lines. On 26 May the evacuation of the British Expeditionary Force (BEF) began from Dunkirk. Almost 340,000 men were rescued from the beaches from 27 May to 4 June but the army lost almost all its heavy equipment. On 4 June Churchill delivered his famous 'We shall fight on the beaches' speech. The Germans entered Paris on 14 June and France finally surrendered on 22 June; a further 144,000 British troops were evacuated from 15–25 June through other French ports. France was then divided into an occupied and an unoccupied zone. Britain was now alone. The USA looked on closely, unwilling to provide support until they were certain that Britain would stand and fight, rather than suing for peace.

It was in the first few days and weeks after Dunkirk that the danger of a successful invasion seemed greatest, with the British army in disarray and with little equipment. Britain was now defended by just eighty, obsolete, heavy tanks! The defence planners considered the possibility of both airborne and seaborne landings, and the potential for an invasion via Ireland. They also feared a collapse of morale due to aerial bombing and the consequences of political division. The Chiefs of Staff formally warned the War Cabinet on 19 June that a risk of invasion was imminent.

> Experience of the campaign in Flanders and France indicates that we can expect no period of respite before the Germans may begin a new phase of the war. We must, therefore, regard the threat of invasion as immediate.[4]

The fast-moving events of May/June 1940, which were focussed upon the dramatic evacuation from Dunkirk, provoked a wide range of emotions from steely resolution to wild panic. Future second-in-command of the Auxiliary Units, Major Peter Wilkinson, described the main reaction as a 'numbing incredulity'.[5] The widespread enthusiasm to join the LDV showed a widespread determination to resist by whatever means, but there were still those in government prepared to consider a peace settlement. This is the time that Lord Halifax and Neville Chamberlain led a concerted campaign to convince the War Cabinet that a negotiated peace was the only option. By 28 May it seemed as if the peace party had the upper hand, but Churchill outmanoeuvred Halifax by calling a meeting of the Outer Cabinet, where he had a better chance of swaying opinion. Here he delivered one of his most important speeches, passionately declaring 'If this long island story of ours is to end at last, let it end only when each one of us lies choking in his own blood upon the ground'. Having convinced the Outer Cabinet to agree to fight on whatever the cost, the Inner War Cabinet felt obliged to fall in line and Halifax's peace plan was defeated. At this point, the whole course of the war and the future of Europe seemed to be on a knife-edge. Churchill had won this crucial debate but, as will be seen, Halifax and Chamberlain both acted as brakes on the development of Britain's 'illegal' plans for resistance.

The Menace of the Fifth Column
The speed of the Nazi advance through the Low Countries and France was widely blamed on the collaboration of local fascist sympathisers who, directed by German agents, had provided intelligence to the German armed forces, committed acts of sabotage and subversion and then provided the core of a puppet government. As a consequence there were fears of a widespread fifth column movement in Britain that would sabotage defence efforts and deliver the country to the enemy. Indeed, the Chiefs of Staff saw this as a key element of Nazi invasion planning. It was 'a very dangerous and important part in any operation the enemy may undertake against this country'.[6] Fears were fuelled by scare stories of deliberate breaches of the blackout, flashing light signals to German bombers, crops cut to leave arrows pointing at military installations and other activities.

It was well known that the German intelligence services had been involved in economic espionage in Britain prior to the outbreak of war, but these agents had been withdrawn along with the German embassy staff in 1939. Subsequent agents were sent in 'blind' or to contacts that, unknown to the Abwehr, were either wireless operators that had been 'turned' or had never existed in the first place. As a consequence, the Germans were deprived of up-to-date intelligence and were unable to engage with the small groups of Nazi sympathisers in the country. Equally worrying was the fear of how far British intelligence, the military and government had been infiltrated by Soviet agents, with MI5 believing that, prior to April 1941, any information collected by idealistic communists could be passed straight to the Nazis.

The threat of fifth column activity had been greatly lessened by the effective infiltration of communist and pro-fascist groups by MI5, including their work as agent-provocateurs to draw any likely recruits out of the shadows. One of their agents was actually the person in charge of the secret headquarters of the British Union of Fascists (BUF)![7] They also had access to all of the discussions of the Central Committee of the Communist Party. Nonetheless, although their official bodies were neutralised, the recognition that there was indeed a significant body of potential pro-Nazi sympathisers remained a worry (a threat greater than even MI5 liked to admit in 1940). As well as the 8,700 members of the BUF, a great deal of argument was given over to the treatment of the 78,000 non-interned enemy aliens. There were also 20,000 members of the Communist Party of Great Britain (CPGB) to consider, with their newspaper, *The Daily Worker*, having a much wider circulation of 90,000. The confused attitude of the British

Communist Party to the war was replicated across Europe. It is arguable how far its members would have supported an active resistance in an occupied Britain during 1940. In France, their Communist Party retained an ambivalence towards the war until just before the invasion of Russia. Only then did it launch the National Front whose members soon gained a reputation as one of the best-organised and most aggressive of the various resistance groups operating in France. In Jersey, however, the communists under Norman le Brocq took a lead in resistance from the start of the occupation. Generally, however, in 1940/1 during the era of the Hitler-Stalin Non-Aggression Pact, the BUF and CPGB were seen as two edges of the same sword. There was also the spectre of renewed activity by the IRA. Given the wide range of potential threats, in early May the Chiefs of Staff Committee had wanted to ensure that people known to belong to subversive organisations could be controlled by the police; by the end of June some army commands were already compiling arrest lists which would become the origin of the assassination lists handed to the Auxiliary Units.[8]

The work of the MI5 agent-provocateurs, together with the later SIS and Special Duties Branch agents, was a vital part of the network of covert spying on the British population that kept a lid on the growth of any significant organisation of collaborators. It therefore needs to be considered as an integral part of the complex network of secret activities that helped thwart the invasion threat. It is no coincidence that the mechanism by which SIS continued its top-secret resistance network in Britain from August 1940 (Section VII) was as a partnership with the counter-espionage section of MI5. Similarly, as the invasion threat receded, the SDB of the Auxiliary Units took on a new internal security role to guard against loose talk in the run-up to D-Day.

Fortunately, despite the disaster of the fall of France, the Royal Navy was still intact and the technology of the time made large-scale amphibious landings difficult. The Germans were intending to tow the main invasion army across the channel in flat-bottomed barges, which would have proved a nightmare for the soldiers. Most importantly, perhaps, the German High Command were nervous of the prospect of invasion and Hitler was expecting that the British government would recognise their hopeless condition and seek terms of surrender, which would allow him to turn with minimum effort towards his main enemy – communist Russia. It is only with hindsight that we know that Hitler did not formally begin preparations for invasion until the issue of Directive 16 on 16 July (see Appendix One). At the time, intelligence on German plans was mixed and invasion seemed imminent. This then was the context for the feverish development during May–June 1940 of the plans for guerrilla warfare and resistance in Britain.

A New Consensus on Irregular Warfare
Given the poor state of Britain's defences in May/June, there was a growing consensus that some form of guerrilla organisation was needed to supplement the weak regular formations. The following chapters will examine in detail the mobilisation of the Home Defence Scheme by SIS in late May, the XII Corps

Observation Unit in early June, and Auxiliary Units in early July, as well as the already existing SIS Section VII intelligence organisation. Government acceptance of their need may have been encouraged by a range of similar proposals for irregular warfare that came to them from enthusiastic individuals and which clearly showed the popular mood towards this form of defence, even if on the boundaries of legality. Examples of this pressure towards irregular warfare came from Captain Walker, a Royal Marines officer, guerrilla leader Orde Wingate, Home Guard publicist Tom Wintringham and the unofficial 'Guerrilla Warfare Committee' of the House of Commons.

Captain Walker, Royal Marines, wrote a paper on the subject on 23 May and forwarded it to Lord Hankey, the government advisor on security matters, on 31 May.[9] Under the heading 'Preparations of the nation for total war within this country' he proposed that 'Every citizen of this Country must now be prepared to take an active part in fighting an invader ... There are many men and women who will be prepared to give their lives in order to deny success to the enemy; as were the people of Spain, Poland and Finland.' Ignoring the legal status of such combatants, he went on 'It is submitted that in all our villages and towns men and women must be organized and armed to deal with enemy mobile parties of motor-cyclists and tanks, or troops in lorries'. Significantly, Walker notes 'The organisation of our civilian population must be linked up with the military defence measures but, it is considered, should not be a Service organisation. There must be no unnecessary delays in organising, due to service routine or the necessity for Committee decisions.' Breaking ranks with War Office and DMI policy, he proposed a civilian Chief of Defence responsible only to the Prime Minister. One wonders who he had been talking to as he makes the point 'The Spaniard knew how to deal with individual tanks. We have many men with experience of the Spanish War'.[10] Is this a veiled reference to Tom Wintringham, whose profile was steadily rising at the time, with newspaper articles, lecture tours and the lobbying of Parliament? Walker went on to recommend that throughout the country there should be bands of 'do-or-die volunteers equipped with dynamite and petrol bombs ... These volunteers to be secretly enlisted and organised as speedily as possible'. Given that he was a serving officer and addressed his paper as being from Admiralty Arch, one wonders what his commanding officer thought of this departure from the normal chain of command and his suggesting non-military control of such forces – but both Grand and Wintringham would no doubt have been proud of him! Hankey's reply on 3 June was diplomatic and non-committal: 'The whole of this question has been taken in hand'. The Home Defence Scheme of SIS had, in fact, just mobilised.

After Dunkirk, Orde Wingate, later to achieve fame as founder of the Chindits in Burma, but then a captain in Anti-Aircraft Command, proposed a version of the 'Special Night Squads' that he had raised in Palestine. Ironside was dubious about the idea, but on 2 June suggested that Wingate might raise one of his 'Ironside' units of lightly-armoured mobile columns out of volunteers from his Anti-Aircraft Brigade. Wingate immediately raised 150 men and ten officers for training in guerrilla warfare. By now Wingate had demonstrated his famous knack of irritating his superior officers and his plans floundered. Lord Ismay concluded 'I wonder if there has ever been a man who went so far out of his way to be intolerable to the very people who wished to help him'.[11] Wingate persisted with his ideas for British Special Night Squads, but GHQ demanded to know 'full and exact details of the proposed establishment' and nothing came of it. He did give a lecture on guerrilla warfare at Tom Wintringham's Osterley Training School, where the meeting between fiercely fundamentalist Christian and communist must have been interesting. The likely paranoia of MI5 over this contact with Wintringham's suspected plans to raise a 'red army' can only have been increased when forty-three former members of Wingate's Special Night Squads in Palestine, members of the Jewish Haganah, were arrested for illegal possession of weapons which, it was feared, were intended for future use against the British establishment.[12]

Through his rising public profile in the media and his lobbying of both government and sympathetic military figures, Tom Wintringham (Plate 45 and Appendix 2) had a huge influence in the period following Dunkirk by creating a popular mood that demanded a more aggressive role for the LDV and its expansion into a 'people's army'. On 15 June the first of his rousing articles on civilian resistance was published in *Picture Post*. He outlined the principles of effective road blocks, destruction of petrol stocks, demolition of bridges, creation of village fortresses and how to successfully ambush tanks. At this stage, however, the term guerrilla had not entered his vocabulary (he did not use the term until the opening of the Osterley Home Guard Training School in mid-July). Instead, his focus was on encouraging mass action. For the government, although they took advantage of his practical advice and the positive mood that his articles engendered, he represented the dangerous possibility of a descent into anarchy. He announced 'I am trying to do what I advise everyone to do – get on with the job of defence against invasion, without waiting for official approval'.[13] On the next day he sent a 'Plan of Action' to the government via MP Tom Horabin, calling for Churchill to broadcast an appeal for a citizen army and to promise 100 million hand grenades within a fortnight together with 2 million rifles and 50,000 Thompson sub-machine guns from the USA as soon as possible.[14] Horabin was a radical liberal MP who had been a strong opponent of appeasement. Wintringham, in pragmatic mood, did suggest that Horabin, before circulating the Plan, might prefer to delete his suggestion that the King renounce the title of Emperor and that India should immediately be given its independence! What Wintringham did not know was that MIR had secretly begun to consider how to develop the role of the LDV in guerrilla warfare as early as 25 May, just eleven days after the LDV's formation.

On 2 July 1940 yet another body joined the debate. A group of MPs had formed the unofficial 'Guerrilla Warfare Committee' and produced a report written by the MP for Ormskirk, Commander Stephen King-Hall, RN. The committee wanted more emphasis on 'Totalitarian Guerrilla Warfare' and better coordination of irregular warfare. They looked at (a) raids on the continent, (b) subversive actions, and (c) sabotage. They proposed commando raiding forces up to division strength, but accepted that it might be possible at that time to form units of only 250 – 500 men (effectively what was then in place as the Independent Companies). They wanted an official Guerrilla Warfare Committee, which would include civilian representatives as well as the services, to propose and co-ordinate guerrilla warfare.[15] On 9 July Hankey wrote to King-Hall to congrat-ulate him on his document as being 'quite admirable' and reassured him that plans for a coordinator of such activity were in hand – a hint towards the creation of SOE.[16]

King-Hall was also the Chief Staff Officer to the new Defence Section of the Ministry of Aircraft Production under Admiral Sir Edward Evans. One of his tasks had been to circulate details of a very crude form of petrol bomb consisting of a petrol-filled bottle with a cotton wool wick around the neck (soaked in petrol from the contents of the bottle). He accompanied the report with the note 'This bomb has been described as fool-proof. The Factory Defence Section draws your attention to the fact that it is not B. Foolproof'.[17]

Unknown to the above enthusiasts (it is presumed), on 17 June the Cabinet had agreed to the formation of the Auxiliary Units – in effect a rather panic-stricken response by the War Office to the Section D Home Defence Scheme (HDS) incorporating the results of Fleming's research on the use of the LDV and General Thorne's creation of XII Corps Observation Unit (see below, Chapters Four and Five) as well as borrowing from the HDS. It did, however, take almost another month for the Auxiliary Units to actually mobilise. Meanwhile, if Britain had been invaded, however chaotic, the country would have been largely reliant on the HDS to provide the basis for a national guerrilla network.

Although preparations to counter invasion had begun immediately following the evacuation from Dunkirk, it was not until 25 June that General Ironside (Plate 7), Commander in Chief, Home Forces, formally presented to the Chiefs of Staff his plan for the Defence of Britain, known as Operational Instruction No. 3. The basic idea was for a 'coastal crust' of defences to delay the enemy advance, with a series of static lines behind the coast to provide a defence in depth and prevent free movement of the enemy. Taking advantage of the delays that such defences would cause, mobile columns, 'Leopard Brigades', would then be able to concentrate for a counter-attack. The coastal crust would only be manned by second-line troops and much of the stop-lines would be manned by the poorly-armed LDV. The counter-invasion plan therefore coldly relied on a huge level of sacrifice by 'expendable' manpower in order to exhaust the enemy before the front-line troops mounted their counter-attacks. The last line of defence was the GHQ line, protecting London and the industrial heartland, with the core of the field army ready behind it to mount the main counter-attack once the prin-cipal focus of the enemy attack became clear. Ironside was trying to make the best use of very limited resources, but his plan met with immediate and widespread dismay amongst the general staff, not least because the plan seemed to accept that a large percentage of southern and eastern England might fall, albeit temporarily, under enemy occupation. The concept of static defence lines also brought back uncomfortable memories of First World War trench warfare and the spectre of a long-drawn-out siege on British soil, leaving large slices of the country under much longer-term occupation, a possibility that was brought home to the Cabinet when they were obliged to consider the role of the British police under occupation. (The image of the British policeman giving directions to a German officer did, indeed, become the defining image of occupation on the Channel Islands.) On 26 June the Vice-Chiefs of Staff expressed considerable opposition to the 'coastal crust' concept with comments that the main resistance might only be offered when nearly half the country had been overrun. Indeed, they described the plan as suicidal.[18] In the background, Section D of SIS – despite all later criticism of their efforts – were distributing arms dumps and mobilising civilians nationwide to cause general mayhem across any occupied area (see Chapter Four); XII Corps in Kent and Sussex had already put in place its local plans for a military form of guerrilla warfare (see Chapter Five) and less dramatically, Section VII of SIS were quietly putting into place a scheme for long-term resistance and wireless intelligence (see Chapter Eleven). The Auxiliary Units, not yet ready to mobilise, were at this stage little more than a twinkle in the eye of GHQ (see Chapters Six and Seven).

ISPB Meeting, 27 May 1940

A crucial meeting of the Inter-Services Project Board (ISPB) was held on 27 May to discuss contingency plans for invasion. This not very effective advisory board had been created in early May 1940 to try to coordinate plans for Europe-wide sabotage but was subordinate to the Chiefs of Staff and therefore had little power in its own right. The Board had a floating membership, usually with representatives of the Air and Naval intelligence services, SIS (represented by Lawrence Grand) and MIR (represented by Jo Holland, who was also chairman). As the Nazis continued their steamroller advance through France, the ISPB meeting of 27 May had, for the first time, to consider the real possibility of invasion and the need to plan for irregular warfare within Britain. As a consequence, the meeting had a notably wider attendance than usual, including Captain Peter Fleming from MIR, who had returned from Norway on 6 May and was now researching ways of using the growing LDV as a guerrilla force behind enemy lines, and Captain John Dolphin, a Section D research engineer who had, on 22 May, proposed the idea of what became the Section D Home Defence Scheme to Lawrence Grand.[19]

Colonel Holland prepared a briefing paper prior to the meeting which opened with the surmise 'that we are entering a phase of "total war" and in consequence the civil population of all classes should be asked to make the same sacrifices as the fighting forces'. This comment was aimed particularly at populations on the continent with a view to organising sabotage in advance of further enemy occupation, but the scope was to expand dramatically at the meeting towards the organisation of guerrilla warfare within Britain.[20]

The discussions were led by the analysis of previous German invasions in the war and an identification of the need to disrupt lines of supply and a settled consolidation of the enemy forces:

When a part of the country had been overrun, and at a time when the strain on a loose line of communication must have been great, and the strain on operating personnel in advanced elements must have been greater, little was done either to deny the enemy essential supplies, or to ensure that the invader had no rest.[21]

In their first proposal, the ISPB applied the recommendation of the Hankey Report on division of responsibilities between SIS and MIR (March 1940) to the situation in Britain so that, in the event of invasion, guerrilla troops, as part of the army, would act in concert with the regular forces.

The regular defences require supplementing with guerrilla-type troops who will allow themselves to be overrun and who thereafter will be responsible for hitting the enemy in the comparatively soft spots behind zones of concentrated attack.[22]

These guerrilla troops would comprise the new army Independent Companies (referred to elsewhere in reports of the meeting as 'the MIRs') rather than representing any proposal for new underground guerrilla units. Five companies were currently serving in Norway under Colonel Gubbins and the remaining five were completing their training in Scotland. This element of the ISPB plan was therefore intended as a deployment of regular military units to undertake work behind enemy lines and the focus of MIR on Independent Companies continued into the early days of the Auxiliary Units.

This was not a discussion about creating a resistance movement in an area under firm control of the enemy (as we think of later Second World War resistance movements in occupied Europe). What was under discussion here was short-term military action on the flanks and rear of an enemy as part of the overall military strategy, but at the same time as considering military means of supporting the regular troops, the ISPB also concluded that SIS should simultaneously organise a specialised sabotage programme that preceded any occupation and supported the MIR units. 'The Secret Intelligence Service must be prepared similarly to organize and execute action of a technical sabotage kind requiring special equipment'.[23] This technical element was another reason for bringing Captain Dolphin to the meeting. He was an expert within Section D on sabotage methods, who had also provided counter-espionage advice to MI5 as to potential German sabotage targets in London. Although the meeting might have been thinking along the lines of a very targeted programme of specialist sabotage by Section D agents in support of regular troops, Grand instead interpreted this as an authority to mobilise a nationwide civilian guerrilla movement – the Home Defence Scheme (HDS) – on lines that he had already been planning abroad (see pp. 39–40). Indeed, at the time of the meeting, Section D officers were distributing secret arms dumps in France and trying (unsuccessfully) to get permission from the authorities for a sabotage programme in conjunction with the French secret service. Whether a bluff to establish a *fait accompli* or not, the SIS operations were said to be 'already partially organized'.[24] Grand said that Section D regional officers had already been dispatched to HQ Home Forces and to the Regional Commissioners in order to organise operational areas for the HDS. Whether the HDS was actually in existence or not, what is certain is that Grand began a large-scale mobilisation of the HDS before seeking formal approval and funding on 2 June.

Crucially, the meeting 'after further discussion' agreed that guerrilla activities in England should be controlled *on a military basis*. That this had to be discussed at all is a pointer to the tensions between the War Office and SIS. Here was an attempt to rein-in the expanding ambitions of Section D by a War Office worried that a civilian private army, acting outside their control, was being created by Lawrence Grand. Their fears would not have been eased by the proposals at the same time to expand the SIS Special Communications Units (SCUs) into what was later termed by the Director of Signals at the War Office as an SIS 'private army'.[25] The ISPB had, however, failed to consider that the Hankey Report had also established the principle that SIS would take control of actions in any occupied area where military forces had ceased to operate. Was Grand preparing for the possibility that no one else dared to voice – or at least commit to paper? The final point made by the ISPB meeting was important for what was to occur in the coming few weeks. The ISPB stopped just short of recommending the organisation of civilian armed resistance, but did state:

> The whole population, whether in formed or loose formations, or whether as individuals, must be instructed in the sort of contribution they can make to assist the services, and must be encouraged to make their contribution, should the need arise, with the same ruthlessness we may expect from the enemy, whether he is provoked or not.[26]

The encouragement of civilian subversion was already part of the role of Section D and so Grand could easily take this recommendation of ISPB as further support for his mobilisation of the Home Defence Scheme. Overall, there was plenty of leeway in the decisions to convince Grand that he had a free hand. If the War Office felt that they had finally brought Grand under control where SIS had failed, they were to be swiftly disabused.

The ISPB meeting also considered the need to develop communications to serve guerrilla operations and looked towards what became known as the BEETLE communication system, which began to be distributed in June 1940. The Minutes of the ISPB meeting note 'some form of coordination ... is neces-sary. Orders can be received by any wireless set owner. The issue of orders will almost certainly only be possible by the Military Command'.[27] The idea of BEETLE was that information and instructions could be broadcast from gov-ernment offices and army commands onto ordinary domestic wireless sets, using regional transmitters, thus allowing a simultaneous transmission of orders with-out having to go through normal signals channels, and avoided the problem of normal telephone communications being cut. Murphy wireless sets (Plate 34) became the standard issue to military commands, with instructions not to use them for any other purpose (there being an obvious temptation to use them for recreational purposes!). The system operated on specific long-band wavelengths to broadcast messages and could include coded operational instructions sent from Army Commands to local HQs. The first priority for deployment in 1940 was for the battalions based on the potential invasion beaches, but this was extended in July 1941 to anti-tank islands or other units not in a normal wireless group who were at risk of cuts to their normal communications, and included units of the Home Guard. The Special Duties Branch of the Auxiliary Units was only incorporated into the system in 1943.

At the ISPB meeting there appears to have been no consideration that the guerrilla units might need their own two-way wireless system beyond normal military systems. This was despite the existing use of wireless in SIS's Eire and Section VII networks (see Chapter Eleven) and the deployment of secret wireless sets in Norway by Section D in the previous month. SIS would also shortly install wireless sets in the hides of the XII Corps Observation Unit, but this was clearly an aspect of clandestine operations that SIS wished to keep close to its chest.

Although the focus of the ISPB meeting was on military action and sabotage it did also include a recognition of the need for obtaining intelligence and stated that 'Some form of "watcher" organisation linked with a command centre on the lines of ADGB control is required'. The Air Defence of Great Britain (ADGB) coordinated Anti-Aircraft units and Fighter Command.[28] It goes into no further details and was either being extremely circumspect, or ignorant, as regards the plans already underway in Section VII of SIS, although it is perhaps significant that the term 'watcher' service was already widely used in SIS. This discussion may, however, have set Grand's train of thought in motion for an expansion of his sabotage plans for the HDS that would eventually lead to the Special Duties Branch of the Auxiliary Units.

Chapter Four

Home Defence Scheme of Section D, SIS (May–July 1940)

At our most forlorn moment when our army was pouring back from Dunkirk through gates we could never have shut against an invading enemy, Colonel Grand conceived the plan of organising throughout Great Britain a closely-coordinated sabotage and intelligence network among the civilian population who would be left behind in any territories which the German armies might temporarily be able to occupy.[1]

Section D Closing Report, 27 August 1940

Part of the role of SIS was to prepare for the worst. Its chief, Stewart Menzies, had been obliged to present to the Chiefs of Staff Committee the worst-case scenario that Britain would be occupied and would then rely on the Commonwealth to maintain an economic blockade on Germany to wear it down, but that ultimately it would be the USA that would bring about the defeat of Hitler. If occupied, SIS did, however, need to maintain an intelligence-gathering and resistance network in Britain to prepare for that liberation. The plans of SIS were complex and operated at two levels. The deep-cover resistance organisation known as Section VII will be considered in Chapter Eleven. Although it proved controversial, the 'sabotage service' – Section D – of SIS also began to mobilise a shorter-term guerrilla and resistance organisation. When Britain was at its lowest ebb and most at risk from invasion it would have been the Home Defence Scheme (HDS) that mounted the initial stage of its last-ditch resistance. Mobilised after the ISPB meeting of May 1940, the HDS was short-lived, but had a major impact on the development of the later Auxiliary Units. It is poorly documented, and noticeable that, while the history of Section D by SOE in 1941 contains detailed staffing and structural information on foreign operations, there is no such information for the HDS. Many of its agents were still in place and details were too sensitive to commit to paper, even in an internal document.

Although traditionalists at SIS may have despaired of Grand at a personal level, the creation of the HDS did fit into known SIS methodology, in which systems could be both labyrinthine and ruthless. The most well-known example is Dansey's creation of the Z Organisation as a shadow spy network. Grand had followed the same basic principle when planning a resistance movement in

Norway, immediately after its invasion by the Nazis on 9 April 1940. Orders were given to Gerald Holdsworth of Section D to create two organisations:

1. Short-term sabotage before the Germans fully occupied the country.
2. Longer-term organisation to operate in occupied territory.

Holdsworth was told, as far as possible, to keep the two organisations separate so as not to compromise security. There was also the implication that the organisation responsible for immediate sabotage would be exposed and destroyed, but if so, this would not compromise the longer-term resistance body.[2] It should, therefore, be no surprise to find SIS mobilising on similar principles in Britain just over a month later. Here, Lawrence Grand's Home Defence Scheme (HDS) would provide a mechanism for short- and medium-term sabotage before the Nazis could properly establish themselves. At the same time, Section VII was being expanded, in the utmost secrecy, to act as a long-term resistance organisation which had minimal contact with Section D and the HDS (see Chapter Eleven). HDS was eventually offered up as a sacrifice to the War Office, but Section VII continued as a deep-cover organisation into at least 1943. By then, the Auxiliary Units had taken over the role of the HDS as the short-term guerrilla organisation.

The idea to extend the existing 'D Scheme' for a European resistance network into the 'Regional D Scheme' for a British resistance organisation came originally from a memo by Captain John Dolphin (D/XE) at the Section D research base at Aston House to Lawrence Grand on 22 May 1940. Entitled 'Pessimism', it argued that the previous disasters in the war had been caused by undue optimism. 'It would therefore appear wise to take the most pessimistic view about invasion of this country and prepare for successful invasion by the Germans, even though successful invasion may only be a very remote possibility'. Dolphin proposed firstly recruiting 'everybody's reliable friends plus their friends reliable friends thus forming a basically sound body of men to operate particularly in the event of a successful invasion'. He called for weapons dumps to be distributed for the sabotage of enemy aircraft, bridges, communications, petrol supplies. The dumps would also contain weapons suitable for use by the general public or for British troops that had been disarmed.[3] Grand seized enthusiastically on the idea and made it his own, then took immediate steps to put it into operation before having received official approval. This was variously known as the 'Regional D Scheme', 'D Organisation for Home Defence', 'Home Defence' or (the term used in this book) the 'Home Defence Scheme'. Having taken Dolphin to the ISPB meeting, presumably to outline the scheme, he declared that the ISPB had deemed it as being of 'immediate importance' and quickly mobilised it to become a *fait accompli*.[4]

Organisation
Plans for the distribution of incendiary weapons dumps were drawn up on 31 May and on 1 June Grand produced a briefing document for the thirty SIS Regional Officers who would operate the scheme.[5] The main contact for what was there

called the 'D Organisation for Home Defence' was to be Viscount Bearsted, using the standard SIS postal address of Room 055A, War Office. Bearsted had been Dolphin's senior officer when both were involved in Section D schemes in Scandinavia. Other HQ officers were Major the Honourable L. Montague and Captain W.E. Hope. Grand pointed out that, under current plans, the main opposition to invasion would be provided by the regular forces, and by the 'MIR Guerrilla section', a reference to the Independent Companies as discussed in the May ISPB meeting. The official contact of the Section D officers would be the regional civil commissioner who, it was said, had been asked to assist in any way, and the regional military commanders had also been sent written requests to provide facilities to the Section D officers. A car would be provided for each of the twelve regions; the contents would include a wireless and other specified contents which included a box of cigars or cigarettes and 'Plenty of chocolate'! In June 1940 SIS was beginning to install both hidden wireless sets and mobile wireless stations in its fleet of Packard saloons. SIS wireless engineers 'Spuggy' Newton, Bob Hornby and Wilf Lilburn, who carried out the work, had all been recruited by Brigadier Gambier-Parry (Head of SIS Communications) from his old firm of Philco, where they had worked on the design of two-way radios in cars; Lilburn had installed wireless in cars for the Glasgow police. Gubbins may have intended (but failed) to install the same system in the cars of the later SDB Intelligence Officers (see below, Chapter Nine). There is, however, no further mention of wireless being used by the HDS, only of runners having to pass through enemy lines.

The officers had to supply their own chauffeur – who had to be 'ready for any-thing' – and were issued with a copy of the Section D sabotage manual *Home Hints* (then being distributed to foreign resistance groups) and a revolver. Each regional officer would be given expenses, but the document makes clear that the only paid staff would be the chauffeurs, suggesting that the regional officers were still part of the unpaid 'territorial' network of officers with private incomes that Section D had been recruiting since before the war. Such officers were soon to be given regular army commissions to provide a legal authority for their activities.

In his inimitable way, Grand sought retroactive approval and funding for the scheme on 2 June. A further set of notes dated 4 June clearly identifies this as a work in progress, explaining some of the inconsistencies in the surviving docu-mentation.[6] Later in June Menzies had a meeting with the Foreign Secretary where it was noted 'D's great ideas. Doesn't seek advice before putting out schemes ... schemes not weighed sufficiently ... but C can't control him'.[7] It is tempting to suggest that the meeting was referring to the Home Defence Scheme. It must be presumed that Grand did, in the end, get his approval, but it proved to be the final nail in the coffin of his SIS career.

The plan was a natural extension of work that Bearsted and Dolphin had been involved with in Norway and France before the fall of those countries, where Section D distributed a number of weapons dumps and wireless sets, and tried to recruit a core of resistance workers. In a matter of just days, Grand laid the basis of a nationwide civilian guerrilla and resistance movement. Expecting imminent invasion, he first began distributing arms dumps over as wide an area as possible, hoping that they would seed future resistance. He also began to recruit the core of guerrilla cells who would deliver both short-term guerrilla action and, if necessary, longer-term resistance. Grand was a whirlwind of activity and it was the speed of the initiative as much as anything else that led to criticism. Speed of action did not necessarily go down well with the War Office and comparison may be made with similar complaints made by the War Office over the instant creation of the LDV (see above, p. 6). According to Mackenzie's official history of SOE, 'D Section with its usual energy speedily created a network of local representatives, operating in deepest secrecy'.[8] This new initiative provoked apoplexy in the War Office and is the context for the later opinion of Major Peter Wilkinson from the Auxiliary Units:

> As for Section D, one of Gubbins' early tasks had been to take over Grand's civilian stay-behind organisation, hastily and unofficially set up earlier and providing a source of embarrassment to all concerned.[9]

Not surprisingly, Grand presents an opposite view of events. He claimed he had War Office approval and, after the Chief Regional Commissioner (Neville Chamberlain) raised objections to this civilian army of *francs-tireurs*, Grand went directly to Churchill for permission to proceed.

> I therefore asked permission in principle and for facilities to contact the Regional Commissioners. This was refused by the Chief Commissioner on the grounds that the distribution of arms and explosives would be dangerous. The danger of invasion, however, seemed to me so great that I appealed to the P.M. (as M. of Defence) and he gave permission to go ahead.[10]

On 3 June, Menzies briefed the first meeting of the intermittent Secret Service Committee 'on the part which the SIS might play in the event of an invasion of Great Britain' but, not surprisingly, no further details were committed to writing.[11] If the Home Defence Scheme did prove to be a case of 'more haste, less speed' then it should be remembered that invasion was expected in a matter of days and that behind the scatter-gun efforts of distributing arms dumps almost randomly across the country there was also a more considered mobilisation of recruits. The history of Section D as compiled by SOE after Grand was dismissed to India (but clearly based on his papers) puts a different light on the matter than Wilkinson's account. The SOE report claims that the new Home Defence Scheme was specifically discussed at the ISPB meeting and a clear strategy agreed. In this version of events it was agreed thus:

> At a meeting of the Inter-Services Projects Board held on May 27th it was agreed that a force should be formed, to act in close co-operation with the military authorities, to deal with the enemy in the case of invasion or occupation of parts of England. This force was to be divided into two main sub-sections, – the MIRs who would wage guerrilla warfare, and selected D officers who would be attached for special duty to the twelve Regional Civil

Commissioners. Under this plan a D officer would work under the Regional Commissioner until the area passed under martial law, when he would serve under the military commander. Within smaller areas of the region he would organize a chain of individuals not liable to be called up for military service who would carry out acts of sabotage, and by judicial whispering he would encourage the general public unconsciously to train their minds to attacking the enemy by unarmed methods.[12]

Again, it should be stressed that the 'MIRs' referred to above were intended to be the Independent Companies, rather than any new guerrilla force. Quaintly using the term 'obstruction' to refer to sabotage, Grand's plan for the HDS was:

1. To make as many persons as possible in areas liable to invasion into conscious obstructionists.
2. To have a nucleus of trained persons who, in the event of invasion, will remain behind and direct further obstruction under the direction of the military where such acts could aid military operations.

Recruitment

The 'D officers', notionally attached to the twelve Regional Civil Commissioners for '*Special Duties*', would divide up the regions into sub areas and within these recruit a number of reliable and discrete individuals as 'Key Men'. Some of these were later to become Group Commanders of the Auxiliary Units, although they all kept their previous work a closely-guarded secret. The 'Key Men' would then recruit their own cell members. In an effort to retain the security of a resistance cell, Grand suggested that organisation might be via self-contained units of a family or of estate workers. Grand recorded the process of recruiting the HDS agents:

Recruiting went well. The qualifications were courage, intelligence, and discretion, and the bait was a certainty of execution if caught. The results were the finest body of men that have ever been collected. All classes and trades were represented, bankers and poachers, clergymen and burglars, farmers and lawyers, policemen and shopkeepers, every sort and kind of trade and interest, and the whole representing a cross section of the England that would never submit to being ruled by an invader.[13]

By the third week of July Grand claimed to have recruited 200 'Key Men'.[14] These were not the fit young spies of James Bond mythology, but rather citizens well-established in business or trades within their local communities, not least so that they would not be liable for call-up to the services and could remain in occupied areas without attracting suspicion. It is not known how many men and women were eventually recruited to the HDS, but it is said that one of Grand's last acts was to appoint eighty specialist saboteurs. The scale of the mobilisation may have been much larger than the later Auxiliary Units knew about or chose to acknowledge. The 31 May 1940 inventory of the contents of the arms dumps (Fig. 1) supports the claim that 800–1000 packs were initially made up and distributed. It also suggests that cells of six sabotage agents were envisaged, each armed with a pistol and *c.*130 rounds of ammunition. The scale of ammunition supply compares well with the handful of rounds provided to the Auxiliary Units. HDS were clearly planning for long-term operations.

Grand realised that he might need a human shield for his sabotage cells. To prevent them operating in an empty landscape, in his 4 June *Preliminary Notes on Regional 'D' Scheme* he stressed that the Regional Commissioners had to prevent any general civilian evacuation from threatened areas so that the stay-behind units could hide within the general populace and not be left isolated and obvious. This ethos of sabotage teams remaining within the community would also be the initial methodology of the Auxiliary Units. If, however, there was a general evacuation of the civilian population then the HDS would create a force of what were termed 'narks', hiding by day and operating by night, using weapons in hidden dumps (a precursor of the operational bases of the XII Corps Observation Unit and Auxiliary Units Operational Patrols). If there was to be a civilian retreat from an area, Grand also suggested that licensed victuallers could be given a supply of 'knock-out drops' to doctor supplies of alcohol with which to 'immobilise, hamper or embarrass' enemy troops.

Sabotage

No advice on specific targets was provided to the Regional D officers, but the officers were to carry out an *ad hoc* 'policy of obstruction' towards the enemy. John Dolphin had, however, already carried out a survey for MI5 on likely fifth-column targets and counter-measures and it may be presumed that this list served to highlight key targets for the HDS. Personal arms were basic. Rather than use army regulation Enfield revolvers, or the Special Branch Webley and Scott automatics, the HDS were issued with unattributable Colt revolvers on the basis that the government could not then be held directly responsible for their actions. For this reason, pre-war SIS had a special section that bought up handguns from around the world. Sadly the supplies of Thompson sub-machine guns had not yet arrived from the USA and the HDS were reduced to using decoy 'machine-gun rattles' (Plate 18). The later Auxiliary Units continued this tradition of using mainly US imported weaponry.

Some of the ideas for sabotage by these civilian agents were very basic and required little or no training – nothing more than what was being openly proposed in the *Picture Post* by Tom Wintringham, 'e.g. putting a pick through a petrol tank, slashing tyres, piles of stone on the road, felling trees, etc.' This was an organisation intended to develop if time allowed before invasion. Explosives had been requisitioned for distribution at a later date, and some cells were to be more specialised. The 1 June briefing stated: 'They will also, in special cases, be instructed in the use of certain aeroplane-destroying devices in case of enemy landings in their areas.'

It was suggested that the arms dumps should be hidden in galvanised rubbish bins, buried and turfed over; delivered in cardboard boxes called 'Auxiliary Units'. The name of the latter harked back to the much-feared 'Auxiliary Division' assassination squads of British intelligence that operated in Dublin in 1920 and of which SIS officer David Boyle, a key figure in wartime plans for British resistance (Plate 16, Chapter Eleven and Appendix 2), had been a prominent member.[15] The name was inherited by the GHQ Auxiliary Units, although Colin Gubbins never publicly acknowledged this ancestry.

The 1 June briefing and inventories of the arms dumps (Fig. 1) suggest that the sabotage element of the Home Defence Scheme was different in concept to that of the later GHQ Auxiliary Units, due partly to the shortage of explosives. In March 1940 Grand had been sharing information with the Finns on irregular warfare and he clearly borrowed some of their ideas about arms dumps.[16] The latter were primarily for incendiary activities designed to be easily concealed in the home from enemy searches and requiring little training. The saboteurs were, therefore, clearly intended to work from home and under enemy occupation.

> Some 30 Officers of this Section went to work at high pressure and completed this organisation and distributed in several thousand secret dumps throughout the country a vast quantity of incendiary materials.'[17]

Materials for Molotov cocktails were distributed as widely as possible, including pint bottles of sulphuric acid 'labelled so as to appear to be innocent'; and a supply of chemical time-delay capsules, which Grand suggested be labelled as 'dog medicine' or similar. The capsules were described by Oxenden as being a gelatine capsule filled with potassium chlorate and sugar, which acted as a crude time delay to a petrol bomb in which a small quantity of sulphuric acid had been added to the petrol/tar mix.[18] Hence the inclusion of two pints of acid in the arms dumps. The device was placed on the target and two of the capsules were added to the bottle. The acid would expose the chemical in about two hours and a violent ignition would follow. Placed so that the fire would quickly get out of

Figure 1. Inventory of Home Defence Scheme Dumps, dated 31 May 1940.

('D Organisation for Home Defence', 1 June 1940, with thanks to Stephen Sutton)

Per crate	Item	Total distributed
25	Flare, Type M, fitted with 1ft of Bickford	2,000
30	Match-headed Tyesules (paraffin)	24,000
1 dozen	Battery Pills	800 dozen
2 dozen	Capsules	1,600 dozen
2	Pint bottles of Sulphuric Acid	800
2	Small Hooded Torches	1,600
4	additional batteries for torches	3,200
1	spare bulb for torch	800
6	rubber truncheons	4,800
6	sheathed knives	1,800
1	Crowbar	1,000
1	each machine-gun rattles	800
1	packing case opener	1,000
6	pistols with 500 rounds	

control, such crude incendiary devices could have a more powerful impact than explosives, cause additional confusion, and could be used to create effective diversions. They also had the advantage of being easily supplemented from everyday domestic items. The battery pills were a failed attempt to destroy vehicle batteries by adding tablets of platinic chloride, but issue was discontinued in July 1940. The dumps also contained Tyesules (paraffin bombs), which were five-inch-long gelatin capsules filled with paraffin and with one half coated in the chemical used to make match heads (Plate 17). As well as being incendiary devices in their own right they could be tied around the magnesium flares (Flares, type M) to increase the effectiveness of the latter. There were also L delays (Plate 32) for use by more specialist saboteurs. Units based near airfields or flat ground potentially useful as landing sites were to be given special instruction and supplies, probably including explosives. As well as individual arms dumps, regional dumps were also established under military guard.[19]

The distribution of explosives appears to have been very limited, making sabotage more sustainable after occupation and easier to disguise. It was, however, the distribution of a number of explosives dumps in June that became notorious and proved the death knell for Section D. This was a last ditch, if not panic-stricken, scatter-gun approach to distribute as much material beyond the existing networks as possible in the hope of seeding at least some additional resistance units. Nonetheless, as Grand rationalised a dual working arrangement with the Auxiliary Units, a final 300 incendiary arms dumps were distributed in July, alongside the explosives dumps being distributed by Section D to the new Auxiliary Units.

By the time that Grand wrote the closing report for Section D in August, he was undoubtedly exaggerating his successes and claimed that 'several thousand' dumps had been distributed.[20] Warwicker records in *Churchill's Underground Army* how MI5 somewhat petulantly reported that the HDS had left 'dumps of explosives all over East Anglia and the southern counties', but the caches had been spread nationwide.[21] The panic was obvious; in Hornsea, Yorkshire, a man was approached during May/June 1940 by a 'mystery man' in civilian clothing, was given a box of explosives and was asked to form a resistance organisation if the Germans invaded. The box was buried in the garden and was only rediscovered in 1968.[22] Captain Eustace Maxwell, an early Auxiliary Units Intelligence Officer, also relates a tale of a Lord – delivering midnight supplies to an old woman in a Scottish village, knocking loud enough on her door to risk waking the neighbours and so arouse their curiosity.[23] Bickham Sweet-Escott, former member of Section D and later SOE, wrote how 'One of our emissaries arrived, complete with black hat and striped trousers, in a remote Scottish village, and on asking the postmaster if he would accept a parcel of stores, was promptly handed over to the police'.[24] Some of the SIS officers clearly found it difficult to shed their stockbroker image. Peter Wilkinson, second in command of the Auxiliary Units in 1940, also reports how:

In early June 1940, army units re-forming in the south of England after their evacuation from Dunkirk reported the presence of mysterious civilians behaving suspiciously in their divisional areas. These were members of Section D who had been given the task of recruiting an underground organisation to carry out subversion and resistance behind the German lines in the event of an invasion...

The appearance of these strangers in their city clothes, sinister black limousines and general air of mystery caused alarm amongst the local inhabitants and infuriated subordinate military commanders since they refused to explain their presence or discuss their business except to say that it was 'most secret'.[25]

Limousines travelling the country delivering arms dumps might seem unusual but in 1940 SIS bought up the entire stock of Packard saloon cars from the UK distributor for conversion to wireless cars.[26] Many of the senior SIS officers, having just left careers in the city, were wealthy enough to purchase their own! The 1941 History of Section D points out that the more plutocratic officers loaned their cars to the Section, gaining only moral reward.[27] Pin-stripe city suits apart, eccentricity in dress seems to have been a feature of the SIS. John Todd, later Auxiliary Units IO for South Wales, Herefordshire and Worcestershire and a former stockbroker, tended to wear tweed fishing gear including a deerstalker hat festooned with fishing flies, which might pass for an attempt at camouflage in rural England (although his large black Pontiac car rather stood out), but he carried on wearing the same outfit in South Africa when he commanded the SOE East Africa mission in 1941–2. Todd was, however, an eccentric in more ways than one. His standard tests for prospective Auxiliers were to (a) drop a stick of plastic explosive at their feet and judge their reaction and (b) entertain a group of them in a public house and only recruit the last one who had to visit the lavatory (a strong bladder being a useful consideration whilst out on patrol).

Passive Resistance

The second 'obstructionist' arm of the HDS would involve Section D officers working in the community to broaden the range of civilians willing to oppose occupation by 'turning conversations' to the subject of resistance and thereby encouraging other persons to 'unconsciously turn their minds to the problem of dealing with the Enemy by unarmed methods'. This would include such simple tactics as misdirecting enemy troops, but it has also been misinterpreted at times to suggest that Britain was training people to act as double-agent collaborators. Some idea of what such a 'whispering campaign' of unarmed resistance might involve comes from the Channel Islands, which were the only part of the British Isles to be occupied by the Nazis. The size of the Channel Islands meant that any military resistance was impractical and discouraged by the civil government for fear of reprisals, and, indeed, the official instruction from the British government upon occupation was for 'passive cooperation'. Instead, at least in the initial stages of occupation, there was passive resistance in the form of shunning the troops or making them wait to be served in shops. Anti-Nazi graffiti appeared on walls, even though painting the V sign on a wall was denounced by the civil authorities as causing unnecessary aggravation to the Nazis and it risked the death penalty. A number of underground newspapers were produced and circulated; listening to the BBC became an act of rebellion. Some residents went further and hepled those engaged in slave labour on the islands to hide and escape. An organised resistance slowly grew but there were also inevitably collaborators – neighbours denouncing others for monetary reward or out of spite. If the mainland had been invaded it is unrealistic to suppose that there would not have been British collaborators – both those who shared the fascist ideology and those who simply accepted the status quo in the hope of minimising the brutality of the occupier. In general, political events are shaped by small groups of activists and Grand saw the task of the HDS as being to identify, encourage and develop those anti-fascist activists and make links with foreign help to the point that the hold of the occupying forces would become untenable.

Intelligence Gathering
In line with the discussions of the May ISPB meeting, Grand stressed that, as well as sabotage, the other purpose of the organisation would be to feed intelligence from temporarily occupied areas back to the British army. On 4 June he maintained 'The communications side of our work to be stressed equally with the "obstruction" side.'[28] As with the later Auxiliary Units Special Duties Branch, this role was not so well documented but appears to have been the specific responsibility of the original coordinator of HDS, Viscount Bearsted.[29] The SOE history of Section D declared that this operation had been transferred '*en bloc*' to the Auxiliary Units, implying that by then it existed as a distinct section of the HDS (see Chapter Nine).[30]

Grand implied that the suggested methodology relied simply on runners from each cell who would pass on information to its neighbour and thence through the front line as a 'grape vine telegraph'.[31] There is no further mention of the wireless sets originally planned for the cars of the Section D Regional Officers, or those sets now being distributed for Section VII (see Chapter Eleven). Was Section D waiting for Schröter's research on a simple duplex wireless system to bear fruit? This crude communication system would clearly have been difficult to maintain as a reliable source of information during an active invasion campaign and has an air of desperation about it. Nonetheless, the intention of HDS in its latter stages was to become:

> a closely coordinated sabotage and intelligence network among the civilian population who would be left behind in any territory which the German armies might temporarily be able to occupy.[32]

'Standfast Club'
Captain John Dolphin was still enthusiastically seeking to extend the scope of the organisation that he had originally proposed on 22 May in 'Pessimism' and on 1 July wrote to Grand with the suggestion of expanding the 'Home Defence Scheme' (as he called it) to include the 'Standfast Club'. His extended plan would

comprise citizens prepared to stay in their homes in the event of invasion. Grade A would be given weapons and instructions on how to make defences. Grade B were people prepared to undertake sniping and minor sabotage. Grade C were those who were prepared to stay in their homes under any circumstances, their value being they would not clog the roads with refugees, but their presence would ensure that the civilians of Grades A and B would not stand out in an empty landscape. Dolphin's ideas seemed to be merging in a confused fashion with the existing LDV. Like them, his 'Standfast Club' would be clearly identified with badges or armlets and Dolphin hoped that the movement would snowball into very large numbers.[33] There is no evidence that this suggestion was taken any further. If so, it would only have reinforced fears that SIS were attempting a take-over bid of home forces. Grand had already proposed a reorganisation of home forces regional command. The Dolphin plan does, however, have points of similarity with the unofficial ideas of Captain Tommy Davies of MIR, presented to General Ismay's staff on 18 June (see below, pp. 53–4).

Opposition to the HDS

The Home Defence Scheme was, potentially, a fearsome addition to the defence plan and a development of warfare that, as seen in Chapter One, did not meet with universal approval. One Dorset LDV officer, who appeared to have been approached by a regional officer of Section D, took the unusual step on 3 July of writing directly to the Prime Minister to complain.

> Sir,
>
> Since it seems unlikely that the matter is within your knowledge, I must respectfully beg to direct your attention to the fact that L.D.V. officers in this and presumably other areas have been approached by persons stated to represent the War Office, with a view to the organisation of a system of sabotage which could be brought into operation within the enemy lines in the event of his establishing a foothold in this country.
>
> For the carrying out of this sabotage it is proposed that caches of explosives and the like shall be established at certain secret points, these to be utilised for *franc-tireur* operations by selected members of the LDV, who would remain behind in the occupied area for this purpose.
>
> Quite apart from its questionable aspect under International Law, in view of the brutal retaliatory measures which action of the kind has already evoked from the enemy, in occupied territory both in this war and in that of 1914–18, and the certainty that it will similarly bring death and untold suffering to innocent non-combatant members of the community if embarked upon in this country, I cannot think that the ill-considered proposal has been made with your knowledge or approval.[34]

The letter excited a furious denial of any responsibility by the War Office for civilian sabotage operations. In a letter of 30 July General Paget, the Chief of Staff of the new C-in-C, Home Forces, General Alan Brooke, instead blamed SIS for the activities in Dorset and distanced the new Auxiliary Units from the concept of organising civilian sabotage and working in an 'occupied' area.

Mr MacLeod's misapprehension may, on the other hand, be due to the fact that there was until recently an organisation working under the SIS, of whose activities he may have heard, which was charged with the task of organising sabotage and obstruction by civilians who, in the event of invasion, would remain behind and operate locally. Special stores for this purpose were issued to selected individuals.[35]

MacLeod's letter may well have been circulated at the meeting of the Chiefs of Staff Committee of 8 July 1940, which declared that there was 'no effective control of the operations of D', being outside the remit of the Joint Intelligence Sub-Committee. This complaint was not, however, specific to the HDS but was instead part of a wider complaint about a tendency for irregular operations to be carried out without the knowledge of the chiefs of staff who, they stressed, were responsible for providing strategic advice to the government.[36] Menzies had explained to the Hankey Inquiry 'that from the earliest days S.S.[Secret Service] had, for vital reasons of secrecy, deliberately been kept aloof from regular Government Committees such as the Committee of Imperial Defence and the Chiefs of Staffs organisation'.[37] The chiefs of staff may also have been piqued at being excluded from discussions by their own senior officers in the War Office. For instance, how far were the chiefs of staff aware that the CIGS had earlier approved the European-wide 'D Scheme' on the specific understanding that knowledge was strictly limited and was beyond the knowledge of the Chiefs of Staff Committee? Similarly, Hankey had discussed with Anthony Eden the possibility of using SIS wireless as an emergency communications system, but likewise agreed that the chiefs of staff need not be informed.

Lawrence Grand's HDS now became the focus of the resentment of the chiefs of staff over their perceived isolation from the planning of irregular warfare. They made the reasonable point that there would be particular problems if the army was expected to fight an anti-invasion campaign on the same ground as a civilian army acting outside its control and outside of international conventions. This argument was part of the difficulty of established bodies in coming to terms with a new form of para-military warfare. Colin Gubbins, the later CO of the Auxiliary Units, was aghast at what he saw as the amateurishness and extravagance of some of the wilder projects of Section D when he began to work alongside them in MIR, but at the same time he found the risk-taking attitude of the young ex-businessmen refreshing in contrast to the ponderous hierarchy of the War Office.[38]

Grand's ideas excited opposition from all quarters. For the army, the whole concept appeared to be an attempt to create a private army acting in competition to both the regular forces and the LDV/Home Guard with the potential to cause massive confusion as a series of private armies ranged across the battle front. For the government this offered the fear of a mass arming of civilians as *francs-tireurs*. For SIS there was also the threat of damaging their other intelligence-gathering capabilities in a wave of uncontrolled sabotage. The War Office seized on the embarrassing incidents in which arms dumps were discovered as part of the campaign to take over Section D and create a military alternative – the Auxiliary Units. Sadly the lack of 'public triumphalism' (as John Warwicker has put it) within SIS has meant that only limited publicly-accessible accounts survive to provide a more balanced view. The fact that it is now known that the organisation had spread beyond the south-east coast and East Anglia across the country into Scotland puts these isolated incidents into a wider context of more successful secrecy.

The difficulties in dealing with Lawrence Grand in the UK and in the worldwide operations of Section D stimulated a quickly-moving consensus in the War Office and SIS that the various initiatives for conducting irregular warfare needed to be better coordinated and be given a higher priority in government by being placed under ministerial control. The ISPB had failed because its members were not sufficiently senior and did not have decision-making powers. Although the principle might be agreed, the sticking point was, unsurprisingly, which ministry would control any new coordinating body. Naturally the War Office believed that any new form of warfare should be under their control, whilst SIS believed that any clandestine operations fell within the realm of the secret service. At the time, no one realised that Hugh Dalton at the Ministry of Economic Warfare was also flexing his muscles to take direct control of any such new venture. If they could not agree among themselves, they could at least agree that Grand's increasingly wild and ambitious schemes had to be curtailed. The War Office made determined efforts to take over Section D. On 3 June 1940 DMI proposed that Section D should come under control of a new Directorate of the War Office under a senior officer also responsible for commandos, irregular warfare schools and all plans for sabotage in occupied countries. On 6 June MIR commented that commando units, the propaganda organisations of the Ministries of Information and Economic Warfare and the sabotage service of SIS 'should be co-ordinated and the co-ordinating authority should be the General Staff as it is a matter of strategy'. Whilst they argued over organisation, and as yet with no active competition on the ground, the HDS still went its own way, recruiting and distributing arms dumps in anticipation of imminent invasion.

There was plotting for change from within the Foreign Office (responsible for SIS), led by Lord Cadogan and Gladwyn Jebb. Cadogan suggested to Jebb in June that the latter should become Controller of all D plans, putting Grand effectively under his supervision. Jebb rejected the idea, firstly on the basis that the sabotage organisation should be under the control of a 'tough and intelligent soldier', and secondly because he feared that Grand would avoid telling him what was going on. Sir Campbell Stuart had tried to reassure Jebb about the plan by saying that such an appointment was merely a stepping stone to getting rid of Grand completely and then he would be in full charge.[39] Cadogan took note of Jebb's views of the desirability of bringing Section D under military control and on 28 June formally proposed that it come under DMI. This proposal was, however, rejected on 1 July by a meeting of Lord Halifax (Foreign Secretary),

Sir Alexander Cadogan and Gladwyn Jebb (Foreign Office), Lord Lloyd (Secretary of State for the Colonies), Lord Hankey, Hugh Dalton (Minister of Economic Warfare), General Beaumont-Nesbitt (Director of Military Intelligence), Sir Stewart Menzies (CSS), and Desmond Morton (Security Adviser to the Prime Minister). Although there was considerable support at the meeting, the opposition to the proposal was led by Dalton, who held that 'war from within' was better led by civilians rather than by soldiers. Not surprisingly, this conclusion was dismissed by MIR as being amateurish.[40] Dalton was no friend of Grand but had his eye on Section D within his own plans for the new SOE. Hankey also defended the present system, blaming the Foreign Office for its delays in authorising action by Section D until it was too late to execute successfully. The attacks on Section D continued at the Chiefs of Staff Committee meeting on 5 July. A chart prepared by the Director of Combined Operations still showed Section D as being responsible for the 'Organisation of civil resistance and sabotage in the UK' but there were complaints that there was 'no effective control of the operations of "D" who might well be brought under the control of the Joint Intelligence Sub-Committee'.[41]

The War Office were over-confident in their claim on irregular warfare, and were to be disappointed. Dalton manoeuvred to take the ministerial coordinating role over the existing work of Section D, MIR and Electra House that all agreed was necessary.[42] At this stage, all other parties seemed to have believed that the new Special Operations Executive (SOE) would be merely a coordinating body. Dalton had other ideas and went on to absorb the above establishments within a new independent organisation under his direct control. The War Office were as irritated as SIS by the emergence of the new organisation. Holland, forever the champion of uniformed irregular warfare, commented in the MIR War Diary for 22 July 'It looks a little as though the Army has missed the bus, so to speak, and has allowed para-military activities to be carried on outside its jurisdiction'.[43]

The Final Stage of the HDS: Joint Working with the Auxiliary Units (July 1940)

The modern assumption has been that the HDS was a chaotic aberration, quickly absorbed by the more organised Auxiliary Units once they became operational in July 1940. According to Mackenzie's official history of SOE, the HDS 'had to be dissolved, and there were many complications, humorous and otherwise'.[44] Following this simple statement, and constrained by the limited information available at the time, David Lampe rejected any idea that there may have been any significant contribution of the HDS to the new Auxiliary Units:

> A few of the men who had been in Section D's resistance set-up were asked to join the Auxiliary Units organisation, but most were politely thanked for what they had been prepared to do for the nation and told simply that their organisation no longer existed.[45]

This dismissive attitude has been followed by most later writers and it may have been originally promoted to historians in order to bury the continuing contribution of SIS in the story. In truth, GHQ could not afford to dismiss so easily the expertise of SIS and its civilian agents and saboteurs during the dangerous days of 1940. Nigel Oxenden, originally Intelligence Officer for Norfolk and then the Training Officer for the Auxiliary Units from 1941–44, provided a more informed contemporary opinion (which only survived as a publicly-accessible document by accident). He acknowledged in the draft official history of Auxiliary Units, that:

> most I/Os [Auxiliary Units Intelligence Officers] were assisted by introductions to one or two men who had already been chosen by MI5 [*sic* – actually MI6] ... These were generally outstanding individuals, who eventually became group commanders. Meanwhile their local knowledge made them invaluable in finding the right recruits.[46]

During July, despite the complaints from the War Office over their behaviour, there was a significant overlap when HDS continued to be supplied and to operate as before, driven by necessity and by a short-lived policy of joint working. Section D also supported the new Auxiliary Units by supplying them with thirty demonstration demolition sets, 400 small weapons dumps and ten large weapons dumps. They also supplied the first training manual to the Auxiliary Units – 200 copies of their *Brown Book* on the use of explosives. It seems likely that this formed the basis of Wilkinson's *Calendar 1937* (Plate 29).[47] Section D also organised some of the first training for Auxiliary Units Intelligence Officers, including the Scottish CO, Eustace Maxwell, at Aston House.[48] The difference in concept between the Auxiliary Units and co-existing HDS can clearly be seen from Fig. 2; here, the Auxiliary Units were heavily supplied with explosives whilst the HDS were supplied exclusively with incendiary devices that were easier to replace and to conceal under occupation. The distribution of explosives to HDS took place in a very narrow band of time in June 1940, but is reflected in the provision of crimping tools and detonators in the July inventory.

As resources from the HDS were gradually handed over during the summer of 1940, its existing arms dumps were, wherever possible, transferred to the Auxiliary Units, although some were lost forever. Nonetheless, Section D's base at Aston House remained the main supply base for the Auxiliary Units for the rest of the war, continuing this role after being absorbed by SOE.[49] 'Aux. Packs' were assembled at Aston House and packed for distribution across the country; in February 1941 they received an order for 1,000 cases of stores for the Auxiliary Units. A storeman at Aston later recorded loading Auxiliary Unit 'Dumps' into large A12 ammunition crates during the winter of 1942/3: the heavy and unwieldy metal A12 crate was $25.2'' \times 17.3'' \times 8.5''$, originally used to pack six charges for the now obsolete 8″ Livens gas projector.[50]

Grand fought back against the attempts of the War Office to absorb the HDS. As an appeasement, Grand made every effort to stress that the HDS would fall under military control during the phase of an active military campaign, although without wireless, any form of strategic control after invasion would have been difficult (as the Auxiliary Units were to find). By the end of July, Grand had come

Figure 2. Material simultaneously supplied by SIS to the Home Defence Scheme
and the Auxiliary Units in July 1940. (TNA HS 8/214)

	Home Defence	Auxiliary Units
Time fuzes	4,060	46,380
Safety fuze (ft)		14,016
Safety fuze, lengths match ended	1,810	
Detonating fuze (ft)		27,000
Instantaneous fuze		4,950
Detonators		27,020
Blasting Gelignite (lbs)		5,600
High Explosive (lbs)		5,246
Medium – Large Incendiary Bombs	450	5,270
Medium Incendiary Bombs	1,610	5,450
Tyesules (paraffin incendiaries)	29,479	10,124
Petrol Paraffin Mixture (gallons)	400	
Capsules for Petrol Bomb	63,540	
Acid for Petrol Bomb (quarts)	206	
Magnets		2,336
Fog Signals		1,560
Crimping Tools	42	540
Tape (15-yd reels)		1,538
Vaseline (tubes)		950
Fuzes (boxes) [Detonators]	1,540	1,571
Striker Boards	1,668	
A.W. Bombs		1,200
Pressure Switches		50

to a clear division of function which would place the HDS outside the remit of the War Office as per the earlier agreement with Hankey. Based on his earlier model of a dual-level resistance organisation in Norway, Grand was now looking beyond the counter-invasion phase into a phase of longer-term resistance. In this scenario the HDS would now only be fully activated after the destruction of the Auxiliary Units (which was assumed to be in around ten to fifteen days), with the HDS remaining 'quiescent' during the actual invasion period. Nonetheless, the reference below to seconding a number of his officers to the Auxiliary Units may have been an attempt to demonstrate cooperation and a degree of integration of the two schemes. There are a small number of early Intelligence Officers in the Auxiliary Units who do indeed betray signs of being former, or current, officers of SIS (see below, Chapter Six).

I allotted one or more officers to each area and directed them to contact and recruit suitable persons, lay down concealed stores of food, arms and devices to make a frame-work that would remain in place if, and when, the Germans occupied the area.

At the same time I detailed officers to my D.M. group to work with a second organisation of special units allotted by the War Office for the same type of work. In this way we had two organisations available and one would be brought into action when, as was inevitable, the other was discovered and broken up. The D organisation was the one that was to remain quiescent at the outset.[51]

Only if the GHQ defence plan failed and large parts of the country were occupied would the HDS emerge as the basis of a longer-term resistance movement. The revised purpose was now going to be quiet intelligence-gathering during the invasion period 'for the purpose of obtaining information for our own forces', but there was also a subsequent phase 'and later for carrying out resistance projects of all sorts'. The contents of their arms dumps suggest that activity would be centred around fire-bombing of strategic targets and industrial capacity. This is a rare contemporary use of the term 'resistance'.[52] It may be that this more calculated plan had been devised with Menzies and Dansey as a means of incorporating the HDS into their wider plans and bringing Grand under firmer control. Having identified that he was, indeed, uncontrollable it is hard to imagine that SIS HQ did not take some steps to control his enthusiasm rather than risk his ideas in an actual invasion.

Thus, in the darkest days after Dunkirk it was Section D of SIS who had mobilised most quickly and was able to provide a para-military shield, however chaotic it might have seemed to the military mind, whilst the Auxiliary Units were being formed and equipped. In even more secrecy, SIS also continued its plans for a deep-cover resistance network in Section VII.

Exile of Lawrence Grand

Under Hugh Dalton, Gladwyn Jebb was appointed as the Chief Executive Officer of the new Special Operations Executive (SOE). It was not until 16 August that Dalton and Halifax agreed that SOE should take over direct responsibility for Section D. Until then Grand had continued to operate in his maverick fashion. Apparently no one bothered to mention this agreement to Menzies at the time, but initially it seemed as though operational control of the new body by SIS might, in any case, still be maintained. On 28 August, the 58 year-old Sir Frank Nelson from SIS was appointed head of the sabotage element of the new Special Operations Executive (initially called SO2), with Lawrence Grand as his deputy. SOE had as much difficulty in controlling Grand as had SIS. The reorganised Section D, still under Grand (as Nelson's Deputy) remained a semi-autonomous body until it was finally absorbed into the new SOE after 18 September 1940.

> D is a separate, secret organisation, forming part of a larger organisation [SOE] under the control of Mr Dalton. The function of this organisation is the promotion of subversion.[53]

Significantly, MIR managed to avoid full absorption by SOE through pre-emptively dividing most of its responsibilities amongst other sections of DMI. SIS may well have done something similar with elements of Section D.

Having inherited Grand from Section D, Dalton barely concealed his dislike for the man he called 'King Bomba', finally lost patience and, on 18 September, brusquely dismissed him. More generously, a note was appended to the letter of dismissal by a civil servant in the Ministry of Economic Warfare to say 'a word of thanks would not have come amiss'.[54] Kim Philby later maintained that there was a general purge of Section D staff by Nelson and that the dismissal of Grand and his 'closest henchmen' was 'gleefully' assisted by Claude Dansey and David Boyle in SIS.[55] Philby undoubtedly exaggerated the situation. There was no great purge of Section D by SOE and indeed the new organisation relied heavily on its staff in the early years. Grand was succeeded in late September by his former deputy, George Taylor, thus providing continuity as the officer in charge of country sections. Viscount Bearsted also transferred to SOE rather than, as might have been expected, to the Auxiliary Units. It is, however, quite possible that Dansey and Boyle wanted Grand out of the way as quickly as possible and that this was the result of more than their personal dislike of the man. It was entirely consistent with Dansey's methodology to 'publicly' sacrifice Grand and lend added credence to the story, if German intelligence were aware of it, that SIS had abandoned any involvement in a British resistance movement and so switch enemy attention to the Auxiliary Units. Whilst Bearsted followed instructions in transferring the bulk of the HDS to the Auxiliary Units, the decks were now cleared to allow SIS to discretely continue the intelligence-gathering work under the name of Section VII, whilst still maintaining, under quieter hands than Grand, a contingency plan under Boyle for armed resistance in the event of enemy occupation.

Postscript: the Davies Plan

A curious example of just how secret the HDS was in its early stages comes from correspondence of 18–27 June in which members of the Chiefs of Staff Committee and the new Ministry of Defence excitedly discussed an unofficial proposal from Captain 'Tommy' Davies of MIR to create a civilian resistance movement under War Office control. This may have been seen as an attempt to hijack the concept from SIS. On 18 June Davies submitted a proposal on the *Need for Organising Civil Resistance* to Lieutenant-Colonel A.T. Cornwall-Jones in the Office of the War Cabinet, who forwarded it to Colonel L.C. Hollis (Secretary of the Chiefs of Staff Committee), who in turn forwarded it on 20 June to General 'Pug' Ismay, Churchill's Chief of Staff, Deputy Secretary of the War Cabinet and also a member of the Chiefs of Staff Committee. Davies sought to clarify the role that civilians should have in resisting the enemy 'whether we are to encourage industrial opposition, acts of sabotage, espionage, etc., in our civilian population, and whether behind our troops we are to leave regular or irregular units entrusted with the task of making a German occupation difficult or even dangerous'. He also raised the need to consider options 'if the possibility of the government and armed forces leaving for a Dominion were considered', one of the clearest statements of the possibility of a national defeat of British forces and an evacuation of government.[56]

Davies called for 'constant organised civilian opposition to the invader in the back areas and even in the fighting zone' and believed that the vulnerability of the German lines of supply had not been sufficiently tested in previous campaigns.

After any occupation 'of any locality, or even of the whole country, some form of resistance and of secret organisation would be essential, which would both tie up large numbers of enemy troops and also preserve the morale of the population'. He dismissed the argument that this would only encourage reprisals by pointing out that this was likely to happen anyway and that there should therefore be 'organized and active resistance from the start'. He also believed that the acceptable rules of warfare had already been changed by the present war, and that the country was only waiting for some concrete application of the principles that Churchill had proclaimed in his 'Fight on the Beaches' speech of 4 June and 'Finest Hour' speech of 18 June. He wanted each army Area Command to have a 'Civil Resistance Section' to recruit saboteurs and guerrillas and to determine local targets. In his covering letter to Cornwall-Jones, Davies admitted that his scheme was unconstitutional and unorthodox and also recognised that 'certain steps' had already been taken on these lines, but thought that it was not comprehensive enough. At the same time Cornwall-Jones was proposing using civilian populations to turn small towns and villages into strong points, prepared for all-round defence. This is essentially Dolphin's 'Standfast Club' and would evolve into the Home Guard nodal points.

In his note to General Ismay, Hollis declared the proposal of Davies to be 'forceful and logical' but had doubts on how it could be implemented.[57] Ismay passed the proposal on to Victor Cavendish-Bentinck (Chairman of the Joint Intelligence Committee) who doubted the immediate practicality of the scheme but noted, in what was possibly a veiled reference to the HDS, that 'from a remark made by the Home Secretary the other day, I gather that something on these lines is being done'. Cavendish-Bentinck recommended that schools for spies and saboteurs should be established in likely areas for invasion.[58] Hollis also forwarded the Davies scheme to H (Lord Hankey?) who saw the core of saboteurs as previously-trained LDV who had been able to merge back into the civilian population after the tide of battle had passed over them. (This is how Albert Toon in Birmingham was recruited: see Chapter Eleven.) Civilians in 'subjugated areas' could then 'keep the enemy continually on the jump as we were in Ireland'. They would have roles in (1) assassination, (2) sabotage, and (3) intelligence, the latter run by SIS. He seemed quite enthusiastic about 'Assassination on the Irish model' suggesting the use of an undetectable poison.[59] On 23 June General Ismay forwarded the plan to General Henry Pownall, now Inspector-General of the Home Guard, and Sir Samuel Findlater-Stewart (Chairman of the Home Defence Executive) with the interesting comment from someone in his position 'We here are not, of course, fully in the picture about all that has been done and is being done to organise civil resistance'. Ismay underlined 'the fundamental question of *whether the civil un-uniformed population is to be encouraged to fight.*'[60] Pownall and Findlater-Stewart cast the first dampening voices on the argument: Pownall saying that this went beyond his responsibility and Findlater-Stewart querying the availability of resources.[61] In the end, Hollis had to recommend to Ismay on 27 June that it was probably too late to start to create such an enterprise.[62]

The whole sequence of correspondence over this proposal is extraordinary given that SIS had begun mobilising its civilian resistance in late May, the Cabinet agreement for the creation of the Auxiliary Units on 17 June and the widespread opposition of other sections of the General Staff and Cabinet to the very principle of the participation of civilians in warfare. General Ironside, then C-in-C Home Forces, went on to send a firm rebuttal of the concept of civilian resistance to the War Cabinet on 8 July. There appears to have been an infectious enthusiasm amongst those corresponding on the topic, countered by some rather restrained and polite rebuttals from those outside Ismay's staff. Davies was a member of MIR, but the proposal was submitted in his own name and in many respects it is counter to the view of his superior officer, Jo Holland. Nonetheless, it certainly did not do his career any harm as he was promoted shortly thereafter and went on to become head of SOE Research under his friend, Colin Gubbins.

Chapter Five

XII Corps Observation Unit
(June 1940)

As the situation on the continent deteriorated rapidly in May 1940, Captain Peter Fleming of MIR (Plate 8 and Appendix 2) was attached to Home Forces on 25 May 'for the purpose of training LDVs, etc., in fighting behind the German lines in case of invasion of this country.'[1] The stated official purpose of the LDV was to act primarily as an observation body. The nickname 'Look, Duck and Vanish' was a good summary of their function and there was no intention to arm all of the volunteers. Nonetheless, just eleven days from their foundation, MIR was already exploring ways of using some of them as guerrilla troops, a major departure for MIR, the primary focus of which was in military missions and the use of regular forces in irregular warfare. Fleming did not, however, have a mechanism with which to implement his ideas. This came with the independent initiative of General Thorne, commander of the new XII Corps created on 8 June to defend Kent and Sussex. His XII Corps Observation Unit provided the first military model for a guerrilla organisation to resist invasion.

General Thorne (Plate 9 and Appendix 2) was very much in the front line of the invasion threat and could not wait for the War Office to sort out its national plans for irregular warfare. He created his own local solution in the area most at threat from invasion. Not for nothing was the biography of General Andrew 'Bulgy' Thorne entitled *Forgotten General*; few people now know his name or his contribution to the war effort. Thorne was a forward-looking regular officer who had commanded a battalion of the Grenadier Guards in the First World War and in 1932 became Military Attaché in Berlin, seeing the rise of the Nazis to power at first hand. His reports on the German army were well-informed and in particular he was able to predict its increasing mechanisation as well as its plans for long-range rockets. Thorne had a particular concern for army education; he wanted officer cadets to undergo normal recruit training before going to Sandhurst and for senior NCOs to be given more responsibility. He supported many of the ideas (if not the politics) of Tom Wintringham, whom he first met on the publication of the latter's *How To Reform The Army*; they subsequently developed a shared interest in guerrilla warfare. Thorne would have found little to criticise in Wintringham's call in March 1940 to encourage initiative in NCOs and private soldiers, the necessity to be able to fight in small groups and the importance of infiltration as a tactic. 'And for the development of these tactics, a new spirit and discipline in the army, a release of the initiative and independent energy of the men who are our soldiers'.[2] Thorne sent a number of his officers from XII Corps on to the Osterley training course and corresponded with Wintringham throughout the rest of the war. Thorne also took a personal interest in the army career of Hugh Slater, another ex-International Brigade instructor at Osterley, and after he was commissioned (much against the wishes of MI5), had him transferred to Scottish Command and appointed as an Instructor at the Company Commander's Training School.

Thorne became a Major General in October 1938, commanding London District and the Brigade of Guards together with a responsibility for the development of civil defence. In October 1939 he took command of 48th (South Midlands) Division and in May 1940 was fighting along a twenty-six mile front as part of the British rearguard to Dunkirk before being evacuated on 1 June. A week after the Dunkirk evacuation, on 8 June, Thorne (now a Lieutenant General) took command of XII Corps in the key areas of Kent, Sussex and parts of Hampshire and Surrey; despite being on the frontline of any invasion threat, they suffered from very weak resources. He desperately needed to find ways of strengthening his regular forces with whatever resources were at hand and to use them to disrupt the seemingly unstoppable flow of the German *blitzkrieg*. The basic idea was to slow down their advance as much as possible towards the GHQ 'stop-line' in order to give more time for a major counter-attack to be launched and to cut off the crucial German supply lines to the sea. This was not a purely defensive strategy: his new guerrilla units were to disrupt any retreat to the sea and so ensure the enemy's complete annihilation.

The decisive Thorne put his plans for what became known as the XII Corps Observation Unit into place immediately after completing the first survey of his command, and it was operational in its most basic form within a matter of days from 8 June. He is reputed to have got his inspiration from a visit to an East Prussian estate in 1934, where the staff had traditionally been trained in this role against the possibility of invasion from the East, and it is hard to escape the conclusion that he came to XII Corps with the idea already formed in his mind.[3] He immediately asked the War Office for a specialist officer to lead the Unit and Peter Fleming was the obvious choice; it gave Fleming a mechanism with which to implement the ideas that he had been considering over the previous couple of weeks. In the MIR diary for 17 June is the entry

> Colonel Gubbins to be in charge of 'Auxiliary Units' for Home Defence, with Major Wilkinson as a G2. Much the same methods as Captain Fleming is using in Kent with his little headquarters.[4]

Fleming acknowledged that the original idea came from Thorne, but he subsequently developed it into a form that was to become recognisable as a pilot for the later Auxiliary Units. One crucial element was a request for a detachment of Lovat Scouts to be brought in as a regular army scout section and the core of a training unit. The Lovat Scouts might be considered to be one of the earliest of Britain's 'special forces'. Originally raised in 1900, they were recruited from hardy Scottish ghillies (gamekeepers) and were experts in camouflage, sniping and stalking. In 1916 the Lovat Scouts (Sharpshooters) were formed to provide nine 'Observation Groups' for the Western Front, each consisting of one officer and twenty-one other ranks; they specifically recruited older men, including the redoubtable 62-year-old Lieutenant Macpherson. Their principal task, usually working in pairs, was patrolling and reconnaissance through no man's land in order to collect intelligence. It is no coincidence that the name given to Thorne's new unit was 'Observation Unit'; Fleming had recently been involved in discussions during mid-April 1940 between DMI, MIR and the Lovat Scouts as to the role of the latter in the new Independent Companies. MIR had proposed a 'Composite Battalion' comprising the 5th Battalion, Scots Guards and 400 men of the Lovat Scouts, which would then be subdivided into ten companies who would act as independent commando units in Norway. Colonel Melville, CO of the Lovat Scouts, was opposed to the idea as it would risk the end of the regiment's independent existence. During the course of the conference it was discovered that the 5th Battalion, Scots Guards had already been disbanded without the meeting being told (ironic given the high-ranking intelligence staff that were present). Instead, it was suggested that the Lovat Scouts would act as an independent commando unit – a proposal overtaken by events but which indicates the special skills of the regiment. Fleming had a personal connection to the Lovat Scouts as his brother Richard was an Acting Captain in the regiment and its Training Officer; he had just returned from a specialist course in sniping and observation. Peter Fleming badly wanted to incorporate the Lovat Scouts into the new Observation Unit, but securing their participation was to be no mean task and was a tribute to Fleming's well-known reputation as a talented and determined 'scrounger'. Since his discussions with Colonel Melville in April, the regiment had been dispatched to garrison the remote Faroe Islands, 200 miles north of Scotland, where they were under great pressures due to shortage of personnel and persistent illness. Fleming persuaded the War Office to agree to a detachment of Lovat Scouts under his brother to be recalled from the Faroes, resulting in an irritable entry in the Lovat Scouts War Diary for 19 June 1940, the CO fearing another attempt to dismember the regiment:

> A cable came from the War Office to dispatch by the first available ship Captain R.E. Fleming, 1 Sergeant and 13 Other Ranks to report to XII Corps at Tunbridge Wells for special duty under GHQ Home Forces. The Other Ranks to be stalkers and good shots. This can be done once or twice, but will be impossible to comply with often.[5]

The attempt to get the Lovat Scouts back from the Faroe Islands is a clear indication of the importance attached to the XII Corps Observation Unit by the War Office. The regiment tried to find a means of circumventing the order. On 20 June the movement order for Richard Fleming and his men was cancelled when the Commanding Officer of the Lovat Scouts depot in Edinburgh sent a cable to say that as an alternative he had sent twelve men from the Home Detail to XII Corps. Had they managed to outflank the attack on their Faroes garrison? Peter was still desperate to involve his brother and maintained the pressure on the War Office. On 30 June the regiment received another cable from the War Office ordering Captain Fleming to report to XII Corps as soon as possible, but this time there was no way out. Fleming and his batman eventually left the Faroes for Tunbridge Wells on 2 July. Such was the importance of the Lovat Scouts detachment, that on 7 August 1940 orders to transfer the Lovat Scouts personnel away from XII Corps were cancelled.[6] Richard Fleming's service with the Observation Unit only lasted four months and he returned to the Faroes on 11 November to command B Squadron as an Acting Major. Nonetheless, on 13 November another small detachment of Lovat Scouts left for services in an un-named 'Observation Group', also presumably referring to XII Corps.[7] Eventually the Lovat Scouts contingent was reduced to just two NCO training instructors in the Scout Section. Major Simon Fraser, the Lord Lovat, was reported to have visited the XII Corps Observation Unit along with other dignitaries interested in this novel approach to warfare.[8] By this time he had left the Lovat Scouts regiment, first to be first Chief Instructor at the Lochailort Commando Training School, where Mike Calvert had been his demolitions instructor, and then to the new Combined Operations HQ.

The original methodology of Thorne did not include the use of hides, but Fleming believed the absence of such bolt holes would limit the operational life of the cells, and introduced the idea of fixed hides, some of which were made from enlarged badger setts. General Thorne visited one and was delighted: descending a rope ladder he found some Lovat Scouts and half a dozen Home Guard sitting on barrels of explosives.[9] The hides were constructed by 172 Tunnelling Company, Royal Engineers and two-man sapper teams from 262 Field Company, Royal Engineers. Other labour was drawn from XII Corps troops. The hides were then carefully camouflaged by the Lovat Scouts. The most spectacular hide was dug into the bottom of what was known as The Airship Hole, in King's Wood above The Garth, Bilting in Kent; it was a large oval hole some 30m long, 10m wide and 5m deep and originally dug as a mooring sub-station for British airships during the First World War. The gondola of the airship would nestle into the pit to give protection against the wind. Fleming reasoned that the last place the Germans would look for a hide was in the bottom of an existing hole. It became a command centre and redoubt, with food, water and sleeping accommodation for around 120 people.

The hides were linked to observation posts by field telephone, but Fleming arranged for some of the hides to be linked by wireless, very much in the spirit of Gubbins's guerrilla warfare pamphlets of 1939 (but ironically not taken up by Gubbins in his 1940 Auxiliary Units). Initially two mysterious men wearing RAF uniform were attached to the unit, equipped with portable wireless sets. For fixed communications he sought the assistance of Section VIII, SIS, who provided one of their top wireless engineers 'Spuggy' Newton (Plate 10), lately back from France having built and delivered the first of SIS's mobile communication units, installed in a Dodge car. Newton then installed wireless sets inside a number of the underground hides constructed within Ashdown Forest, pre-dating the installation of the Auxiliary Units pilot wireless network in the same area by around three months.[10] The fact that the wireless had to be installed by a specialist suggests they were using the standard SIS combination of HRO National Receiver and Mk III long-range transmitter that Newton had installed in embassies and secret radio stations all over Europe, and was now building into the Packard cars and trucks of the SIS Special Communications Units. The long-range wireless sets could report to a central receiving station at Whaddon, rather than having to use the type of IN/OUT Station relay system as used by the later, less powerful, SDB system of the Auxiliary Units.

The other key recruit to the Unit was Captain Mike Calvert, a Royal Engineers officer, an expert in explosives who would go on to command a Chindit brigade and then the SAS. He was brought down in mid-July from the Commando Training School at Lochailort where he was a Demolitions Instructor. Like many others, he was shocked by the reality of the preparations for invasion: 'I had been caught up, along with everyone else, by the invasion fever, but this official recognition that desperate measures might soon be needed brought home, as nothing else had, the full gravity of our situation in 1940'.[11] He mined bridges and railway lines and filled the basements of country houses liable to be used as German HQs with explosives ready to be detonated if occupied by the Nazis. He also enthusiastically booby-trapped Brighton Pier. Unfortunately an inquisitive seagull set off one of the charges, which produced a spectacular chain reaction. The seagull survived: the pier did not![12]

At the strategic core of the XII Corps Observation Unit were the regular army Battle Patrols and the Lovat Scouts training unit. The Battle Patrols were formed in each battalion of XII Corps and would act independently as guerrilla units, attacking the rear and flanks of the enemy. The twenty Patrols were typically units of twelve men under an officer and each sub-divided into two patrols. They had hidden hides and, crucially, many were equipped with wireless and so could be directed more strategically. From February 1941 Henry Hall, a former student at the Lochailort Commando School, commanded the Battle Patrol of the 4th Battalion, Dorset Regiment with three NCOs and thirty other ranks (probably to be divided into three sub-units of ten men each under an NCO). They were trained in close-quarters combat and demolition skills, with orders to go to ground upon invasion and create as much havoc as possible. In the meantime they would test the security of HQs, ammunition dumps and communication systems and act as the 'enemy' on brigade exercises. Hall went on to assist the Auxiliary Units Intelligence Officer in Kent. One NCO who served with the Battle Patrols was Tom 'Chalkie' White. He was recruited by Peter Fleming into a patrol of the West Surrey Regiment with seven other NCOs from the reserve depot. One thing that struck him was that Fleming insisted they all be treated as equals and call each other by their Christian names – a tricky line for an officer to follow whilst retaining both his authority and their respect. Fleming acknowledged that he did not naturally have the common touch with his men and as a consequence made great efforts to talk and listen to them, taking their advice on choice of weaponry and encouraging them to use their initiative. He also warned his men that their life expectancy would be just forty-eight hours.[13]

These Battle Patrols went on to provide the inspiration for the Scout Sections of the Auxiliary Units (see Chapter Eight). They were supported by additional LDV/Home Guard patrols recruited by Peter Fleming: he was armed with a letter of authority from the general commanding Tunbridge Wells Home Guard to choose whatever men he needed 'which may necessitate their going with Captain Fleming or his subordinates in the event of an emergency.'[14]

Fleming described their respective roles in 1952:

> This [Battle Patrols] was a nucleus to which in time we precariously linked a network of picked sub-units of the Home Guard, who would in theory – after fighting like lions in their normal role – withdraw to well-stocked hide-outs in the woods when their localities were overrun by the Germans. The whole scheme in its early stages was typical of the happy-go-lucky impro-visation of those dangerous days, and though we gradually built it up into something fairly solid I doubt if we should have been more than a minor and probably short-lived nuisance to the invaders.[15]

It is curious that the LDV patrols were only expected to go to ground after having defended their allotted posts with their battalion. How many would have survived to join the Observation Unit is therefore debatable. Fleming established a training centre in a farm, The Garth at Bilting; his HQ was in a hut where the officers dined on a crate of explosives, using other crates of explosives as chairs. There they entertained curious generals and even the Prime Minister.[16]

The XII Corps Observation Unit was a tighter structure, more directly inte-grated with the regular forces, than that which developed in the Auxiliary Units; with a battle plan that made guerrilla warfare an integral part of the Corps strategy. What made this possible was that it was directly administered at Corps level. The Auxiliary Units struggled to find a mechanism that achieved the same ends until 1942. Peter Fleming had a huge admiration for Thorne's common-sense approach to irregular warfare, but was more scathing about what he later saw as the romanticism of Gubbins and his staff 'for whom an enemy is hardly worth killing unless he can be killed with a tarantula fired from an airgun by a Bessarabian undertaker on Walpurgis night'.[17] This from the man who tried to re-introduce the longbow to the British army via the Observation Units! 'We had not been there very long before I procured, at the taxpayers' expense, two large bows and a supply of arrows and told the Lovat Scouts to learn how to use them'. They found that a detonator and short length of fuse taped to an arrow made an effective distraction device when fired over the top of an enemy post.[18]

Although XII Corps Observation Unit was absorbed into the Auxiliary Units in late 1940, they still retained their original title until their stand-down in 1944. General Montgomery succeeded Thorne as commanding officer of XII Corps on 25 April 1941 and Thorne became General Officer Commanding, Scottish Command. Although this was technically a promotion, few could understand why he had been moved to what was considered to be a backwater. There were suspicions that Montgomery (then commanding V Corps) might have engineered the move to increase his own profile, but Thorne was too much of a gentleman ever to make public comment on the matter.

Chapter Six

Foundation of the Auxiliary Units (June–July 1940)

> In July it was decided by the authorities that the risk of reprisals incurred by allowing civilians to engage in sabotage activities was too great. It was therefore decided that M.I.R. and D Section home activities should be united and called G.H.Q. Auxiliary Units (under Colonel Gubbins) and the members would be selected from Home Guard Units.[1]
>
> *Section D, Early History to September 1940*

Despite the perceived risk of imminent invasion during June/July 1940, the government took a clear decision to reject the existing concept of a civilian resistance that was at the heart of the Home Defence Scheme (HDS), and which was already in the process of being mobilised and supplied, in favour of a radically different military model to operate purely as an anti-invasion force: the Auxiliary Units. They were named after the ammunition dumps (Aux. Units or Aux. Packs) at the time being supplied to the HDS by Aston House. These, in turn, had probably been named after the British intelligence Auxiliary Division operating in Dublin in 1920 and undoubtedly well known to Colin Gubbins, although he never acknowledged the SIS connection. The Operational Branch of the Auxiliary Units went through a series of rapid changes in its early months; these are considered in this chapter and in Chapters Seven and Eight.

According to Major Peter Wilkinson, General Ironside 'read the Riot Act' after learning of the chaotic distributions of arms dumps by Section D and demanded that all such activities should now be under military control.[2] Having been briefed by Jo Holland, the CIGS and C-in-C Home Forces successfully won the approval in principle of the War Cabinet on 17 June for the formation of the Auxiliary Units.[3] They had little idea of how it would operate; the agreement was only a few days after the creation of the XII Corps Observation Unit, its closest model. Two days later Colin Gubbins, who had only returned from Norway on 10 June, was in his new post. The Chiefs of Staff Committee discretely noted that Gubbins had been transferred from CO of Independent Companies to 'other duties connected with home defence'.[4] Gubbins was already known to General Ironside, having been his Aide de Camp in Archangel in 1919.

Gubbins gathered around him a staff of men that, in the main, had worked with him before (principally in MIR or in the Independent Companies) or who were otherwise known personally to him or to his second in command, Major Peter

Wilkinson. Despite its history in researching guerrilla warfare, MIR had no direct involvement in the development of the Auxiliary Units after Holland's briefing to the CIGS, beyond supplying some staff and subsequently making available its explosives stores, which was in line with its primary role as a theoretical think-tank rather than a management body. As late as the document of 2 June 'Duties of the MIR' there is no indication of any germ of an idea concerning the Auxiliary Units. Nonetheless, by 22 July Jo Holland was listing Auxiliary Units in 'Duties and Activities of MIR' as one of the projects MIR set in motion 'through an inter-change of personnel and ideas'.[5] There was, however, no pre-conceived masterplan.

According to Wilkinson, the organisation evolved as they went along, over the following two months. Gubbins said:

> I had in fact been given a blank cheque but was there any money in the bank to meet it? Everything would have to be improvised. Time was the essence … at the shortest we had six weeks before a full-scale invasion could be launched; if we were lucky we might have until October …[6]

Changes in structure were inevitable as Gubbins's ideas developed and the organisation moved from providing a desperate response to an immediate threat of invasion into something more sustainable. Initially, the organisation was not expected to survive beyond the first two weeks of any invasion and many of the later problems were caused by the subsequent need to create a longer-term structure acceptable to the War Office. The quiet-spoken Gubbins was an ideal person for the task with his experience in working in MIR with Section D on the theory of guerrilla warfare and his development of the Independent Companies.

Gubbins wanted to extend Thorne's model of guerrilla warfare using small regular army and LDV patrols, under the supervision of county Intelligence Officers, as a means of providing defence in depth into all of the coastal areas judged vulnerable to the threat of invasion. In May 1940 the beach defences were thin and weak. They were mainly defended by second-line troops whose role was simply to delay the enemy for as long as possible, with the main front-line infantry and armour being held back in the mobile reserves – 'Leopard' brigades. The precious armoured division was not expected to be deployed until the third day of landings – when the main focus of invasion would hopefully be clear.[7] Although the beach defenders were ordered to hold their positions at all costs there was a real danger that the enemy would break through before the 'Leopard' brigades could properly engage them. The main battlefield would be the territory between the coast and the GHQ line, within which there may have been considerable areas of temporary occupation. Gubbins therefore created the Auxiliary Units, initially extending out along the east and south coast, from the existing organisation of XII Corps Observation Unit in Kent and Sussex. Whether known by GHQ or not, SIS simultaneously continued to build its organisation of last resort in Section VII, with a top-secret wireless that extended beyond a coast-watching service and the GHQ stop-line into the industrial heartland.

At the heart of Gubbins's initial concept was the basic principle of Jo Holland, as expounded at the ISPB meeting in May 1940, that 'irregular warfare should be controlled by, and undertaken in conjunction with, the actions of regular forces'.[8] This was already being provided within XII Corps by Thorne's specially-trained Battle Patrols, which operated under his direct chain of command. Gubbins did not have the authority to create similar patrols across other Corps areas. Instead, coming directly from command of the Independent Companies, it was natural that he should turn to them first of all for his new model. Five of the Independent Companies had sailed to Norway under Gubbins as Scissorforce, but in the event there was only limited opportunity for their specialist role in the Norwegian campaign. Now seemed to be the chance to use them as originally intended.

Initially Gubbins saw the role of Auxiliary Units HQ and its Intelligence Officers as being only an advisory and supply body to encourage the formation of guerrilla units that were under the control of the local LDV and army commander. These would in turn support the new Independent Companies (MIRs) as they moved through the enemy lines. Only subsequently were the Auxiliary Unit Operational Patrols of six to eight men created. Speed was everything, with Gubbins warning LDV commanders that 'The present situation obviously necessitates speed at the expense of security, but at the same time it is important that, whatever else be known generally, the names of the operatives, the existence of dumps of stores, their location, etc., should be kept as secret as possible'.[9]

The first HQ of the new organisation was at 7 Whitehall Place in London. Major Peter Wilkinson was appointed as GSO2 in charge of Organisation, Planning and Liaison with SIS, but was only able to take up his post from 25 June. Alongside him was Major Bill Beyts, formerly of the Rajpuntna Rifles but latterly training officer for the Independent Companies and a natural choice as Operations and Training Officer for the Auxiliary Units. He had previous counter-insurgency experience in Burma where he had gained a reputation for ruthlessness. Captain, the Honourable Michael Henderson (16th Lancers and latterly a staff officer at GHQ) was the Quartermaster. After these early appointments, the Auxiliary Units officially came into being on 2 July 1940 when the War Office circulated an advance notice of the War Establishment (the document that established the official composition of the unit) of the Operational Branch. The formal establishment of the HQ, Special Duties Branch (SDB) followed on 11 July 1940, with the cryptic comment that the organisation had already commenced activities but was now 'attached to' the HQ of Auxiliary Units, a discrete reference to the pre-existing intelligence operations of the HDS.[10]

Intelligence Officers

Local organisation would be undertaken by a number of Intelligence Officers, each responsible for an operational area, and the first eight met in Whitehall on 13 July. Others quickly followed, with a rash of almost simultaneous promotions to acting captain for those not already at that rank (Fig. 3).

The mix of the early Intelligence Officers is interesting. At least 20 per cent had been personal friends of Wilkinson from Cambridge days and had latterly

Figure 3. Auxiliary Units (Operational) Intelligence Officers, 1940.

Name	Age in 1940	Previous service	Rank	Area	Later service
*Stuart Edmundson	45	Territorial Royal Engineers	Temporary Captain, 16 July 1940	Devon and Cornwall	SOE
Nigel Oxenden	45	Royal Northumberland Fusiliers	Temporary Captain, 24 July 1940	Norfolk	Remained with Aux Units
Guy Atkinson	43	Royal Fusiliers (formerly Coldstream Guards) MIR	Promoted Captain, 3 July 1940	North Yorkshire	RAOC / Royal Fusiliers
John Todd	41	General List (SIS)	Temporary Captain, 22 July 1940	Monmouthshire, Herefordshire and Worcestershire	SOE
W.W. Harston	41	Dorset Regiment	Lieutenant, Sep–Nov 1940 Captain, 10 Nov 1940		
*Lord Ashley	40	Major, Territorial Reserve (Wiltshire Yeomanry)	Gazetted Captain, Intelligence Corps, 22 July 1940	Dorset	Intelligence Corps to Royal Tank Regiment
*Donald Hamilton-Hill	39	Queens Own Cameron Highlanders / MIL(b)	Acting Captain	Lincolnshire	SOE
*John Gwynne	35	Royal Artillery	Acting Captain	Sussex	SOE
*Peter Fleming	33	Grenadier Guards / MIR	Captain	Kent	SOE
*Andrew Croft	32	Essex Regt / MIR / Independent Companies	Captain	East Anglia	SOE
Ian Fenwick	30	King's Royal Rifle Corps	Lieutenant (Special Emp, 30 June 1940; Acting Captain, 11 Dec 1940)	Somerset	SAS
*Alan John Crick	27	Foreign Office General List (comm. 20/4/40)	Temporary Captain, 2 Oct 1940 (Int. Corps)	Somerset	Intelligence Corps
Eustace Maxwell	27	Argyll and Sutherland Highlanders	Temporary Captain, 27 July 1940	Angus, Fife	Argyll and Sutherland Highlanders
*Hamish Torrance	24	Highland Light Infantry / MIR / Independent Companies	Captain	Forth, Berwick and Northumberland	SOE

*Present at initial meeting of 13 July.

served with MIR or with the Independent Companies in Norway. Others had earned their reputation in the retreat through France, such as John Gwynne, who had become known as a fiercely determined artillery officer. Some were friends or family of Gubbins. More surprising is how many were in their late thirties or forties. These were older men who could be spared from front-line service and later there was to be a clear policy of only retaining IOs over 38 years old and of 'B' medical grade or lower. Overall, the average age of the 1940 IOs was about 35 years old; Edmundson, Todd, Atkinson and Lord Ashley were 40 years or older; the youngest was Torrance, aged 24. If not young commando officers, the older men were confident, self-assured individuals who, in the main, had already proved their ability to lead men in civilian life without being too rigid in military thinking. As a consequence, they were exactly what the intelligence services were looking for, and most of them were later recruited into SOE, Intelligence Corps or, in the case of 30-year-old Ian Fenwick, into the SAS.

The oldest was Nigel Oxenden, aged 45, who had seen service in the First World War with the Welsh Regiment and Machine Gun Corps. He was recalled from the reserves in November 1938 and was commissioned into the Royal Northumberland Fusiliers. On the basis of his First World War experience, in November 1939 he was promoted to acting captain and was seconded to 341 Machine Gun Training Centre based on Alderney, Channel Islands, until they were evacuated in June. Oxenden left Jersey on 20 June and was, at least temporarily, out of a job, with his age making future employment and promotion unlikely. He was, however, a cousin of Gubbins and whilst staying with relatives in Sussex asked one of Colin's sisters to mention to her brother that Oxenden was looking for a post. Oxenden joined the Auxiliary Units a few weeks later on 13 July, as Intelligence Officer for Norfolk, and as with most of the IOs, he was promoted to temporary captain. He later became Training Officer and also the official historian of the Auxiliary Units.

Another older man, Stuart Edmundson, was also in the first wave of Auxiliary Units IOs. Edmundson had special skills in demolition and engineering which were an obvious attraction to Gubbins. He had worked pre-war for a fertiliser company in Devon, which probably gave him a knowledge of the ingredients in improvised explosives. He joined the Territorial Army and in August 1937 was commissioned as a second lieutenant in the Devon & Cornwall (Fortress) Engineers TA at Plymouth. Promoted lieutenant in January 1940 in the Royal Engineers, he set up a production line of Molotov cocktails for the LDV at Fort Austin, Plymouth, in May and travelled the region to instruct the LDV on their use. Edmundson was recruited to the Auxiliary Units on 13 July and received his promotion to temporary captain on 16 July 1940. Fort Austin then became the regional HQ of the Auxiliary Units, although initially the local corps commander was not informed and as a consequence he surrounded the base with armed troops after reports of explosions inside. Edmundson left the Auxiliary Units in November 1943 and continued his engineering research first with SOE at Station XII and then in the Far East with Force 136 and the School of Army Ordnance South East Asia.

The Yorkshire Intelligence Officer was 43-year-old Captain Guy Atkinson. Born in 1897, he had joined the Bedfordshire Yeomanry straight from school in 1915 and was then commissioned into the Coldstream Guards and won a Military Cross on the Western Front in 1918. Like Gubbins and Holland he served in North Russia in 1919. Remaining in the army, in 1926 he was seconded as a lieutenant into the Colonial Office where he was promoted captain in 1929. He retired from the Coldstream Guards in October 1931, but it is not known how long he remained with the Foreign and Colonial Office or what his job with them entailed. Atkinson was recalled from the reserves into the Royal Fusiliers in August 1939 and served with Gubbins in MIR. He was promoted back to his old rank of captain on 3 July 1940. He finally retired from the army in 1956 as a major and died in 1964.

John Todd was aged 41 at the time he joined the Auxiliary Units. He had served in the Honourable Artillery Company during the latter part of the First World War and then became a successful London stockbroker. His City career may, however, have hidden a more secret occupation; on 31 May 1940 he was suddenly gazetted as a second lieutenant on the General List – 'without pay and allowances' – a classic indicator of an SIS officer. Indeed, he was commissioned and listed in the same batch as other known SIS officers including Sweet-Escott. In the absence of any other obvious qualifications it seems likely that he was seconded to the Auxiliary Units as one of Grand's officers from his 'D.M. group' (see above, p. 51) and was already recruiting men for the HDS. He was recruiting saboteurs in Herefordshire in June and recruited the first Auxiliary Units patrol in Worcestershire during late July 1940.[11] It was only on 26 July that a report of HQ Auxiliary Units noted that an intelligence officer had been dispatched to South Wales and was expected to organise fifty weapons dumps there by 4 August, but there is still no mention of any authorised activity in Herefordshire or Worcestershire.[12] Neither are these counties mentioned in the August Progress Report of the Auxiliary Units, and throughout their lifespan the organisation in the inland counties for which he was initially responsible remained a sparsely-documented oddity.[13] Worcestershire had been surveyed as early as 1938 for the eventuality of a move of government offices into the county following invasion – the 'Yellow Move'. If the capital became untenable then 'Black Move' would bring the Prime Minister, Cabinet and Royal Family to Worcestershire, along with emergency communication HQs of the three services, making the county of great strategic importance. It would therefore have been an obvious area in which to create an early HDS network and a decision could, likewise, have been made to extend the coastal distribution of Auxiliary Units into these areas in anticipation of any attack. Such units in Worcestershire and Herefordshire would then also help provide an outer ring of defence on the southern approaches to Birmingham.

Todd left the Auxiliary Units in August 1941 with a promotion to lieutenant Colonel to lead the SOE Mission in East Africa. It was only from this point, having finally left SIS, that he was badged as a member of the Intelligence Corps. On his return in 1943 he was promoted to a colonel in the Intelligence Corps but in 1944 he suddenly returns to his old haunts in Monmouthshire and presents

SDB member, George Vater, with his stand-down letter of thanks from Colonel Douglas. In true Todd fashion he then burnt the letter in front of George![14] The HQ records of the Auxiliary Units are notably blank when it comes to any direct reference to John Todd. Nonetheless, he was well-remembered by Willie Wilmott, the former secretary to the CO, Colonel Bill Major. Willie Wilmott joined the ATS at the outbreak of war and became secretary to the CO of the Auxiliary Units, living at Coleshill House, an idyllic setting where she would spend the mornings sunbathing and being brought cups of tea by the NCOs until she got bored. When in the summer of 1941 the 'IO from Cardiff' announced he was leaving, Wilmott asked if she could go with him as his secretary – although she had no idea as to his posting. After first being threatened with disciplinary action for daring to communicate directly with a superior officer, she was allowed to go and found herself in the offices of SOE in Baker Street where Todd was preparing the East Africa Mission.

Village Cells
The first known action of the new Auxiliary Units was for Quartermaster Captain Henderson to be dispatched in late June on a reconnaissance mission into Essex and Suffolk. This would establish the location of the main arms dumps in the region (Warley Barracks, Brentwood and the Cavalry barracks, Colchester) and to make initial contact with local LDV commanders and local landowners who would agree (on the HDS model) to be local 'dump owners' and who would also suggest suitable recruits. He reported back on 30 June.[15] On 5 July, just three days after the circulation of the War Establishment, Gubbins sent out a letter to LDV Area Commanders to advise them of the existence of the new organisation.[16] The overall sense of the letter is that at this stage the formation of the Operational Patrols was regarded as very much an LDV responsibility with his Intelligence Officers providing support and supplies. He explained that the purpose of the new units was to harass the flanks of the enemy and that it had been decided to embrace such units within the LDV organisation. 'The personnel will consist of existing LDV volunteers and others who will be enrolled therein for the purpose.' Gubbins went on to state that 'The raising of these special sub-units will be decided between the local military commander and the LDV commander'. In this initial concept the role of the Intelligence Officer was simply to 'work in the closest touch with the military commander and the LDV commander so as to assist in every possible way the selection, training and organisation of these sub-units, and the provision and storage of equipment'.[17] The Intelligence Officers were therefore conceived as having a mainly advisory and supply role, a concept very much in line with the thinking of Jo Holland in MIR, which was not to run operational units.

This purely advisory model did not survive more than a week, but the letter was to cause some problems later with LDV/Home Guard commanders who would use it to claim that the later Operational Patrols should come directly under their command. In September 1940 there were difficulties in the Portsmouth area, where Brigadier General Bryan Curling (retired), CO of the local Home Guard, believed that it had been agreed that the Auxiliary Units patrols should be under the command of his platoon commanders and not the Auxiliary Units Intelligence Officer (Major Saunders). He had already made plans for guerrilla units of his own and believed that the Auxiliary Units should be regarded merely as 'specialists' of his own command.[18]

It is highly unlikely that the LDV at this stage were capable of managing such guerrilla units. By 13 July and the first meeting of the Intelligence Officers the ideas of Gubbins had developed considerably. The new concept was, as in the original XII Corps Observation Unit plan, to recruit a number of village sabotage cells as quickly as possible, making best use of the existing HDS and their network of weapons dumps. Gubbins produced a briefing note for the Intelligence Officers on 17 July which gives a very clear summary of his strategy at this early stage. It relied heavily on the existing methodology of the HDS. One of his first points was that 'decentralisation therefore is initially forced upon us. If time allows, organisation, and hence control of these cells, can be more and more centralised; eventually larger units can be formed'. These 'larger units' were Gubbins's concept of Home Guard commando units.[19] The Intelligence Officers were to recruit 'key men' (the same term as used in the HDS and quite possibly the same people), who would recruit the remaining members of their cells, and then train and supply them. Explosives would be supplied for small acts of sabotage – vehicles, dumps, sentry posts, HQs, signal communication, etc. (Fig. 4). They would act in the period where the invading forces were forming up and advancing through any bridgeheads. Their window of opportunity to engage the enemy before being destroyed was seen as being very limited and it was therefore stressed that as many cells as possible needed to be formed in the shortest

Figure 4. Auxiliary Units Explosives Dumps (Small), July 1940.
(TNA CAB 120/241)

Time fuses, Red (½ hour)	16
White (1½ hours)	11
Green (4 hours)	11
Yellow (12 hours)	11
Blue (20 hours)	11
Fuses	1 box
Adhesive tape (¾in × 15 yards)	
Detonators	35
Bickford fuse	24 ft
Instantaneous fuse	12 ft
Cordtex fuse	50 ft
Crimping tool	
Vaseline	1 tube
Large magnets	4
Magnesium incendiaries	10
Fog signals	4
Plastic explosive	83 sticks
Paraffin incendiaries	12
Medium–large incendiaries	4

possible time. Their key strategic role was to act as guides to Independent Companies commando units, which would infiltrate the enemy lines and harass the flanks and rear. The main task of the Intelligence Officers after recruiting the village cells was therefore to lay down large weapons dumps ready for the commandos to use behind enemy lines and to ensure coordination between the two bodies (Fig. 5). Gubbins said that a new War Establishment was being prepared that would superimpose these new Independent Company units onto the existing LDV organisation and so relieve the IOs of administrative detail. This never happened.[20]

Some of the existing HDS volunteers who were absorbed into the Auxiliary Units may have not been aware of the change. At this stage the HDS were still independently recruiting and supplying their saboteurs (see p. 49). In South Wales and the South Midlands, Intelligence Officer John Todd is believed to have been one of the SIS officers attached to the new Auxiliary Units by Lawrence Grand. He began the tradition in this area of having a single intelligence officer control both Operational Patrols and the Special Duties Branch of the Auxiliary Units and some of his methodology has close links to the HDS. His SDB unit in Monmouthshire was a hybrid of intelligence-reporting and operational activity. They went out on stalking exercises, had an emergency HQ, and one of them was issued with a .22 sniper rifle and a 'hit list'. George Vater's rifle was given to him by a 'Mr Graham'. Todd was unhappy about this but accepted the situation, suggesting that 'Mr Graham' was senior to Todd. 'Mr Graham' was an alias used by Lawrence Grand.[21] In Herefordshire, Geoffrey Morgan-Jones recalled being contacted by telephone 'about the time of the Dunkirk evacuation' by someone asking if he was willing 'to do something to help his

Figure 5. Auxiliary Units Explosives Dumps (Large), July 1940.
(TNA CAB 120/241)

Time fuses, Red (½ hour)	180
White (1½ hours)	120
Green (4 hours)	120
Yellow (12 hours)	120
Blue (20 hours)	240
Fuses	51 boxes
Adhesive tape (¾in × 15yards)	28
Detonators	210
Large magnets	16
Magnesium incendiaries	10
Fog signals	12
Bickford fuse	95 ft
Instantaneous fuse	50 ft
Cordtex fuse	100 ft
Plastic explosive	83 sticks
Blasting gelignite	400 lb
Paraffin incendiaries	180
Small Magnesium incendiaries	150
Medium–large incendiaries	110

country'. A meeting was arranged where he met Alex Beck and John Todd. This would pre-date the creation of the Auxiliary Units and is much earlier than any documented Auxiliary Unit activity in the region. It suggests that the men were initially recruited into a unit of the HDS, which then morphed into Adam Patrol of the Herefordshire Auxiliary Units. Other patrol members were recruited and armed, but at this time there was no Operational Base.[22] Alex Beck became patrol leader, but his view of action after invasion was that each member would act independently, so they all kept individual supplies of equipment, and again this was very much in the spirit of the HDS. In Worcestershire the spy cell at Upton was linked directly to the Operational Patrol HQ at Wolverton Hall where there was already an SIS interest. Other shadowy intelligence and guerrilla units operated in Worcestershire and the Midlands during the war and it is possible that in 1940/41 John Todd was still working to an SIS agenda that was tolerated and only partially absorbed by the Auxiliary Units.

In Devon, Edmundson established the early Auxiliary Units village cell system, but his account of the organisation at this stage is highly redolent of the HDS and their frantic distribution of its arms dumps. He recruited teams of a leader and two men who were expected to operate discretely from home as civilians. 'These early recruits were told nothing about being in a special unit of the Home Guard – or indeed about being in any formal organisation – and their names were never committed to paper.' Each team was given a cardboard box containing a sabotage kit; initially these were delivered to Edmundson's garden. 'His wife, who had been let in on the secret, rushed frantically around, trying to find new hiding places in the neighbourhood'.[23]

Like the original XII Corps Observation Unit and HDS before them, these early cells did not have buried Operational Bases. Samson Patrol in Broadheath, near Worcester, used the local scout hut (most of the original team were Boy Scouts). Here local butcher, Peter Price, gave them weekly instruction in unarmed combat (he later became an instructor at Coleshill). They also used the army rifle range at Tyddesley Woods, Pershore, with grenade instruction at Norton Barracks, Worcester. They continued to use the scout hut until 1941, even after their underground base was constructed in October 1940, but when obliged to move out by the local Home Guard they booby-trapped the entrance with a detonator![24]

The Village Cell scheme in support of putative regular army commando units only lasted around one month. A shortage of manpower meant it was not possible to allocate large numbers of regular troops to the scheme. The plan was abandoned in August 1940 in favour of the more ordered system that had been devised by Fleming in XII Corps Observation Unit and which became the standard model of Home Guard teams of six to eight uniformed men who had withdrawn to underground hides. The intention was still that the teams would support regular units who were now to be on the model of the small Battle Patrols/ Scout Sections as used in XII Corps Observation Unit. In the event, it was only possible to introduce Scout Sections from November, just as Gubbins and Wilkinson left for SOE (see Chapter Eight).

In the urgency of the situation, Gubbins had been obliged to abandon key elements of his 1939 pamphlets on guerrilla warfare. His ideas on 'Planning and Action' prior to enemy invasions stressed not only the need for early planning, nomination of local leaders and provision of arms dumps, but also for wireless communications and a means of liaison with HQ. However, the Operational Patrols of the Auxiliary Units did not work from within the community, were not linked by wireless and could only have uncertain contact with higher authority once they had gone into action.[25] A progress report from Duncan Sandys, a member of the new Ministry of Defence, to Churchill on 8 August on the new 'Home Guard – Auxiliary Units' mentions that 'selected units are also being provided with wireless and field telephone apparatus', probably referring to the Scout Sections of XII Corps and the hopes for their expansion.[26] The lecture notes for the patrol leader's course of 1941, however, downplayed the need for outside communication and stressed that there would be few times when the Patrol Leader would need to send a message and that trying to do so might jeopardise the security of the patrol: 'Do not, therefore, let intercommunication become your master, when it should be your slave'.[27] Wilkinson recognised that communications would have been one of the weak spots if the patrols had indeed gone to war. At the time he left, he knew the Auxiliary Units were experimenting with wireless sets, but he had little confidence in this because he believed that once invasion took place they would be isolated to do what they could until they were quickly discovered, therefore any sophisticated set-up was unnecessary; this only became a problem when the organisation took on a longer-term existence.[28]

The members of the Auxiliary Units Operational Patrols were under no illusion as to their chances of survival beyond two weeks. Long-term survival was not part of the agenda of GHQ in 1940; they were purely a short-term military expedient to hinder the invasion army. Because of the popular mis-labelling of the Auxiliaries as a resistance organisation, it is worth quoting the contemporary opinion of this role. Gubbins himself concluded that the Auxiliary Units 'were designed, trained and prepared for a particular and imminent crisis: that was their specialist role.'[29] Basically, they were considered a short-term and expendable option, all the more so because they avoided taking army scout sections and instructors from front-line units. Gubbins explained 'they were something additional – don't forget we hadn't taken men from regular formations, but from depots. We were expendable. We were a bonus, that's all.'[30] His second-in-command, Peter Wilkinson, shared this sentiment, writing: 'any suggestion that Auxiliary Units could have provided a framework for long-term underground resistance is, in my opinion, absurd'.[31] In an earlier interview he had explained the confusion of purpose:

Originally, there was a slight muddle in the concept because nobody could quite make up their minds whether we were trying to set up something for immediate action against the Germans in the event of an invasion. Or, whether we were trying also to set up a nucleus of an English secret ... a British Secret Army. If it was the former, which I think was probably the idea of the War Office and probably GHQ Home Forces, then security was not a paramount consideration. On the other hand, if you were trying to produce a 'long-term' organisation, then obviously one had to deal with an entirely different sort of clandestine technique. I certainly in the initial stages, adhered to the latter. Gubbins, I think, was about half way in between ... The War Office, and indeed GHQ Home Forces, I believe, saw the thing in the early stages, in the former sense.[32]

Duncan Sandys's progress report of 8 August 1940 only refers to their function of acting offensively on the flanks and rear of an enemy army with no mention of any longer-term resistance function.[33] His careful wording may well have been in response to the furious letter that he had received only a few days before from General Paget, Chief of Staff to the new C-in-C Home Forces, General Alan Brooke, a letter (30 July) which was, in turn, a response to the concerns expressed by Lieutenant MacLeod on 3 July about the attempts of the HDS to recruit members of the LDV for acts of civilian sabotage (see above, pp. 46–7). Paget begins by stressing that the Auxiliary Units Operational Patrols are uniformed members of the Home Guard:

The object of these fighting patrols is to provide within the general Home Guard organisation small units of men, specially selected and trained, whose role is to act offensively on the flanks and in the rear of any German troops who may obtain a temporary foothold in this country. Their action is to be directed particularly against tanks and lorries in laager, ammunition dumps, small enemy posts and stragglers, etc., and their main activities will be under cover of darkness ... These men, being members of the Home Guard, will of course fight in uniform.

He begins to get more agitated when having to stress that the role of these patrols was not 'sabotage' and neither did it imply that there was official recognition of a possibility of 'occupation'.

Mr MacLeod refers in his letter to preparations for 'sabotage' in an 'occupied area'. The action of these units is not sabotage, but offensive action by fighting patrols against military targets. As regards the expression 'occupied area', this is an entirely wrong conception. As you know, the policy in the event of invasion is to fight the enemy on the beaches wherever he tries to land. He may, if in sufficient force, secure a temporary footing in places until counter-attacked and driven out, and it is during this phase of confused fighting that the action of these special Home Guard units will be of great value in preventing the establishment of a secure bridgehead; but there can be no question of an 'occupied area' behind the German line where civilian life will continue peacefully.

Paget finally distances Home Forces from the previous operations of the HDS in organising civilian sabotage operations and moreover states that any such organisation would be impractical and undesirable.

This organisation [HDS] was recently transferred from the SIS and put under GOC-in-C Home Forces, but as several indiscretions immediately came to light showing the impossibility of maintaining the necessary degree of secrecy, and as in any case the military value of such an organisation, based as it was on the misconception of an 'occupied area', was insufficient to warrant the reprisals its activities would inevitably evoke, it was decided that the organisation should be closed down forthwith and its activities suspended. This has been done.[34]

For Paget, the use of the term 'occupied area' implied defeatism; something that would be fresh in the mind after the surrender of France and its division into occupied and unoccupied zones. Indeed, the 1941 Nazi blueprint for invasion implies throughout that there would indeed be occupied and unoccupied zones.[35] The fact that SIS were even contemplating planning for the failure of the army to immediately throw the enemy back into the sea seems to have raised the blood pressure in some quarters of the War Office, made worse by the fact that they were going to use civilians and operate outside the traditional rules of war. This reaction of the General Staff was not dissimilar to that regarding the contemporary creation of SOE in order to 'Set Europe Ablaze'.

Paget was explicit about the wearing of uniform by the Auxiliers, but this matter has nonetheless aroused some denial and consequent confusion as to the status of the Auxiliary Units. Stuart Edmundson wrote:

> There was no uniform in 1940. They were given denims to protect their clothes ... I never trained a man in uniform and we never intended them to fight in Home Guard uniform.[36]

Likewise, Herman Kindred, an Auxilier from Suffolk, said 'Our "real uniform", if you like, was just plain army denims, but they were only really to protect our ordinary clothes'. Both Edmundson and Kindred seem to have forgotten that, when the Auxiliary Units were founded, the only uniform for most LDV/Home Guard was an armband worn with civilian clothes. The Home Guard uniform for the rest of 1940 was army-issue plain denim overalls, about which Edmundson and Kindred were so dismissive; the Auxiliary Units were therefore dressed in step with the normal Home Guard and, for the War Office at least, had equal legal status. Unfortunately the Home Guard was regarded by the Nazis as a terrorist organisation, uniform or not! Even after the issue of battledress in 1941, it is likely that the denim uniform was retained for use on operations (as indeed a percentage was retained by the Home Guard for dirty working). Although shapeless, the denim overalls were practical and quick-drying, which made them the favoured dress of the D-Day assault troops in 1944. The issue of uniform in order to bring the Operational Patrols within international law was considered so serious that the August progress report to the Prime Minister was delayed until 11 September when the supply issue could be resolved.[37] The official position is therefore absolutely clear: the Operational Patrols were soldiers of the Home Guard and would wear uniform. Given that the Intelligence Officers and the individual patrols had considerable latitude in the way that they operated it would not be surprising if some patrols did decide to fight out of uniform – although their long disappearances into the Operational Bases would have meant that it would not have been as easy to blend back into the local community as under the village cell methodology. It would have only been human nature for them to hope and plan for a longer-term role than that envisaged by GHQ. In Kent, Fleming and Calvert did organise additional dumps of hidden supplies to try to extend their operational life. In Worcestershire during 1941 the men were given vague hopes of resupply by the new Group Commanders, although no one was sure how this was actually going to be achieved.[38]

The intention is clear from the start that the Operational Patrols were to be formed from, and be part of, the LDV/Home Guard. The instructions to IOs of 27 July make this clear.

> Auxiliary Units will be created within existing LDV units. Suitable men you have found not in LDV should be brought into it.[39]

Further explanation was provided in a letter of April 1941 from the War Office to the local Territorial Army Associations that managed the Home Guard and who sometimes found themselves holding the supplies of weapons for the Auxiliary Units:

> Approval has been given for the enrolment of selected men into special patrols of Auxiliary Units, the personnel of which is mainly drawn from the Home Guard. Individual selection is made of the men required. They retain their Home Guard status and operate in their home localities but come under the control of Headquarters, Auxiliary Units.[40]

The above letter has frequently been taken as evidence that any connection to the Home Guard was purely nominal, with the latter having an organisational responsibility but with operational control being in the hands of the Coleshill Auxiliary Units HQ. As will be seen, that operational control was itself quite nominal and in action the Auxiliary Units patrols would come under the same Corps control as the Home Guard or regular forces. The relationship between the Auxiliary Units and Home Guard is more fully discussed in Chapter Twelve.

Chapter Seven

Auxiliary Units (Operations) (August–November 1940)

In August, the HQ of the Auxiliary Units began its move out of London, first to Northgate House, London Street, Farringdon (shared with the RASC Company of the 1st Armoured Brigade) and after 20 August to Coleshill House, Highworth, Wiltshire, a move which coincided with a significant shift in direction for the organisation. This phase ended with the departure of Colonel Gubbins and Major Wilkinson to SOE in November 1940.

From 15 August, the concept of village cells was changed to form well-armed patrols of six to eight men operating from hidden Operational Bases, with a chance of survival that could now hopefully be measured in terms of a couple of weeks rather than a couple of days. This followed the precedent set by Fleming's earlier changes to the XII Corps Observation Unit. The Auxiliary Units HQ was taking on a distinct identity of its own and was moving further away from the concept inherited from the HDS. This was the point at which Major Wilkinson lost faith in the organisation as it moved from its origin as a secret guerrilla force to a much more military commando arm of the Home Guard.

The work of constructing the new Operational Bases (the term 'hide' was rejected for being too suggestive of a defensive role) was usually carried out by army engineering units brought in from a considerable distance in order to improve security, although they might be based in the area for a year or more and be billeted in local houses. Some of the work of constructing the Operational Bases (OBs) in Northern and Southern Command was carried out by 184 Special Tunnelling Company of the 4th Special Tunnelling Engineers, whose template plan for an OB has survived, as well as their detailed schedule of works on building Auxiliary Units OBs during 1942, in their war diary.[1] Unfortunately, during their work in north-east England in October 1942 there was a security leak and a pegging-out plan for the local OB was left in one of their billets at Wheatley Hill, County Durham; it was found by local police and returned to Chief Engineer, IX Corps. The fall-out from this embarrassing incident is not known.

The Operational Bases (Fig. 6) would contain beds and supplies for up to a month, and stores of weapons and explosives. Some patrols objected to sharing their accommodation with the volatile No. 76 self-igniting phosphorous grenade and so buried them some distance away – some of the crates were never found again. They had no wireless, but usually had a field telephone (Mk V, Type D) linked by cable to an Observation Post up to half a mile away. To stop the enemy following the cable directly to the base, the cable entered the ground through

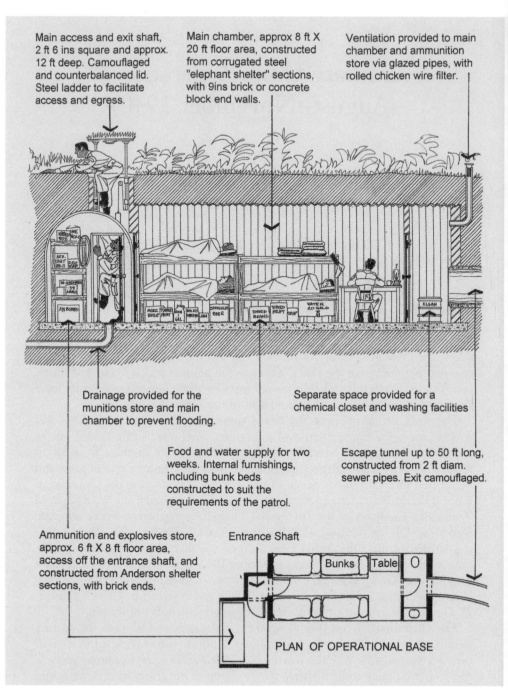

Main access and exit shaft, 2 ft 6 ins square and approx. 12 ft deep. Camouflaged and counterbalanced lid. Steel ladder to facilitate access and egress.

Main chamber, approx 8 ft X 20 ft floor area, constructed from corrugated steel "elephant shelter" sections, with 9ins brick or concrete block end walls.

Ventilation provided to main chamber and ammunition store via glazed pipes, with rolled chicken wire filter.

Drainage provided for the munitions store and main chamber to prevent flooding.

Separate space provided for a chemical closet and washing facilities

Food and water supply for two weeks. Internal furnishings, including bunk beds constructed to suit the requirements of the patrol.

Escape tunnel up to 50 ft long, constructed from 2 ft diam. sewer pipes. Exit camouflaged.

Ammunition and explosives store, approx. 6 ft X 8 ft floor area, access off the entrance shaft, and constructed from Anderson shelter sections, with brick ends.

Entrance Shaft

Bunks   Table

PLAN OF OPERATIONAL BASE

Figure 6. Reconstruction and plan of Auxiliary Units Operational Base, based on that at Alfrick, Worcestershire. (Mick Wilks)

a pipe around five metres away, which would give precious minutes' warning to allow the patrol to exit along an escape tunnel, leaving a booby-trap behind them.

Training

Major Beyts had experience in training the Independent Companies for guerrilla warfare and so was well placed to organise the training routine. Some of his earlier counter-insurgency work in Burma had been unorthodox to say the least; he later admitted carrying out mock hangings of prisoners in order to convince their fellow villagers to reveal information.

With invasion in July 1940 expected in just a matter of weeks, training was a key priority. Wilkinson recounts how he was in the London office from 8.30am– 5.00pm and was then driven out to meet a patrol; he would give a lecture or instruct on a night exercise, finishing around midnight, sleep in the car and then be back in the office again at 8.30am.[2] In early August, Gubbins managed to beg a small temporary training staff from Southern Command. Brigadier Richie of HQ Southern Command asked for help for this from 3rd Division.

There exists an organisation, in reality a part of the H.G.s, [Home Guard] which works under one Brigadier GUBBINS and whose role is highly secret. GUBBINS you may possibly know already as he was in Norway.

The Chief is most anxious to help GUBBINS's show by getting hold of five good young officers, one from each of our areas, to train this personnel in intensive scouting and battle patrol training.[3]

The 3rd Division consequently provided five training officers: Captain Perry-Knox-Gore (1st Battalion, Grenadier Guards), Second Lieutenant Goss (2nd Battalion, Grenadier Guards), Second Lieutenant Stanley (7th Guards Brigade Anti-Tank Company), Lieutenant Shepherd (1st South Lancashire Regiment) and Captain Bredin (2nd Royal Ulster Rifles). Further support was provided from 20 August by the tank-hunting platoons of 1st and 2nd Battalions, Grenadier Guards. These were regular army officers with no experience in irregular warfare.[4] At this stage it is, therefore, no surprise to find Scottish Intelligence Officer Eustace Maxwell quoted as saying he believed the training provided at Tom Wintringham's Osterley Park Training School, staffed by veterans of the Spanish Civil War, was better than that provided for the Auxiliary Units.[5] From 22 August Coleshill HQ built up its own training establishment of instructors in patrolling, explosives and unarmed combat, providing weekend courses for patrol leaders. When the Scout Patrols were introduced on a general basis from November, part of their role was to provide local training (so avoiding the trips to Coleshill); first, however, they too had to be trained in the techniques of irregular warfare as they were drawn from ordinary regimental depots.

The progress report to 1 September gives a summary of the standard of training achieved during the period that they were most likely to have faced invasion:

By the 1st September all members of the Home Guard enrolled have had preliminary instruction in the use of the special weapons. At least 50%, in some areas 90%, of them have had practical experience in using High Explosive, in pistol firing and dummy Mills Bomb throwing. 70% of the patrols have had training in field stalking and at least 50% have carried out two or more night schemes.[6]

The level of training was therefore by no means complete, and the question was, would it have been enough to meet the threat of imminent invasion? It is interesting to reflect that this training covered the 2,300 members of the Auxiliary Units Operational Patrols; during the same period, around 4,000 members of the Home Guard attended an intensive weekend course in explosives handling and manufacture, stalking, tank-hunting and camouflage at Osterley Home Guard Training School.

Early Weapons and Explosives

The Auxiliary Units were given the best equipment available in 1940 to allow them the greatest chance of completing their desperate task. Churchill famously said that 'these men must have revolvers' at a time when they were in very short supply. Most were of US origin: by November 1940, 2,500 pistols had been issued, mainly American Smith and Wesson or Colt .38 revolvers, some still in their US police surplus holsters (Plate 22).[7] The first hand-guns issued, however, included a batch of 400 .32 Colt semi-automatic pistols, small calibre weapons which were withdrawn in 1943 (Plate 21). Small numbers of Beretta .32 semi-automatic pistols were also issued. They could not afford to get into firefights as this would only bring further enemy forces down upon them; their firearms were, therefore, to be used only as a matter of last resort. They were expected to travel light and silently, so some of the weaponry that was initially rushed to them – such as the heavy Browning Automatic Rifle (BAR) or P17 rifle – proved to be totally unsuitable (Plate 25). Even their Thompson sub-machine gun, valuable in providing short-range fire support and a huge status symbol, was considered a luxury (Plate 26). 'The tommy gun may be required to cover a withdrawal, but will not always be necessary'.[8] The Auxiliary Units did not receive the first Thompson SMGs in British service as is sometimes believed. The Phantom unit probably deserves that accolade, receiving a number of the 'gangster guns' in February 1940 for the protection of their forward intelligence patrols operating with the BEF in France.[9] Neither is there mention in the 1941 patrol list of the silenced .22 rifle, issued to every patrol but in practice too long and clumsy to carry on sabotage missions and not reliable in securing a silent kill (Plate 28). Although it had a known assassination function, it was perhaps most useful operationally against guard dogs, but was mainly used throughout the war in shooting 'for the pot'. By contrast, the later Scout Sections had the standard army .303 sniper rifle (without a silencer).

The above weapons were simply a means of allowing the patrols to place their explosives in the required position and withdraw safely. The instructions were that 'Each man should be a complete demolition unit in himself', which could be taken literally: the explosives were often carried in pouches sewn into the inside of their battledress blouses, with a length of cordtex instantaneous detonating fuze wrapped around their waist![10] Thus the training notes for 1941 recommended that they only carried:

- revolver with 12 rounds,
- Mills grenade,
- demolition materials,
- truncheon or fighting knife,
- first-aid dressing.

The earliest knives carried were commercial sheath knives; some Rogers knives were bought in bulk by intelligence officers. Many patrol members made their own, including versions of the army issue 'punch knife'. The Fairburn-Sykes fighting knife did, however, become an icon of commando forces and was carried proudly by the Operational Patrols (Plates 19 and 20). The gung-ho approach in the initial stages of the Auxiliary Units can be seen in the changing attitude to explosives. In 1940, Wilkinson's manual for the Auxiliary Units (*Calendar 1937*) contained no restriction on the use of the new plastic explosive supplied by Section D, with the advice that if in any doubt as to the quantity of explosive to employ – double it (Plate 29).[11] Amendments were sent out in April 1941 and by the second edition of 1942 (*Calendar 1938*) plastic explosive had been restricted to use as a primer and a unit charge of 1 lb had been introduced (Plate 32).[12] An amendment of January 1944 recommended a unit charge of only 8oz; a covering note from HQ was careful to stress that the reduction in the size of the charge from 1 lb had been tested and did work.[13] The final, and most famous, edition of the manual was the *Countryman's Diary 1939*, compiled later in 1944 by Royal Engineer Captain Philip Tallent (Plates 30 and 31). At this stage in the war, with increasing puzzlement from the War Office as to why the Auxiliary Units were still in existence, Tallent could afford a little wry humour. The '*Diary*' was supposedly produced by 'Highworth Fertilisers' with the rider that 'You will find the name Highworth whenever quick results are required'. It would not take too much research to identify Highworth as the location of the Auxiliary Units HQ at Coleshill House!

The smaller unit charges could be linked together as necessary, but there was clearly a concern to avoid unnecessary noise and expense. An example from Worcestershire serves to illustrate concerns over the enthusiasm of the Auxiliers in using high explosives. Samson Patrol decided to help out the father of one of their members, John Boaz, by blowing up a tree in the middle of a field that needed to be ploughed, but overestimated the charge and not only scattered fragments of tree all over the field (which they had to spend the next week clearing up) but also cracked the ceilings of a nearby house. Fortunately the house belonged to the mother of a former patrol sergeant, who could be appeased with minimum fuss.[14]

In 1944, after a period when the Auxiliary Units were presented with a multitude of booby-trap devices and new weapons including the Sten gun (Plate 27),

Training Officer Nigel Oxenden recommended that the patrols returned to the basic kit list of 1940/1 and only carry the new Welrod silenced pistol (Plate 23) and No. 77 phosphorous grenade (Plate 24) as weapons.

Roles

The primary role of the Operational Patrols was to engage in night-time operations that would disrupt the enemy supply lines. Auxiliary Units were trained to be selective and calculating in choosing their target, both to provide maximum effect and not to sacrifice their lives unnecessarily. The ideal was seen as one target per night for what they were told would be a three-week campaign of invasion. Discussions as to how long they might survive into winter time when their Operational Bases would be more exposed or how the Nazis might retaliate were considered irrelevant at the time.

The major problem in the system was that there was no means of using the patrols strategically once they had first gone to ground. Some targets could be pre-selected by the Intelligence Officer – bridges, airfields, railway lines etc. – although Geoffrey Morgan-Jones of Adam Patrol in Herefordshire maintained that the only instruction his patrol received from Captain Todd was to be a 'bloody nuisance' to the Germans.[15] Often the siting of the Operational Bases gives an indication of the intended primary target; for example, the Worcestershire patrols were clearly located to destroy the local railway network and airfields, and one patrol was sited to overlook the BBC shadow broadcasting facility at Wood Norton. Some of the targets required considerable forethought. In Kent, Mike Calvert filled the basements of country houses liable to be used as German HQs with explosives ready to be detonated by local volunteers if occupied by the Nazis.[16] At Clater Pitch in Herefordshire, Jacob Patrol cut slots in trees ready to receive charges which would blow them across the A44 and create an ambush for passing German staff cars. They were so thorough that the trees had to be felled post-war as a safety hazard and the resultant gaps in the woodland bounding the road can still be seen. If the Auxiliers survived the attacks on the first wave of pre-ordained targets they could go on to more opportunistic ones. For this purpose, patrol members would take turns to go out during the day on reconnoitring missions. A well-sited Observation Post might also be useful in identifying targets, as well as giving some warning of an approaching enemy.

One of the most notorious secondary roles of the Operational Patrols was that each held a letter giving the details of local people who were to be assassinated following invasion; they might be suspected local collaborators, someone who had accidentally stumbled onto the location of an Operational Base or even a former member of the patrol who might be considered a security risk (as happened in one Worcestershire patrol). In some cases at least, patrols were simply handed a letter with no prior knowledge of its contents. Geoff Devereux, patrol sergeant of Samson Patrol in Worcestershire, decided not to open his so that he would only learn his targets when he actually needed to kill them. Like the HDS before them, all patrols were issued with a .22 silenced rifle, usually with a telescopic sight. The intention of the weapon was clear when George Vater from Monmouthshire was handed such a rifle together with a sealed envelope containing the names of his victims. In truth it was a poor tool for long-range assassination as it had an effective range of only 100m. In order to ensure a silent kill, it was not enough simply to aim for a 'head shot' as the bullet would only penetrate the skull through the eye socket; it was, however, the only silenced weapon available at the time.

This role of assassination should be seen within the context of regional Army HQs repeatedly asking MI5 to release to them its lists of possible fifth columnists for arrest. In June 1940 MI5's head of counter-espionage, Guy Liddell, recorded:

9 June 1940: The fighting services are becoming more and more restive about the 5th Column. In some cases they are taking the matter into their own hands, but generally the wrong cases.[17]

20 June 1940: Mawhood, our Security Officer Eastern Command, says that Fifth Column jitters in his area are extremely serious. The military seem to be taking the law into their own hands. They arrested a perfectly inoffensive ex-officer with a fine record in the last war and kept him and his wife under detention for seven days without any justification whatever except that his name was Landsberg or Landsberger. Some of the local units appear to have prepared a kind of Black List of their own. When the balloon goes up they intend to round up or shoot all these individuals. The position is so serious that something of very drastic kind will have to be done.[18]

24 June: Maude [John Maude, MI5 officer] has discovered that the military, particularly the 55th Division in the Eastern Counties, have badgered the local police into giving them a list of people with whose bona fides they are not altogether satisfied. If and when the balloon goes up the military intend to take the law into their own hands and arrest these people. We have got hold of these lists which do not seem to have much in the way of a common-sense basis. One man's only crime appears to be that he is a dentist.[19]

Despite the best efforts of MI5, it seems that GHQ had decided upon a policy of using the Auxiliary Units as assassination squads to deal with the lists of suspected fifth columnists that they had compiled themselves. One problem with such vigilante action was that MI5 had widely infiltrated the British Union of Fascists and other suspect bodies, and their agents might well have been caught up in any purge. If so, their fate may have been horrific. Jim Caws, an Auxilier from the Isle of Wight, explained how they were taught to deal with fifth columnists: 'We could either sort of tear them to bits to start with or shoot them first and then tear them to bits ... The purpose of that, I presume, was that if someone was helping the Germans and you could catch up with them we would make a mess of them and leave them on the side of the road to deter other people from doing it'.[20] This ruthlessness was not an isolated case or confined to dealing with fifth columnists. In Worcestershire, the Intelligence Officer, John Todd, arranged for a local butcher (probably Peter Price, who was to become an unarmed combat instructor on the staff of Coleshill) to demonstrate the technique of evisceration, to be used against German sentries in order to unsettle their comrades.[21] John Thornton from Jacob Patrol in Herefordshire similarly remembers 'After killing the enemy we were told by Todd to cut their "knackers" off to demoralise the rest'.[22] A local bloodbath would surely have ensued.

Such barbarity follows suggestions in SIS's 1939 D Scheme for European Resistance for dealing with captured members of the Gestapo; Grand coldly reasoned that reprisals for guerrilla warfare would usefully create a number of martyrs.[23] Mike Calvert (XII Corps Observation Unit) believed that this became a deliberate part of the government anti-invasion strategy as widespread reprisals on the civilian population would have hardened the British resolve and might have convinced the Americans of the justice of joining the battle.[24] Looked at objectively, the Auxiliers were being ordered to commit war crimes. One has only to look at the horror of war on the Eastern Front, where Soviet partisans took brutal revenge on German prisoners for Nazi atrocities, followed by further Nazi retaliation against whole communities, to see how quickly guerrilla warfare could degenerate into barbarism.

This blood-curdling response to invasion must be seen in the wider context. If the Germans had survived being gassed on the invasion beaches then the whole British plan was to deny the enemy any chance of successfully mounting their lightning strike – *blitzkrieg* – that would drive columns deep into British territory before hooking round to encircle the defending forces. This tactic had served them well in France and the Low Countries where there had been no sustained opposition, but in England they would have faced opposition at every crossroads, village and town.[25] The terrifying *fougasse* would have blown seas of burning petrol across approaching columns of vehicles; Home Guard were publically announcing through the press that they were going to ambush tanks with petrol bombs and home-made explosives, or kill paratroopers with scythes as they hit the ground.

Memories would still have been fresh in 1940 of the brutal reprisals carried out against even minor civilian resistance in 1914, as the German army advanced through Belgium. The Nazi invaders were unlikely to have distinguished between the body of a dead Auxilier found after a night-time sabotage mission and wearing his denim overalls, and the body of a Home Guard wearing the same denims who was killed whilst throwing petrol bombs at a German tank. Even use of the common Home Guard shotgun constituted a war crime in the view of the German army. Massive reprisals would have followed in both cases.

Whilst demonstrating the uncompromising strategy that was being prepared to resist invasion, the role of assassination may have been overemphasised subsequently for dramatic effect. Remaining alive for as long as possible meant acting quickly, quietly and focussing on their strategic mission rather than engaging in more random violence. By 1941, the situation was calmer and the Auxiliary

Units had been more fully absorbed within the military sensibilities. The Patrol Leaders training course now cautioned them against the temptation to be blood-thirsty.[26]

The Directorate of Military Intelligence had considered the greatest risk of invasion lay between 8–10 September and on 7 September the code word *Cromwell* was issued, indicating that invasion was imminent and troops should take up battle stations. New instructions were even issued to the police on how to behave in occupied areas. By 1 September 1940, 2,300 men had been recruited to the Operational Patrols of the Auxiliary Units in over 370 patrols in the coastal counties (Figs 7 and 8).[27] Herefordshire and Worcestershire were not included in the official list, although it is clear that small-scale recruiting had been started as early as late July. The Midlands patrols were perhaps needed to help counter an attack on the emergency government, army and navy command centres in the county and the southern approaches to Birmingham, linking to the SIS Midlands resistance network. An odd omission is Gloucestershire. The county TAA was included in circular letters regarding the Auxiliary Units throughout the war but no evidence has yet been found for any Operational Patrols or Special Duties Branch. This left a curious gap in distribution on the south bank of the Severn estuary north of Bristol, in contrast with the distribution along the South Wales coast into Monmouthshire and Herefordshire.

Even as the Auxiliary Units were expanding, but with the immediate crisis over, in mid-September questions were being asked about the future of the Auxiliary Units. GHQ told Wilkinson and Gubbins that they believed there was now little likelihood of invasion in 1940. The defence landscape had changed radically from the time that the Auxiliary Units were conceived. There were more troops and equipment, better beach defences and a new dynamism in the form of the replacement C-in-C, General Alan Brooke, who could take full advantage of resources that Ironside could only have dreamed of in order to construct a more mobile form of defence and better field intelligence.

Wilkinson in particular was increasingly disillusioned about the direction of the organisation and the contribution that he could make. As the Operational Patrols had been set up to be self-supporting and to act independently, once they had been equipped Wilkinson believed that there was not much more for HQ at Coleshill to do except to maintain on-going training.[28] As will be seen, the intelligence-gathering arm of the Auxiliary Units, the Special Duties Branch, was still largely under SIS control and there is a sense that the organisation was already floundering before it had really begun to be fully operational (although the volunteers on the ground were not to know this). Gubbins is rumoured to have ensured the survival of the organisation through this difficult time only through a timely lunch with War Office staff at the Cavalry Club.[29]

Nonetheless, the Operational Patrols would, arguably, have most proved their worth in 1940. Writing post-war, the opinion of contemporaries such as Gubbins, Wilkinson and Fleming could be quite dismissive, yet at the time the army were desperate for any means possible to slow down the *blitzkrieg*. This included

Figure 7. Contemporary tally of Operation Patrols created up to 1 September 1940 (it does not include Herefordshire and Worcestershire, which by this stage had one patrol each).
(TNA CAB 120/241)

County	Patrols	County	Patrols
Caithness and Sutherland	20	Sussex	11
East Highlands and Aberdeen	35	Isle of Wight	13
East Riding	37	East Hampshire	13
Lincolnshire	23	Dorset and West Hampshire	40
Norfolk	23	Somerset	40
Suffolk and Essex	42	Devon and Cornwall	34
Kent	25	South Wales	15

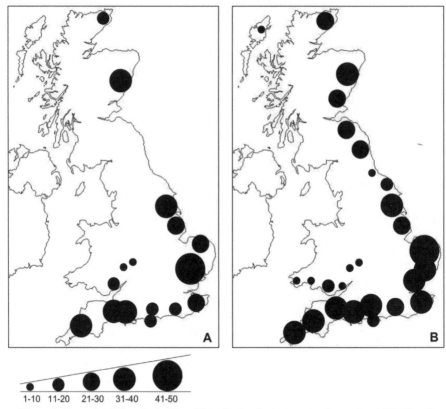

1-10   11-20   21-30   31-40   41-50

Figure 8. Operational Patrols, Auxiliary Units by density in counties, September 1940 (A) and June 1944 (B). (Data from TNA CAB 120/241)

accepting huge casualties from the beach troops and the Home Guard. The scale of 'acceptable losses' must be seen in their context. In May 1940 Brigadier Claude Nicholson was ordered to hold Calais with his 3,000 men to the bitter end, in order to protect the flank of the Dunkirk evacuation.[30] The Auxiliary

Units cost little to operate and could be used in what amounted to suicidal operations in order to slow down an enemy advance without risking precious front-line troops. Of the original XII Corps Observation Unit, Fleming wrote:

> reprisals against the civilian population would have put us out of business before long. In any case, we would have been hunted down as soon as the leaf was off the trees ... I doubt if we should have been more than a minor and probably short-lived nuisance to the invaders.[31]

Peter Wilkinson had an even more crushing assessment of the Auxiliary Units:

> at the very best they would have been a 'flea-bite' behind the enemy lines. They might have sown a certain amount of confusion and insecurity but they were never on a scale that could have been of any decisive importance. And, I think that in the cold light of reason, it is at least arguable, as many senior officers held, that they were not worth the effort that was put into them![32]

He did, however, admit that they might have been able to influence operations in the early days of any bridgehead, when any delay, however small, to a German breakout might have proved significant in buying time for the limited British armour to organise a counter-attack.[33] Wilkinson left the Auxiliary Units in November, despondent about the way they were already developing, away from the HDS concept of a secret resistance organisation toward commando units of the Home Guard. His answer lay in a return to the more covert ideas of Section D and the unofficial scheme of his ex-colleague in MIR, Tommy Davies.

> I think that both Gubbins and I took a very realistic view of the limitations of Auxiliary Units and their very short-term nature. It was for this reason that before I left in November, 1940, I was, with Gubbins' knowledge and approval, planning a sort of 'inner-circle' of specially selected members of Auxiliary Units who would be really secret and who might form the nucleus of a future Resistance Organisation if they survived the first month. I saw myself as the Chief of Staff of this super-secret organisation and had planned a secret hideout for myself whilst masquerading as an engineering apprentice at Rugby ... But this plan had not gone beyond a pipe-dream by the time Gubbins and I left Auxiliary Units and I doubt if the concept would have been acceptable to Colonel Bill Major.[34]

By November, the structure of the Auxiliary Units was so embedded in the Home Guard that Wilkinson's idea for an 'inner-circle' resistance organisation was no longer practicable, and there is no evidence that it was ever put into operation. As Wilkinson realised, it was diametrically opposite to the ordered military structure that Gubbins's successor, Colonel 'Bill' Major, was to introduce. A version of the idea had, however, been taken up by SIS. There are a number of instances of individual Home Guard being recruited for work after occupation in other super-secret sabotage operations which have been gathered within the discussion on Section VII of SIS (see below, Chapter Eleven).

It seems right and proper to give Colin Gubbins the last word on an assessment of the Auxiliary Units in 1940.

> they would have justified their existence ... But my judgement is based heavily on the fact that they were costing the country nothing either in manpower or in weapons ... their usefulness would have been short-lived, at the longest until their stocks were exhausted, at the shortest when they were caught or wiped out. They were designed, trained and prepared for a particular and imminent crisis: that was their specialist role.[35]

Chapter Eight

Auxiliary Units (Operations) (November 1940–44)

For a time it seemed that the Auxiliary Units might not outlast the Battle of Britain and the abandonment of Operation Sealion on 12 October 1940. On the basis of subsequent developments, the deal that Gubbins negotiated for survival in the September Cavalry Club lunch is likely to have included three key elements: (a) the long-awaited introduction of a regular army component to the operational structure via Scout Patrols, (b) a tighter military organisation to the Operational Branch and (c) the development of a more military iteration of the Special Duties Branch. These changes were implemented in late 1940/early 1941 and with them, despite mounting scrutiny and criticism, the Operational Branch of the Auxiliary Units survived until November 1944. By then it was a very different organisation to that originally envisaged by Colonel Gubbins.

Gubbins had never considered the need for a long-term structure for the organisation when it was established. It was only from November 1940 when more orthodox officers began to take control that it took on more of the characteristics of a permanent fixture in the army establishment. Nonetheless, it remained somewhat out of step with the rapidly changing war situation; some historical inconsistencies remained, as did a continuing confusion over its purpose. Together these served to confound the contemporary War Office and modern researchers.

Scout Sections

Thorne's original model of guerrilla operations in the XII Corps Observation Unit was built around a nucleus of regular army 'battle patrols', amounting to one per battalion, which would act as 'stay-behind' units. In all, twenty such patrols were created.[1] His LDV patrols were to play a support role, trained by a Scout section that was initially built around the contingent of Lovat Scouts (eventually reduced to two NCOs but with additional troops brought in from other regiments).

The timetable for the introduction of a similar regular army component within the Auxiliary Units proved difficult. Donald Hamilton-Hill, one of the first wave of Intelligence Officers, remembers being told at their introductory meeting of 13 July that they should recruit two subalterns from local regiments in their areas, who would in turn each recruit the twelve best men from their regiment and form two scout sections.[2] These would combine the properties of the XII Corps Observation Unit Battle Patrols and Scout Sections as both fighting and training units. Gubbins put this proposal on a more formal basis in a War Establishment report of 26 July 1940, in which he clearly articulates his vision for the eventual expansion of the Scout Sections to create a new version of the Independent Companies as commando units of the Home Guard.

> As and when time allows of more centralisation, increased training, and greater efficiency, the sections can be organised into platoons, and the platoons into something in the nature of Independent Companies of Home Guards.[3]

A report of 30 July again refers to the XII Corps Scout Section as an experiment that would hopefully be expanded.[4] Despite such clear ambition, no mention is made of the recruitment of Scout Sections in the August progress report to Churchill, and Oxenden documents that they were not introduced until November.[5] A delay in mobilisation across the rest of the Auxiliary Units areas may have been because Gubbins was not in the position of Thorne as a corps commander to order the regiments under his command to comply. Although Gubbins had successfully negotiated the loan of five training officers from 3rd Division by the end of August, it may well be that commanders were reluctant to lose some of their best officers and men in the face of imminent invasion, and perhaps no one believed the assurance of Gubbins in July that the Scout Section officers would be returned to their unit if invasion occurred. By November, with the immediate invasion crisis over, such secondment could have been seen as a useful training exercise, and it was agreed that the men for the new Scout Sections would be taken from reserve units and depots rather than from the front line, providing a better integration of the Auxiliary Units with the rest of the army, and avoiding any concern that Gubbins (like Grand before him) was building up a private army. Increasing corps control of the Auxiliary Units was to be a feature of the organisation throughout the war.

The introduction of Scout Sections, whose tasks were to include training, construction of hides, distribution of arms dumps and as special fighting patrols, greatly increased the strategic potential of the Operational Branch of the Auxiliary Units. Two Scout Sections were to be allocated to each Intelligence Officer, each one consisting of twelve men, including an officer and often a Royal Engineers sapper.[6] Their distribution was specifically stated to exclude the inland counties north of the Bristol Channel, i.e. Herefordshire and Worcestershire, although the reason for their official absence is not clear; except to repeat that these counties remained an anomaly throughout the whole organisation of the Auxiliary Units. The Scout Sections were drawn from personnel of locally-based regiments who had a good knowledge of the local areas but who did not necessarily have any specialist training in irregular warfare. Their own training, therefore, was initially just one step ahead of the Home Guard patrols that they were expected to train. They had a higher percentage of NCOs than normal, reflecting their intended use in small teams and in a training role.

In action, the Scout Sections would go to ground like the Home Guard patrols, but they had the significant advantage that most seem to have had regular army wireless communication, meaning they could act more strategically on behalf of the local corps and be retasked as the campaign developed. There was, however, no claim (unlike in the Special Duties Branch) that such wireless communications were secure. They were equipped to act as an offensive strike force on the flanks and rear of the enemy rather than as the covert sabotage unit of the Home Guard patrols. Some, at least, had additional hidden dumps of supplies scattered around their area in order to extend their operational life.[7] The official War Establishment of a Scout Section in October 1940 comprised:

1 second lieutenant
1 sergeant
1 corporal
1 lance corporal
8 privates
1 batman
1 car
1 motor cycle
19 bicycles

Their weaponry was initially basic, reflecting the shortages of the time: two revolvers (twelve rounds on man) and eleven .303 rifles (fifty rounds on man). By March 1942 the weaponry for each twelve-man Scout Section had increased dramatically in firepower and is listed in Fig. 9.

Oxenden was dismissive of the quality of the early Scout Sections and particularly by the youth of their inexperienced officers, although their improvement is best judged by the high percentage recruited into the SAS and other special forces from August 1943, after stand-down began.[8]

At the height of the organisation, there may have been up to fifty Scout Sections. By September 1942, reductions were already being considered as demands on front-line manpower increased across the war fronts.[9] In January 1943, eighteen Scout Sections were abolished which left just eight. They were finally withdrawn in late 1943.

Changing Circumstances

In the summer and autumn of 1940 the priority had been to find any means of disrupting the German *blitzkrieg* and giving the regular forces time to concentrate and counter-attack. The Home Guard was to fight to the last man in the face of the German advance, to slow it down and to force the enemy to use up precious

Figure 9. Weapons for twelve-man Scout Section, March 1942. (TNA WO 199/337)

Weapon	Number	Rounds, carried	Rounds, total
Pistol, .38	12	12	576
Sniper rifle, .303	4	50	200
Thompson SMG, .45	2	200	2,400
Bren Gun, .303	1	1,000	1,500

supplies of ammunition and fuel. At the same time, the Auxiliary Units patrols would operate on the rear and flanks of the enemy, cutting lines of supply and communications, destroying airfields (ideally with planes on the ground) and generally cause confusion by guerrilla tactics that the German army had not previously been obliged to face in their stampede through Europe. The hope was that the Nazis could be held and then forced to retreat, during which time, as the planning for the XII Corps Observation Unit makes clear, they would be hit again by renewed guerrilla attacks and finally annihilated before they could evacuate.

The departure of Gubbins and Wilkinson in November heralded a significant change in emphasis for the Auxiliary Units. Commanding Officers henceforth would have no expertise in irregular warfare and the post eventually appears to have been treated as a sinecure before retirement, as the War Office tried to 'normalise' the organisation. Lieutenant Colonel Cyril 'Bill' Major (formerly Directorate of Military Intelligence), aged 47, took over from Gubbins on 20 November 1940 and introduced a more ordered pyramid-style military hierarchy throughout the whole organisation (both Operational and Special Duties branches).[10] Major was a long-time staff officer with no experience of irregular warfare. This left Beyts and Henderson of the original senior management team to maintain continuity until they too left in 1942.

The previously independent Operational Patrols were now organised under a Group Commander, commissioned from the Home Guard. Oxenden records that some of them were recruited from former members of the HDS: 'These were generally outstanding individuals, who eventually became Group Commanders'.[11] A possible example are the Van Moppes brothers in Worcestershire, British-born diamond merchants of Dutch descent who had SIS connections. When they moved their diamond-processing factory to Worcestershire from Norfolk they brought with them a fit young 'gardener' who also joined the Auxiliary Units and may well have been their 'minder'.[12] The basic principle of Major's 'group attack' philosophy was for a number of patrols to rendezvous under the Group Commander and together attack a single target. As some of the Group Commanders were in late middle age, the post was eventually relegated to one of administration. Wilkinson was appalled at this divergence from the idea of small sabotage teams working in isolation. In an interview in 1992 he recorded:

> In my opinion, the greatest weakness of Auxiliary Units after we left, was that Major tried to organise it along military lines which, in my experience, is almost invariably fatal for a clandestine organisation for reasons of security.[13]

Nonetheless, Major's scheme may have been the product of an orthodox military mind, to partially resolve a fundamental weakness of the existing system. The early compartmentalisation of the Operational Patrols provided security but, without wireless communication, prevented patrols from acting strategically after they had destroyed their pre-determined primary target. The Group Commanders could act in lieu of the Intelligence Officers (who may, or may not, have gone to ground with the patrols) in coordinating the subsequent action of the patrols over a sub-county area. It is no coincidence that the new pyramid system of responsibility had a symmetry with that being put in place for the Auxiliary Units Special Duties Branch (see Chapter Nine).

Why did the Auxiliary Units survive at all after Hitler's Operation Sealion was finally cancelled in October 1940? The C-in-C Home Forces, General Alan Brooke, took some heart from the Nazi invasion of Russia on 22 June 1941 in removing the immediate threat to Britain, but he considered this was a temporary respite, believing that Russia would only be able to resist for three or four months.[14] The Joint Intelligence Sub-Committee assessment of invasion believed that Hitler would be obliged to invade in 1941 if he stood a chance of winning the war or dragging it to stalemate. The main attack was expected somewhere between the Wash and Portsmouth and at a time after 1 April. Advance warning might be twenty-four hours up to three weeks, but invasion would still depend on achieving air and naval superiority. The first wave of invasion was expected to suffer 50 per cent casualties and to land with supplies for only four days operation and fuel for 100 miles, which explains the importance attached to cutting the enemy supply lines and bogging down its advance for as long as possible.[15]

The speed of the initial stages of Operation Barbarossa in invading Russia only served to reinforce the sense of invincibility of the German forces. As a consequence, General Brooke believed that the contingency against possible invasion still had to be maintained. Churchill was less convinced of the possibility, but he had a calculating political motive for maintaining public concern over it, as a useful tool in keeping the country united and in continuing the pressure to draw the USA into the war. His machiavellian outlook did not stop him from drawing off forces from the UK defences to serve elsewhere. As early as 16 September 1940 – at the height of the RAF's Battle of Britain – Brooke complained that Churchill was intending to remove one quarter of his infantry strength for service in the Middle East. Fears of invasion continued even after the entry of the USA into the war in December 1941 and on 16 January 1942 plans were discussed for Ulster forces to move into Eire in the event that German forces landed there in preparation for an invasion of Britain; Gubbins planned for SOE to send in sabotage teams, working in conjunction with SIS and the Irish Intelligence Service (G-2); the plan was eventually dropped in favour of providing technical support to G-2.[16]

The threat of invasion after what was assumed would be a rapid collapse of Soviet Russia is the context for an expansion programme of the Auxiliary Units (both Operational and Special Duties branches) agreed by the War Office in August 1941, which mainly concerned expansion in northern England and Scotland, reflecting concerns of a possible invasion via Norway.[17] The number of Intelligence Officers in the Operational branch doubled, reaching its peak of twenty-two in 1941 before falling to nineteen in 1943, and finally to four in the drastic reorganisation of August 1944.[18] But the Commanding Officer no longer had the free hand given to Gubbins in building the Auxiliary Units; approval now had to be obtained for each new patrol so that it fell within the total agreed establishment costs. The accountants were now in control of the war effort! Nonetheless, despite grumbles from the War Office quartermaster's department, the Operational Patrols and Scout Sections continued to get whatever stores they demanded, on the basis that, because the Auxiliary Units were classed as top secret, few officers in authority felt able to ask what exactly they were up to or why they needed a particular piece of equipment.

In the event, Britain was not invaded in 1941 and was increasingly unlikely to be so thereafter, which left the Operational Patrols without a primary purpose, and facing official scrutiny and a renewed threat of disbandment. The first reaction of HQ at Coleshill to the diminution of the invasion threat was the traditional British army response of keeping the men busy. They were supplied with an array of booby-trap and delay devices, which served to keep their imagination alight. Coleshill organised inter-patrol competitions and, when all other options were exhausted ... introduced parade-ground drill. The concept of an irregular guerrilla force was steadily being eroded.

In February 1942 Colonel Major left to found the RAF Regiment, whilst Major Henderson left to join the Directorate of Military Training, leaving only Major Beyts from the original senior management team. Colonel Major was replaced as CO of the Auxiliary Units by Colonel, the Lord Glanusk, aged 51. He had originally retired from the army in 1924 but was still on the reserve list; now in ill health but well-connected, he was clearly given the post to assure his promotion to full colonel with a consiquent increase in his pension before retirement. Such an appointment clearly indicates the changing attitude of the War Office to the organisation and its fall in status. Glanusk was a former Guards officer and brought a number of his fellow old-Etonian and Welsh Guards officers onto the staff, including Captains Lord Delamere and Marcus Wickham-Boynton. His driver and batman were also imported from the Welsh Guards. The first question Glanusk asked the then Intelligence Officer for the Scottish Borders, Peter Forbes, was 'Do you have any Gentlemen, Forbes?'.[19] Intelligence Officer Anthony Quayle in Northumberland believed the superior and patronising manner of his new commanding officer interfered with the smooth running of his patrols, and the dislike appears to have been mutual. Glanusk summoned Quayle to tell him that he had formed a 'dim view' of him; Captain Quayle told his commanding officer that he could only reciprocate his feelings. Quayle then started looking for another posting (which eventually led him into SOE).[20]

Reports indicate that the wine cellar improved enormously as the officers mess became more of a social club and less a hub of clandestine warfare. The traditional military background of Glanusk is reflected in some of the changes he introduced, including drill competitions, and during residential courses Wickham-Boynton (Camp Commandant) insisted that the kit of the participating Auxiliers had to be laid out in Guards fashion. Anonymity disappeared: on 25 April 1942 Auxiliary Units patrols were authorised to wear the Home Guard county flash and a distinctive battalion number representing their official cover within the spurious GHQ Reserve Battalions, Home Guard. The patrols therefore became visually recognisable and, in an age when every small boy had become an expert in identifying unit insignia, identifiable as a special oddity.[21] This was especially ironic as Intelligence Officer Captain Todd had instructed his SDB agents in 1940 on the important intelligence to be gained from recognising German units by their uniform distinctions. Much to the relief of traditionalists, the Auxiliary Units had become a military organisation far from the original maverick guerrilla dreams of Grand or Gubbins.

More positively, Glanusk abandoned the system of group patrol action in favour of the original, more secure, independent patrol action and streamlined the principle of 'hit and run'. The Group Commanders now had a purely administrative role, which would increase as the number of regular army Intelligence Officers was reduced in 1944. The then Training Officer, Nigel Oxenden, was coldly analytical in his appreciation of these changes: 'From now on the patrol was self-contained and would fight alone; from now on the rank and file would not be asked to think.'[22] Oxenden may have been reasoning that the widening range of booby traps and timers supplied to the Patrols had only complicated their options in destroying targets. He wanted to simplify their approach to sabotage, and minimalise the weapons that they should carry. Importantly, Glanusk clarified the lines of responsibility should the Operational Patrols have to go to ground, which had always been vague and left more or less to personal choice. The role of the local army Corps was strengthened. A cynical mind might suggest that the Coleshill staff could now spend less time on tiresome operational matters about which they increasingly knew very little, especially so after Major Beyts left in August 1942 (to help form SOE Force 136 in Burma), but it was really only returning to the original July 1940 concept of Gubbins. As Training Officer, Beyts had been a lynchpin of the organisation since its original inception; his replacement was the former Intelligence Officer for Norfolk, Major Oxenden. It should be borne in mind that the HQ establishment had always been small. In 1944 it comprised just ten officers and eighty-seven other ranks, with the main responsibilities being in administration and training rather than any operational function.[23]

The issue of strategic control had always been a problem within the structure of the Auxiliary Units. Even prior to the arrival of Lord Glanusk, Norman Field (then Intelligence Officer for Kent) had said that the Operational Patrols were expected to operate more or less independently, with only hints from Coleshill. From May 1942, however, the control of operations by local army corps was tightened. Formal responsibility for the patrols would pass from GHQ to regional corps commanders once they prepared to go into action, in effect, giving the corps commanders the strategic control over the patrols that had been lacking except in the original XII Corps area.[24]

The headquarters of the Intelligence Officer (IO) was structured to act, if necessary, as an additional operational patrol, consisting of:

Intelligence Officer
clerk
corporal, Royal Engineers
2 drivers
2–3 NCO instructors

The role of the Intelligence Officer HQ was left to the discretion of the corps commanders and in the majority of cases the IOs were ordered to go to ground with the rest of the patrols, having already given them instructions for operations.[25] But some IOs were ordered to remain with Corps HQ and one had even been tasked with acting as Police Liaison Officer after invasion. The long-standing confusion over the role of IOs is seen in the fact that as late as May 1942, hidden Operational Bases had not been built as IO control centres and not all IOs had wireless communication to Divisional or Corps HQ or to the Scout Patrols. Indeed, some wireless sets had been removed from the IOs. In May 1942 Beyts asked for nineteen WS17 sets for the IOs for them to go to ground, and for underground hides to be built for the IO unit. But by June, the WS17 was out of production and the Auxiliary Units were told that they would have to source them locally.[26] The WS17s were needed to maintain contact with both military HQ and Scout Patrols; and finally, on 1 June 1942 authorization was given for the construction of nineteen Operational Bases for IO HQs. Such fundamental weaknesses had increased the questioning of the role and efficiency of the Auxiliary Units at corps level and above. Thus, alongside the final decision to build hidden Zero stations for the SDB, it was only in 1942, almost two years after its formation, that the Auxiliary Units system was finally completed. The invasion threat may have receded considerably and the USA was now in the war and beginning to send troops to the UK, but the Japanese were still advancing in the Far East, Rommel was a threat in the Western Desert, and the war on the Eastern Front wavered back and forth. With British troops hard-pressed in action all over the world, the Auxiliary Units still had some value as an insurance policy against invasion, but they were increasingly difficult to justify.

The final abdication of strategic direction by Auxiliary Units HQ to the army corps was perhaps inevitable given the lack of long-range communications available to the organisation. A similar devolution is also evident in the organisation of the SDB where the Coleshill/Hannington HQ had no control over the assessment or dissemination of any military intelligence gathered, because it was in the hands of Divisional or Corps Intelligence Officers. With the Auxiliary Units more directly subject to local army control, scrutiny intensified over their increasingly dubious anti-invasion role and they had to find a new purpose and direction that still made the most of the skills of the volunteers, but better fitted the immediate needs of the generals commanding the army corps.

The Operational Patrols were reinvented as well-armed reconnaissance teams to counter the anticipated threat of German commando and parachute landings (Fig. 10). In describing this new role, Oxenden displays some contemporary cynicism, describing the rumours of raids as 'a gift to IOs' and 'a wonderful tonic for fading enthusiasm in the ranks'. He went on 'Sceptics wondered whether it was ever intended as anything more. The effects, with careful nursing, lasted for the next two years'.[27] This role did, however, become important during the run up to, and during, the Normandy landings. The Allies were intending to use the new SAS to disrupt lines of communication and supply behind enemy lines and so

Figure 10. List of Auxiliary Units Operational Patrol weapons, August 1942 (preceding the request for an issue of 1,416 Sten guns on 4 September 1942). (TNA WO 199/738)

Revolver, .38 ($\times$7)	40 rounds total
Rifles, .300 ($\times$2)	200 rounds total
Knives, fighting ($\times$7)	
Knobkerries ($\times$3)	
Grenades, Type 36M, 4 sec fuze ($\times$48)	
No. 74 S.T. Grenades (Sticky Bombs) ($\times$3 cases)	
No. 76 SIP Grenade ($\times$2 cases)	
Rifle, .22 with silencer ($\times$1)	200 rounds
Thompson SMG, .45 ($\times$1)	1,000 rounds

it seemed logical to suppose that the Germans might have similar tactics in mind to disrupt the build-up and execution of Operation Overlord. Concerns were heightened by the repeated requests in 1944 from German intelligence to their supposed agents in Britain to provide the location of Eisenhower's SHAEF headquarters, but fortunately these agents were under the control of MI5. On 19 May 1944 Guy Liddell of MI5 noted that the Germans had asked double-agent 'Garbo' for information on the street addresses of various HQ which would be sent to the Brandenburg regiment in Arras by special priority.[28] The Brandenburg Regiment was Hitler's English-speaking special forces unit who were trained to operate in Allied uniform. The obvious suspicion was that they were planning a series of commando raids as a spoiling tactic for D-Day. Many photographs show Operational Patrols of this period (especially in coastal areas) heavily armed with an increased allocation of Sten guns (Plate 27), and now they had a purpose for the two long-range P17 rifles with which each patrol had been issued in 1940.

The work involved acting as scout patrols for the local Home Guard and a number of joint exercises were held. Despite the repeated concerns to maintain secrecy and independence from local Home Guard control, the Operational Patrols were steadily coming out of the shadows. The Home Guard were also reorganising to meet the threat of raids and they had the advantage of increasing levels of transport, wireless communication and heavier weapons provided for the purpose. The following is an extract from circular orders sent out a few days after D-Day regarding joint anti-raiding working with local Home Guard.

1. In the event of Enemy Raids by Seaborne or Airborne troops, one of the operational roles to be fulfilled by troops of 201 (GHQ Reserve) Bn. will be to act as scout patrols and observers.
2. Troops of 201 (GHQ Reserve) Bn. will contact, and maintain contact with the Enemy Forces, and will pass any information they thus acquire to XXX Bn. Home Guard Sub Unit Commanders, who will be responsible for the transmission of such information to their Headquarters.
4. The command of 201 (GHQ Reserve) Bn. is entirely independent of the Home Guard, but close liaison will be maintained between the two

Units on 'STAND TO', and in any 'STATE OF EMERGENCY' which may develop. It must be borne in mind that the Command of 201 (GHQ Reserve) Bn. troops remains under the control of the Regular Military Authorities, and that they will be acting on orders received from the Headquarters of such Authorities.

6. The secrecy regarding the formation of 201 (GHQ Reserve) Bn. H.G. will be maintained at all times, and information regarding their existence will not be divulged.[29]

The emphasis in the orders on the Patrols not being operationally responsible to the Home Guard, even though their task was to pass their information on to them, may reflect the concern to protect the special status of the auxiliers at a time when morale was slipping. From the start, they had been promised that if the Auxiliary Units were ever disbanded they would not be obliged to return to normal Home Guard duties, and from 1943 this became a major factor in keeping the Auxiliary Units in existence until the Home Guard was disbanded. In practice, because the Intelligence Officers who had the direct responsibility for the Patrols were themselves now responsible to the corps commanders in action, there was now a unified chain of command that encompassed Home Guard, Auxiliary Units Operational Patrols and regular forces.

In January 1943 the War Office carried out an analysis of the potential future use of the Auxiliary Units.[30] The study decided that the survival of the Auxiliary Units had to be judged against:

(a) likelihood of invasion
(b) the 'vital area' of invasion risk

It concluded that there was no possibility of invasion in 1943 and unlikely thereafter; that the most risky stretch of coastline for attack was the area between Norfolk and Hampshire; that the Auxiliary Units were unlikely to be used in the future; and that the fit officers and men amongst its ranks were needed elsewhere. The consequences of the report were immediate. From January 1943, eighteen of the twenty-six scout patrols were abolished, leaving only eight. They were finally disbanded at the end of 1943.[31] Many of the men transferred to the SAS or Parachute regiment. It was suggested that eleven of the nineteen IOs could be replaced by Home Guard officers and two (Woodward and Sandford) had been given emergency commissions already. It was also thought possible to replace fit Signals and Royal Engineer officers with older or partially unfit officers.[32] The process continued throughout the year. In November 1943 all 'A' medical grade officers and men in the Auxiliary Units had to be listed ready for redeployment. The downgrading of officers extended to the SDB and in late 1943 civilian OUT station operator David Ingrams, of the Devon SDB, was commissioned and promoted to become IO for the county.

The men on the ground may have been oblivious to the problems increasingly affecting the Auxiliary Units at a strategic level, but now their special status was being eroded at a personal level and, as a result, both recruitment and morale suffered. In February 1943 the Auxiliary Units exemption from call-up was cancelled, an important signal as to the declining status of the Operational Patrols, although in practice, this exemption had often been ignored. It was difficult to keep someone in the Operational Patrols if they were itching for more immediate action. Geoff Devereux, patrol sergeant for Samson Patrol in Worcestershire, was called up to the Grenadier Guards in August 1941 and the details were carefully recorded on Home Guard Part II Orders (see below, p. 156). He moved from royal protection duties in London to a commission in an anti-tank regiment. Details such as discharge from the Auxiliary Units, or resignations back into the Home Guard, are dutifully recorded on Home Guard enrolment forms. In the main such movement did not seem to cause problems, although when 'X' asked to resign from Jehu (Alfrick) Patrol in Worcestershire because of stress, the IO politely shook his hand and wished him well – but later told the patrol sergeant, Tony Barling, that he would have to be killed if the invasion occurred. (Barling, a medical student, left the patrol in December 1942 to join the Parachute Regiment as a medical officer and was captured at Arnhem.)

The January 1943 report concluded that if the Operational Patrols were ever used it would be around the flanks of the area from Hampshire and Norfolk.[33] This is indeed what happened in the run up to D-Day. From May to September 1944, volunteers from patrols selected from across the country were sent to the Isle of Wight in relays to guard the vital pump-house for the Pluto Pipeline carrying fuel to the invasion beaches and a secret communications centre rather naughtily disguised as a hospital. The pipeline was considered a priority target for German commando raids and who better to guard the terminal than the poachers turned gamekeepers of the Auxiliary Units. In the bureaucratic way of Whitehall the first inkling of what was about to happen came when on 22 April 1944 the War Office circulated a memo to local Territorial Army Associations, who administered the Home Guard, advising them that they might receive some travel and subsistence claims from 'certain Home Guard units'![34]

Lord Glanusk had to resign his command in August 1943 due to ill health and was succeeded by his second in command, Lieutenant Colonel F.W.R. Douglas (Plate 14), who came from the Inspectorate of the Royal Artillery, although Lampe (who interviewed him for *The Last Ditch*) claimed he had worked for DMI; Warwicker also maintained he had SIS connections. Like Glanusk before him, Douglas, aged 46, was on the List of Reserve Officers. He had the difficult task of steering the Auxiliary Units through fifteen months of increasing scepticism from the War Office and regional commands as to the purpose of the organisation. The Director of Staff Duties commented in August 1943 'It is doubtful whether there is any justification for the continued existence of this unit whose function is essentially of a defensive nature.'[35] Douglas was not well-liked and did not appear to have too high an opinion of his officers, as in a handwritten letter of July 1944 he claimed that his remaining officers were basically unemployable elsewhere. 'Regarding officers for retention I have not suggested anything of very high grade – either mentally or physically – there are no pocket Napoleons!'[36]

In their new anti-raiding role the Operational Patrols faced competition from the increasingly well-armed, and well-trained, Home Guard in their designated role of guarding vulnerable points around the time of D-Day. Gone were the pitchfork days of 1940! The Home Guard were now significantly younger and 40 per cent of them were armed with the new Sten gun (Plate 27). Their reputation had been greatly enhanced as they took over responsibilities for anti-aircraft and coastal artillery and even bomb disposal work. Fighting to preserve the existence of the Auxiliary Units, on 16 August 1943 General Franklyn (the new Commander-in-Chief, Home Forces) explained that in case of raids the Operational Patrols would form fighting patrols to cut off withdrawal of the enemy whilst the SDB could provide alternative methods of information on enemy movements.[37] How the Operational Patrols would be able to organise such a rapid reaction force without the benefit of wireless communications is not clear. Here was the enduring irony of the Auxiliary Units: the local agents of the SDB could transmit information on enemy movements – but not pass it on to their local operational patrol. Instead they would transmit information to division or corps HQs who would then have to arrange a response through regular channels. Their hides had become redundant and it is likely that the new mobile columns of the local Home Guard, equipped with army backpack wireless sets, would have been mobilised and in action before the Auxiliary Units.

Oxenden, in the draft of his official history of the Auxiliary Units, summarised the changes of fortunes in the organisation as being:

- 1940: 'a blaze of wild priority'
- 1941–2: a phase of organised power 'guarded by a security that nobody could get past, however much they might resent it'
- 1943–4: 'a realization that the soundest attitude was unobtrusiveness' in the hope that senior officers might forget their existence.

Here was a new reason for the Operational Branch of the Auxiliary Units to crave secrecy. Operational IOs increasingly sought a low profile and kept away from contact with division or corps HQs in order to avoid hostile questioning on their activities and purpose.[38] As the organisation began to wind down, the final Patrol Leaders course was held at Coleshill in May 1944, ironically at a time when many Auxiliers finally went into active service and were being deployed to guard the Isle of Wight against the threat of German commando raids.

If the local IOs tried to keep a low profile in their dealings with regional commands, the Coleshill HQ could not so easily avoid its critics in the War Office and they did not help their case by trying to maintain their priority status over supplies. The supply branch of the War Office was suspicious. On 27 August 1943 a quartermaster complained 'I am sorry to worry you with these but they are both typical of the type of thing we get from Auxiliary Units'. One of these complaints was an objection to the requests for increased supplies of morphine! The other complaint was that curse of bureaucracy – travelling expenses:

I see no reason why Auxiliary Units should have preferential treatment. I have in the past been told more than once that their duties are so secret that their officers must go by car and not by rail. 800 miles a week does, however, seem excessive and I suggest we take this up with G/Ops, whose protégées they were in the old GHQ.[39]

On 15 September the Quartermaster's Branch of the War Office probed deeper. While accepting that 'In view of the special nature of these units the purpose for which the stores are required is not revealed when the demand is made', they now sought confirmation that the Auxiliary Units were indeed essential for Home Defence and asked for details of the War Office branch where further information on the Auxiliary Units could be obtained.[40] Coleshill seemed unperturbed at such questioning. On 2 October 1943 there were complaints from GHQ that, whilst the allotment of booby trap wire for an infantry battalion was 25yds/six months, the Auxiliary Units had requested 364,000 yds/six months. GHQ commented 'This demand is quite out of proportion'.[41] Such complaints continued into 1944. If nothing else the persistence of the quartermaster at Coleshill has to be applauded. In November 1943 the Auxiliary Units requested 2,000 of the new Type 77 phosphorous grenades for training purposes and a further 50,000 for operational use, and were told they could only have the 2,000 for training. Undaunted they persisted with the request and were told they could have the 50,000 grenades for operational use whenever such quantities were available and the need actually arose. The response was simply to repeat the request, and so it continued. On 2 February 1944 the Auxiliary Units had to be firmly told that they did not have priority for .38 ammunition over field army units.[42] They were not making any new friends in the War Office. Pressure for their disbandment intensified from April 1944, even as some patrols were being deployed to the Isle of Wight. Now there were complaints from the War Office over the continuing priority for Auxiliary Units vehicles, which concluded:

There is a very strong feeling in high places in the War Office that the time must be approaching (if it has not already arrived) when Auxiliary Units will have ceased to justify their continued existence.[43]

The sequence of development from anti-invasion guerrilla force to anti-raiding or reconnaissance patrols begs the question of what role Oxenden had in mind for the future role of the Operational Patrols when he concluded in 1944 that the only weapons the patrols needed to carry from now on, apart from their charges of explosives, were the new Welrod pistol (Plate 23) and the Type 77 phosphorous grenade (Plate 24). The purpose of the Welrod (a bolt action, magazine-fed .32 calibre silenced pistol still in use with the SAS in the 1990s) was for extreme short- to point-blank range assassination, whilst the phosphorous grenade could be used to provide smoke cover and as an incendiary weapon; both weapons would work well for infiltrating targets and blowing them up. But what exactly were they planning to blow up in 1944? Apart from their reconnaissance role, the organisation had become a test-bed for techniques of guerrilla warfare.

Despite all their problems, active recruitment continued well into June 1944, but with sharply declining manpower levels, and many patrols were at half-strength. It was around this time that the *Countryman's Diary 1939* was produced as the final Auxiliary Units training manual. By this stage it had almost a souvenir value! In June 1944 the total strength of the Auxiliary Units stood at 4,200 Home Guard members of the Operational Patrols and 3,250 civilian members of the Special Duties Branch. John Hartwright of Worcester was enrolled into Joshua Patrol on 27 May 1944; John Thomas from Crowle (Worcestershire) was enrolled into the Auxiliary Units even later on 12 June 1944. Such men were unaware that on 17 May the War Office had recommended the withdrawal, by 30 June, of all regular army personnel from the Auxiliary Units and for them to be reorganised on a purely Home Guard basis.[44] On 5 June, as the invasion fleets for Normandy were preparing to set sail, Colonel Douglas was summoned to a crucial meeting in the War Office to discuss the future of the organisation. Events moved rapidly thereafter. The stand-down letter to the SDB from General Franklyn was issued on 4 July 1944.[45] The disbandment of the Operational Branch was given a slight reprieve in order to bring it into the same timetable as the stand-down of the rest of the Home Guard. As an interim stage, the Operational Branch was reorganised in August 1944 into four large regional areas. The number of regular army Intelligence Officers was reduced to just four and the Home Guard Group Commanders took on increased administrative and liaison duties. The time of the Auxiliary Units had passed. As regions took on more responsibilities, the Coleshill HQ was withering and there was a threat to reduce the required rank of the CO from full colonel to lieutenant colonel.[46] It was difficult to maintain the Operational Bases and the priority was to deal with the deteriorating stockpiles of weapons and explosives. The explosives packs (Aux. Packs) began to be removed in July and concerns continued to be expressed about the condition of other

Figure 11. Contents of 'Aux. Unit Mk II' explosives pack, July 1944. (TNA WO 199/937)

24	Copper Tube Igniters
6	Striker Boards
12	Pocket Time Incendiaries
20	1-hour Lead Delays
50	3-hour Lead Delays
50ft	Instantaneous Fuse (Orange Line)
240ft	Cordtex
100	Detonators, Nos 8 or 27
20lb	Explosive (Nobel 808, Polar Gelignite or Plastic)
48ft	Safety Fuse, Mk II Bickford
20	CE Primers (Two tins of 10 each)
24	Tubes, Fuse, Sealing, in those Aux. Units where the fuse is *not* packed in tins
1	Crimping Tool
1	Tube Vaseline
1	Spool Trip Wire .032"
3	Spools Trap Wire .014"
8	Coils Tape
1	Sandbag
6	Pull Switches
3	Pressure Switches

stored ordnance, with some Type 36 grenades being declared unserviceable (Fig. 11).[47] On 18 November 1944 the stand-down letter for the Operational Patrols was finally issued. The HQ at Coleshill remained open until 15 January 1945 in order to manage the final close-down of the organisation.[48] The protracted decline and demise of the Auxiliary Units should not, however, take away the important anti-invasion role that its volunteers were prepared to undertake in 1940–42 and the contribution that it made as a training ground for techniques of 'stay-behind' units and in training individuals who were to go on to serve in SOE and other irregular forces.

Chapter Nine

Auxiliary Units (Special Duties Branch) 1: Anti-invasion Reporting and the Wireless Network

The SPECIAL DUTIES branch of AUXILIARY UNITS is organized to provide information for military formations in the event of enemy invasion or raids in GREAT BRITAIN, from areas temporarily or permanently in enemy control.

All this information would be collected as a result of direct observation by specially recruited and trained civilians, who would remain in an enemy occupied area.[1]

Major Jones, June 1944

The intelligence-gathering branch of the Auxiliary Units – the Special Duties Branch (SDB) – remains the least-understood, and certainly the most secret, element of that organisation. In practice, the Operational and Special Duties branches of the Auxiliary Units functioned as two independent organisations and this lack of integration is, largely, a consequence of their early history, albeit rationalised as a desire to maintain compartmentalised secrecy. It will be argued that even within the SDB, members were not aware of the full range of responsibilities. It is hardly surprising, therefore, that a number of myths have arisen – over its relationship to SIS, the nature of the wireless network, its role as a 'resistance' organisation (or not) and the true function of its agent network. Its history has been distorted by a focus on the physical evidence of the hidden wireless stations, and a reliance on the testimony of the wireless technicians and operators who may have been the people least likely to know the full story of the organisation! The present chapter focusses on the origins of the SDB, its role in any invasion alongside the Phantom Unit, and the development of its wireless network.

The Inheritance from HDS

From its inception it was recognised that, as well as undertaking sabotage missions, the Auxiliary Units had a role in supplying intelligence from behind enemy lines for on-going military operations, a dual function driven as much by the need to bring the entirety of the HDS under the control of GHQ as from being a deliberate policy. This is not to suggest that the intelligence branch (what became the SDB) was designed to provide a 'resistance' organisation after occupation. The summary of duties given by Major Jones, CO of the Auxiliary Units (Signals) at the start of this chapter was written in June 1944, when any real danger had passed and was, to some degree, poetic licence. In 1940 the very suggestion of a permanently-occupied territory would have sent GHQ into apoplexy; it was never in the business of establishing resistance organisations, especially civilian resistance bodies. Over the summer, Gubbins automatically inherited responsibility for Viscount Bearsted's intelligence-gathering section of the Home Defence Scheme (HDS) together with the sabotage wing, but had to find a way of integrating the civilian spies into the military structure and operational priorities of the Auxiliary Units. Whilst by the end of July the still-operating HDS was envisaged (at least by Lawrence Grand) as a longer-term resistance organisation specifically not to get involved in the immediate invasion campaign, the pressing need for GHQ in terms of intelligence-gathering was for a ground-based early warning system that could immediately pass on information to army commands for analysis of the pattern of initial German landings.

There was a major concern in late May 1940 that any advance intelligence of German invasion might be very limited and that the main invasion would be preceded by the scattered landing of small parties of assault troops from fast boats and from inland parachute landings, who would then secure small bridgeheads and cut off lines of communication.[2] In these circumstances, a network of civilian agents able to bypass the normal telephone communication system and report enemy activity by wireless would be very useful. Although this might have been Gubbins's intention when he formally took over the HDS in 1940, plans were frustrated by the lack of a wireless connection to army HQs until the Special Duties Branch (SDB) was effectively re-formed in late 1940/41.

Gubbins received authorisation to create an HQ 'Special Duties' on 11 July 1940, with the cryptic comment that the organisation had already commenced activities, a discreet way of referring to Bearsted's pre-existing intelligence-gathering wing of the HDS (see Chapter Four) which was now supposed to transfer to the Auxiliary Units as part of the process of wresting control of Grand's organisation.[3] The agreed War Establishment for the HQ of what became the Special Duties Branch was impressive and closely mirrored that of the Operational Branch (Fig. 12).

The staff would be responsible for managing the civilian agents already recruited by the HDS and for building a new intelligence network. Significantly,

Figure 12. Extract from War Establishment for Special Duties Branch, 11 July 1940. (TNA WO 260/9)

GSO2 (major)	1
GSO3 (captain)	1
Intelligence Officers(captains)	11
Clerks, (RASC)	2
Drivers (Intelligence Corps or RASC)	12

however, it included no signallers as at this time the SDB had no wireless communication system. Twelve four-seater cars and drivers were to be provided (from Intelligence Corps and RASC); the number of cars was queried by the War Office with the explanation that 'it is the only means by which the officer can carry all his gadgets about the country'. Before the introduction of wireless sets to the SDB, what were these 'gadgets'? Was this simply a bluff to acquire vehicles on the basis that no one could enquire too closely as to the nature of these 'gadgets'? Or was the intention to take over the wireless-equipped cars of the HDS which, however, appear to have remained with SIS? Eventually the Auxiliary Units would overplay the 'secret – don't ask' argument, but in 1940 they were able to get away with a lot. (For comparison, the Operational Branch of the Auxiliary Units had twelve Intelligence Officers at this stage, with fourteen cars, together with five GSOs and the commanding colonel.) The original request was for the SDB to be commanded by a GSO1 (lieutenant colonel) but this was downgraded to a GSO2 (major), perhaps a sneaky attempt to get a promotion for the overall commander of the Auxiliary Units to brigadier (i.e. so Gubbins could retain his temporary rank, awarded at the time of his command of the Independent Companies).

The early references to the intelligence role are, however, brief and vague. Removing control of the HDS from Grand was one thing, but Gubbins had not worked out how the service would be delivered. A progress report to Churchill on 8 August 1940, written by Duncan Sandys on behalf of General Ismay, stated that as well as sabotage, the second role of the Auxiliary Units was to 'provide a system of intelligence, whereby the regular forces in the field can be kept informed of what is happening behind the enemy's lines'. This makes it very clear that the purpose was to provide intelligence during an active military campaign rather than any post-occupation resistance. A subsequent paragraph amplified this by saying 'In order to enable them to carry out their second role, namely, to supply Home Forces with information of troops movements, etc., from behind the enemy's lines, selected units are also being provided with wireless and field telephone apparatus'.[4] There is no mention at all in the report of a named Special Duties Branch (SDB). The progress report on the Auxiliary Units for August, written by Gubbins on 4 September, makes no mention of intelligence-gathering at all.[5] It is most likely that Gubbins was relying on the intended expansion of the still-putative Scout Sections, equipped with wireless, to deliver a means of passing back intelligence. The reference to wireless communication in August can only have been to the trial Scout Sections of the XII Corps Observation Unit. Gubbins was driven by the over-riding need to provide a solution to meet the anticipated invasion deadline of six to twelve weeks; the Scout Sections would offer a practical, no-fuss military mechanism for so doing, but in the event, he was not able to expand the Scout Sections until November.

Just a few days after the SDB War Establishment was agreed, concerns were expressed about any wholesale dismantling of the HDS at this critical time in the war. SIS officer Major Maurice Petherick (Plate 13 and Appendix 2) had been a liaison officer attached to the Paris embassy before the fall of France. He was clearly on personal terms with Lawrence Grand, if not actually employed within Section D, and on 15 July wrote a blunt letter on the subject.

Dear Grand,
I hate to worry you but isn't it time a halt was called before the organisation which you conceived is jettisoned to national disadvantage.
Sincerely
Maurice Petherick 15.7.40[6]

All the criticism of Grand's HDS had been directed at its sabotage organisation but no mention had been made of their intelligence-gathering arm, which appears to have rapidly developed into a distinct section after the first vague allusions to its work in early June. None of the senior officers at Auxiliary Units HQ had experience in running agent networks and they lacked the technical expertise to provide a communications system. The earlier understanding between SIS and the War Office is that it would be the former who were responsible for all agent-based activity, with MIR focussed on military-based operations. To make matters worse, SIS were notoriously protective over all clandestine wireless systems. They maintained a stranglehold over SOE communications until 1942 and so were unlikely to have readily handed over to the War Office their Section VII wireless network, which was already secretly in place to provide intelligence following an invasion (see below, Chapter Eleven). The paucity of references to the operation of any Auxiliary Units intelligence network during 1940 is very noticeable and this is especially true of Peter Wilkinson's accounts, despite the fact that at the time he seems to have been the officer within the Auxiliary Units responsible for liaising with the Special Duties Branch. In his autobiography he also admits that one of his roles as GSO2 (Operations) was 'liaison with my friends in Section D' and with the other intelligence services.[7] Nonetheless he barely mentions the SDB in his summary of the early days of the Auxiliary Units. Whilst a member of MIR earlier in 1940, Wilkinson had worked closely with Section D to the point of having his own SIS identity code and so was ideally placed for the role. It seems that concerns to protect the existence of the secret HDS intelligence network were still uppermost at the same time that he was making scathing comments on HDS inefficiency in distributing their arms dumps.

With such obscuration it is no surprise that misconceptions have arisen over the origins of the SDB. The reality is that GHQ and Gubbins were obliged to accept a working solution from SIS to allow the HDS intelligence network to remain in operation during 1940. Effectively, SIS continued to run the network until it was possible to implement a more military version linked to Army Command HQs. Thus it was agreed between SIS and GHQ in July that:

While obstructive activities of the 'D' organisation are being gradually transferred to GHQ Auxiliary Units, it is considered necessary and desirable by GHQ and CSS that the Intelligence side of the activities should be maintained and developed.[8]

The agreed solution was for Section D officer Viscount Bearsted to continue to operate the existing network much as before, but now under the guise of Auxiliary Units (Special Duties). From the SOE history of Section D:

> Colonel Viscount Bearsted continued his organisation en bloc under the name of 'Auxiliary Units (Special Duties)'. It was not until the danger of invasion was relatively past that the organisation as originally planned by D section was dissolved.[9]

From the available evidence, Gubbins was content to leave Bearsted to his own devices. Lampe records that when the Special Duties Branch began it had 1,000 agents. These were presumably mainly inherited from HDS, but this already comprised around one third of the total 3,250 attained by June 1944.[10] The civilian agents and wireless operators were exempted from military service and also other civil defence duties.[11] Comparatively little is known about these volunteers although a letter of 1947 refers to a full roll having been kept of their names by the War Office. If this was not a confusion with the nominal roll compiled of the Operational Patrols in 1942, such a list has never been released.[12] Oxenden recounts that one of the weekly Wednesday Auxiliary Units progress meetings in July 1940 at Whitehall was attended by 'an equal number of strangers, officers and civilians, and even a woman.' Gubbins declared 'You may as well get to know each other, gentlemen; you are all in the same game'.[13] It is significant that Oxenden described them as strangers, and Gubbins, whilst acknowledging that they were in the same 'game', did not say they were part of the same organisation. As civilians, the agents were particularly confusing to the military mind. This division was never overcome and although the usual explanation was a concern for security, the inherent problem was that the two branches served different masters and had different needs. Bearsted's 'Auxiliary Units (Special Duties)' survived as such until autumn 1940 when he joined SOE and perhaps unsurprisingly, it was Major Petherick who was transferred from SIS into the Auxiliary Units in order to convert the 'Special Duties' into a body that GHQ could manage directly. Petherick was later described by Major Beyts as the genius behind the SDB and it can therefore be assumed that it was he who devised the pyramid structure of IN and OUT stations that would feed back intelligence to army HQs. One of his roles was undoubtedly to maintain a watching brief over SIS interests and also, it may be argued, to ensure that the SDB did not jeopardise the continuing, deep-cover operations of Section VII (see Chapter Eleven). Petherick worked closely with Colonel Major (Plate 12), often closeted in private meetings, and the reorganisation of the SDB fits neatly into the overall pattern of highly-structured military organisation that Major favoured. For a time the SDB had a separate HQ at Hannington Hall, a few miles from Coleshill, but when the Operational and SDB HQs were combined at Coleshill, Hannington Hall became an 'Attery' billet for the ATS.

Recruitment to the SDB War Establishment proceeded in gradual stages as suitable Intelligence Officers were found to take over management of the agent networks from SIS. In the beginning there can have been few in the army who had any experience of running such networks and so naturally they had to rely on Section D and its still-existing regional officers – including the men described as attached to the Auxiliary Units by Grand from his DM group.[14] Three of the four known SDB Intelligence Officers appointed before November 1940 show evidence of having previously served with SIS. They were not serving regimental officers but had originally been commissioned onto the General List and were then promoted almost immediately: John Todd, K.W. Johnson and R. Fraser. All three received their promotions to acting captain on 22 July, which probably marks their formal transfer to the Auxiliary Units.[15] None had any known links with MIR, the most common recruiting ground for Auxiliary Units Intelligence Officers of the Operational Branch.

The surviving 1940 Army List entries for Todd and Johnson include the phrase characteristic of SIS officers 'without pay and allowances', indicating that the men were not paid for out of War Office funds; the entry for Fraser does not survive. The career of Todd and his likely SIS connections has been discussed above (p. 68). K.W. Johnson was commissioned a Second Lieutenant on the General List. He joined the Intelligence Corps on 13 July, but retained the 'without pay and allowances' rider on his commission. He may have transferred from SIS upon his promotion to Acting Captain on 22 July, and served in the SDB until at least May 1944 (having been promoted to Temporary Major in February 1943). Like Todd, he unusually served in the Auxiliary Units as a joint SDB and Operational Patrols Intelligence Officer in South Wales and the Midlands. Were these areas something of an enclave for ex-SIS officers?

Less is known about R. Fraser. He was originally commissioned as Second Lieutenant on 1 July on the General List and was promoted to Acting Captain on 22 July (the same day as Todd and Johnson) in the new Intelligence Corps. In October 1940 he was promoted to War Service Captain and ended the war as a Temporary Major badged to the Intelligence Corps. His promotion to Major on 4 February 1943 was also on the same day as Johnson. He remained the SDB Intelligence Officer for South-East Command area until at least May 1944.

The fourth in the initial round of SDB Intelligence Officers was John S. Collings, who had special skills. He had been commissioned as a Second Lieutenant on 16 September 1939 into 5th (Inniskilling) Royal Dragoon Guards, but he spent little time with his regiment. In November 1939, being fluent in French and having also lived in Belgium, he became a founding member of what became the Phantom Unit (GHQ Liaison Regiment) and was promoted to Acting Captain. He served as Intelligence Officer for the Phantom regiment in France and Belgium, commanding six subalterns and six NCOs, all lightly-armed on motorcycles; skilled linguists and wireless operators, they were responsible for liaison between the forward HQs of the Allied armies. During his evacuation from Ostend on 27 May, his ship narrowly missed being torpedoed by a German E-boat; having to defend themselves with their Thompsons, Lewis guns and even revolvers, they survived without injury, but sadly the accompanying ship, carrying a number of senior officers and other ranks of Phantom, was sunk.[16] Collings then joined the SDB as Intelligence Officer for East Anglia, although it is not clear why he left the understaffed but expanding Phantom Unit. He was promoted to full captain on 16 August 1940. His recent practical experience in gathering intelligence in the face of *blitzkrieg* was no doubt useful, as would be his links to Phantom which was, by then, already deploying across the region. He remained as SDB Intelligence Officer for East Anglia until the spring of 1944, ending the war as a temporary major still badged to the Royal Dragoon Guards.

Three other IOs are known from the start of the reorganisation of the SDB in November/December. The Suffolk IO Frederick Baldwin Childe was first commissioned from his university officer training unit in 1930 (Coldstream Guards), then recommissioned in April 1940 in the King's Royal Rifle Corps and on 3 November was promoted acting captain on special employment. He joined the Intelligence Corps in 1941 and retired in 1945 as a major. The Yorkshire IO, M.J. Farrer, was commissioned into the Royal Sussex Regiment in December 1939. In April 1940 he was promoted acting lieutenant on special employment, rapidly followed by promotion to temporary captain on 24 June and full captain on 27 December. E. Robert Ramage Fingland, the Somerset IO, was another man commissioned onto the General List followed by rapid promotion. Was he also SIS? He was commissioned on 3 August 1940 and was appointed full captain on 14 December; he was still on the General List and only transferred to the Intelligence Corps in 1942. The rest of the SDB Intelligence Officers were recruited from 1941 at the time that the new SDB wireless system was generally introduced around the coast and the network therefore needed more intensive management. However, details of what the Intelligence Officers actually did remains vague and it will be argued that their role went beyond managing the wireless network into more traditional intelligence duties and field security work, perhaps in association with the Field Security Section (FSS) of the new Intelligence Corps.

A few SDB former agents have told consistent stories, about being given leaflets on German army uniforms, insignia and weapons units to study. Ursula Pennell in Norfolk kept the leaflets in her purse or even her bra.[17] Those given to George Vater in Monmouthshire had to be memorised in a week and then burnt. Vater has given one of the most detailed descriptions of the procedures. The fact that he remembers being driven by IO John Todd to a meeting at Hannington Hall suggests that he was a actually a 'Key Man' in the organisation. He was given the names of eight other people who formed his cell by Todd. Observations were made by day, and each night Vater had to collect messages from half a dozen dead-letter drops in the local area. Each message had to contain the safety word 'precisely'. At a later stage in operations a wireless set was introduced, with the Reverend Sluman of Llantillio Croesenny as the wireless operator who was expected to be contactable twenty-four hours a day. Vater was told to expect fourteen days of activity after invasion. Whether this meant that his life expectancy was expected to be fourteen days or that the invasion would be over by then is not clear (although probably the former). Vater's story does include some oddities, as might be expected from an association with SIS officer Todd. The cell had a local HQ (a derelict barn) where, if cut off from Todd, the agents would meet after

. Sir Stewart Menzies (1890–1968). Chief of
he Secret Intelligence Service 1939–52. He left
much of the day-to-day operations of SIS to
Dansey. (Walter Stoneman, 1953; © National Portrait
Gallery, London)

2. Sir Claude Dansey (1876–1947). Assistant
Chief of SIS during the Second World War. The
strategy of SIS secret operations in Britain bears
his hallmark. (Elliot and Fry, 1947; © National Portrait
Gallery, London)

. Lawrence Grand (1898–1975). Head of
abotage section of SIS, 1938–40. Creator of the
Home Defence Scheme and a major influence
n the development of later irregular warfare.
BRO Museum collection)

4. Walter Samuel, 2nd Viscount Bearsted
(1882–1948). SIS officer who managed the
transfer of the Home Defence Scheme into the
Auxiliary Units. (Walter Stoneman, 1942; © National
Portrait Gallery, London)

5. Jo Holland (1897–1956). Head of MIR at the War Office. MIR worked with Section D, SIS but favoured the use of military special forces rather than civilian guerrillas. (BRO Museum collection)

7. General Edmund Ironside (1889–1959). C-in-C Home Forces until 21 July 1940. He was a firm opponent of the idea of armed civilian resistance but argued for the creation of the Auxiliary Units in order to take control of the SIS Home Defence Scheme (© Hulton-Deutsch Collection/Corbis)

6. Winston Churchill (1874–1965) in August 1940. Once Churchill became Prime Minister in May 1944 plans for irregular warfare in Britain accelerated considerably. (© Bettman/Corbis)

8. Peter Fleming (1907–1971). Pre-war writer and adventurer. Tasked with investigating the potential of the LDV in guerrilla warfare in May 1940 and leader of the XII Corps Observation Unit. (Howard Coster, 1935; © National Portrait Gallery London)

General Andrew Thorne (1885–1970). Creator of the XII Corps Observation Unit. (Schroeder archive, Troendelag Folk Museum, Norway)

11. Sir Colin Gubbins (1896–1976). First CO of the Auxiliary Units and later head of SOE. (Walter Stoneman, 1944; © National Portrait Gallery, London)

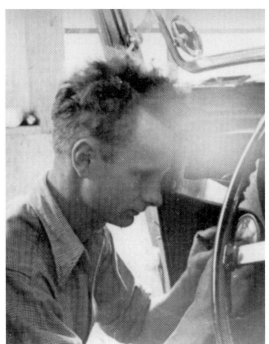

10. 'Spuggy' Newton of SIS fitting a wireless set into a car. Newton installed wireless sets for the XII Corps Observation Unit. (Courtesy of Geoffrey Pidgeon)

12. Colonel 'Bill' Major (1893–1977). CO of Auxiliary Units November 1940–February 1942. Formerly of the Directorate of Military Intelligence, his priority may have been in developing the Special Duties Branch. (A.P. Holmes, 1942; Courtesy of Mick Wilks)

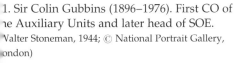

13. Maurice Petherick (1894–1985). Conservative MP and SIS officer. He was one of the architects of the re-formed Special Duties Branch in 1941. (A.P. Holmes, 1942; Courtesy of Mick Wilks)

15. John Todd (1899–1980). SIS regional officer who was attached to the Auxiliary Units as an Intelligence Officer for South Wales and the Midlands. Later head of SOE operations in SE Africa. (A.P. Holmes, 1941; Courtesy of Mick Wilks)

14. Colonel Douglas, last CO of the Auxiliary Units, 1943–44. (Courtesy of Mick Wilks)

16. David Boyle (1883–1970). Lifelong intelligence officer, head of the top secret SIS Section VII network in Britain during the Second World War. From a painting by Don Pottinger. (Courtesy of Piers Pottinger)

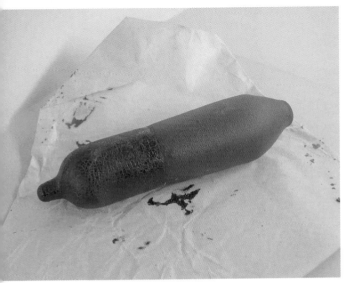

17. Tyesule paraffin incendiary, 5 inches long, as used by HDS and the Auxiliary Units. (Courtesy of David Sampson)

8. 'Machine-gun rattle' as ssued to the Home Defence cheme. (© Kate Atkin)

9. Rogers sheath knife (top) and Fairburn-Sykes fighting knife (bottom) as used by Auxiliary Units. © Kate Atkin)

20. Punch knife. This example is a military issue (1942) but many used by the Auxiliary Units were home-made. (© Kate Atkin)

21. Colt .32 semi-automatic pistol. The first 400 pistols issued to the Auxiliary Units were of this type. Some weapons of this type had been bought by the War Office during the First World War. (© Kate Atkin)

22. Smith and Wesson Model 10 (top) and Colt New Service .38 (bottom) revolvers as issued to the HDS and Auxiliary Units. Many were ex-US police issue. (© Kate Atkin)

23. Welrod bolt-action silenced pistol with 8-round magazine, .32 Calibre. Range point-blank to approximately 23m. It requires a two-handed grip to control properly. (© Imperial War Museums, TR 2979)

24. Type 77 phosphorous grenade. The request for 50,000 of these grenades in late 1943 over-stretched the patience of the War Office in dealing with the Auxiliary Units. Oxenden believed the 1944 Operational Patrols would only need these and the Welrod as personal weapons. (© Kate Atkin)

25. M1918 Browning Automatic Rifle (BAR), 7.27 kg, .30-06 calibre. Effective range up to 1,500 yards (1370m); weight 7.27kg (15.98lb). Too cumbersome for patrol work but the earliest automatic weapon supplied to the Auxiliary Units. (© Royal Armouries, PR.5306)

26. Thompson M1928A1 sub-machine gun. .45ACP calibre. Effective range 55 yards (50m); weight 4.9kg (10.8lb). This example has a simplified rear sight. Although most Thompsons were replaced in the Auxiliary Units by Sten guns during 1942, some remained in use until October 1943. The impressive-looking drum magazines contained 50 rounds but were heavy, rattled and took a long time to reload. The stick magazines containing 20 rounds were usually preferred. (© Kate Atkin)

27. Mk II (bottom) and Mk III (top) Sten guns, 9mm calibre. Effective range 110 yards (100m); weight 3.2kg (7.1lb). Began to be issued to the Auxiliary Units in September 1942. The main virtue of the Sten gun was that it was cheap to manufacture, but it had a poor reputation for reliability. It was well designed for clandestine warfare as the horizontal magazine (32 rounds) allowed it to be easily fired from prone position. (© Kate Atkin)

8. Winchester 74 sniper rifle of the type issued to the Auxiliary Units, .22L Calibre. Effective range 100 yards (91m). These civilian rifles were fitted with sound moderators and most had telescopic sights, although the latter were considered unsatisfactory by the Auxiliary Units Training Officer, Nigel Oxenden, as they kept going out of alignment and had to be adjusted by armourers. Remington and Martini models were also used by the HDS and Auxiliary Units, but the semi-automatic Winchester 74, issued from 1942, was particularly silent in operation as it had a closed bolt. It was also issued to SOE. (© Kate Atkin)

9. Page from *Calendar 1937* training manual for the Auxiliary Units. (BRO Museum collection)

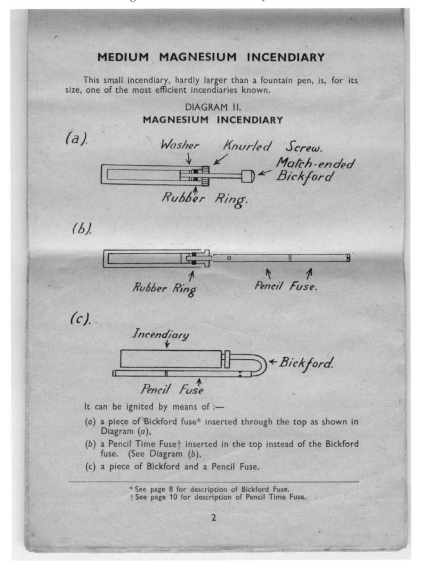

MEDIUM MAGNESIUM INCENDIARY

This small incendiary, hardly larger than a fountain pen, is, for its size, one of the most efficient incendiaries known.

DIAGRAM II.
MAGNESIUM INCENDIARY

(a).
Washer   Knurled Screw.
Match-ended
Bickford
Rubber Ring.

(b).
Rubber Ring   Pencil Fuse.

(c).
Incendiary
Bickford.
Pencil Fuse

It can be ignited by means of :—

(a) a piece of Bickford fuse* inserted through the top as shown in Diagram (a),

(b) a Pencil Time Fuse† inserted in the top instead of the Bickford fuse. (See Diagram (b),

(c) a piece of Bickford and a Pencil Fuse.

---

* See page 8 for description of Bickford Fuse.
† See page 10 for description of Pencil Time Fuse.

2

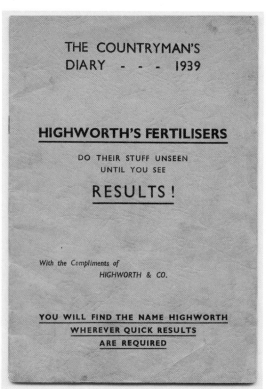

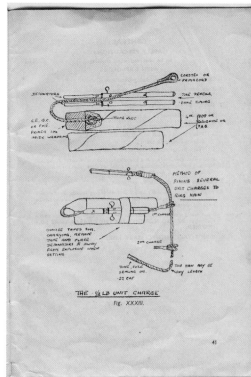

30 & 31. Auxiliary Units training manual *Countryman's Diary* (1944). Instructions for making up a half-pound unit charge. (BRO Museum collection)

32. Time Pencils, early and late with L Delay. Shown with replica unit charge. (© Kate Atkin)

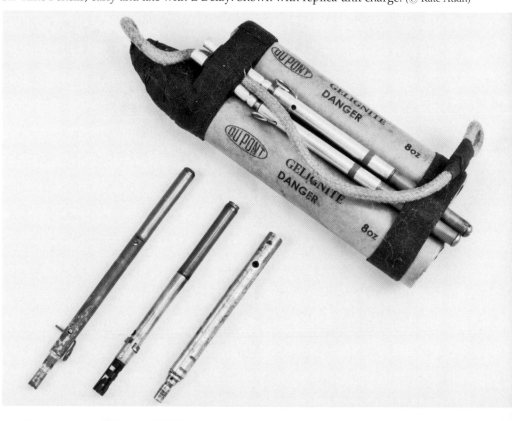

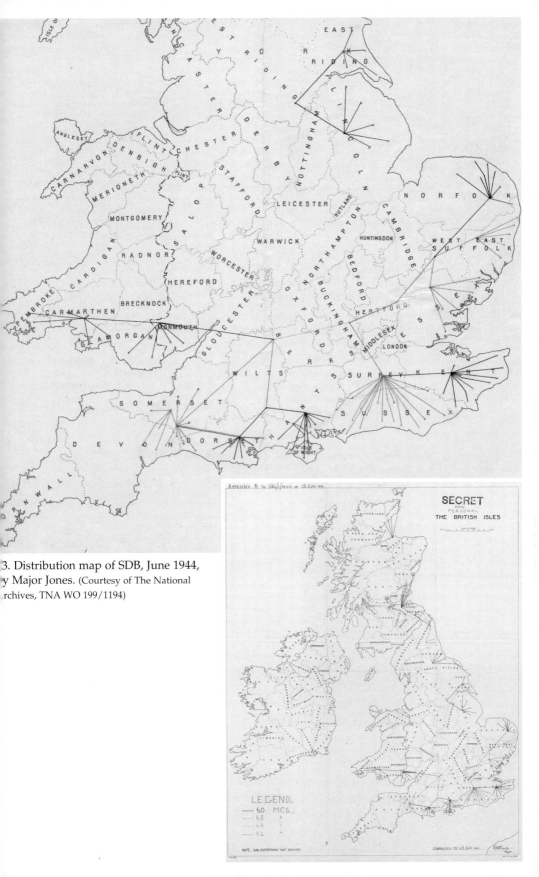

3. Distribution map of SDB, June 1944, y Major Jones. (Courtesy of The National rchives, TNA WO 199/1194)

34 (*Left*). Murphy B81 portable battery-powered wireless (1939). This became a standard issue to the military, including the SDB, to receive the BEETLE emergency broadcasts. (© Susanne Atkin)

35 (*Right*). TRD set (replica by Malcolm Atkin). The main wireless set of the Special Duties Branch, Auxiliary Units from January 1941. It was powered from a 6-volt accumulator battery and operated at 48–52 MHz. It was designed to be easily maintained and to be used with minimal training. The controls simply consisted of an On/Off switch, Send/Receive switch, Receiver Tuning and Volume. This approximation is based on contemporary accounts and research undertaken by Richard Hankins and the VMARS Witney Project. (© Susanne Atkin)

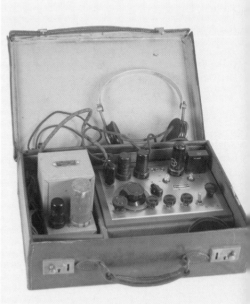

36 (*Left*). WS17 Mk II wireless set as used by Auxiliary Units (Special Duties Branch). It was invented in early 1939 for the control of balloon barrages. The WS17 Mk I operated on the 46–64 MHz frequency range and the WS17 Mk II on the 44–61 MHz frequency range. It had a range of up to fifteen miles and was battery-powered in a self-contained but heavy wooden box. (© Susanne Atkin)

37. (*Right*) SIS Mk VII 'Paraset' transceiver (replica by Malcolm Atkin). A 'suitcase' set used as back-up set by SCUs and possibly by Eastbourne Section VII cell from 1941. (© Susanne Atkin)

8. 'Keep Mum' Poster. To test the effectiveness of the 'careless talk costs lives' campaign, the Special Duties Branch of the Auxiliary Units and Field Security Sections of Military Intelligence spied on both military and civilians, sometimes acting as 'honey traps'. The internal security role of the GDB, although the least well-documented, may have been its most significant contribution to the war effort, especially in the months leading up to D-Day.

Tell NOBODY – not even HER

CARELESS TALK COSTS LIVES

9. Star Brewery, Eastbourne, Sussex. This was the HQ of what is believed to be a Section VII sabotage and intelligence cell, operating throughout the war from March 1940. A wireless set was hidden in the brewery chimney. (East Sussex County Council Library & Information Service)

40. (*Left*) Section VII wireless station on Smedley Street, Matlock, Derbyshire. (*Right*) Entrance to the office of the SIS training officer at the Hydro, Matlock, seen in 2014 with former wireless operator, Peter Attwater. (© Susanne Atkin)

41. A Special Communications Unit (SCU) of SIS in April 1944 posing in front of three Guy 15cwt wireless trucks. Their HRO receivers and Mk III transmitters are laid out on bench. The SCUs could pass on intelligence received from Section VII wireless stations to army commands, as well as intelligence traffic from ULTRA. (Courtesy of Geoffrey Pidgeon)

2. Home Guard Part II Orders, September 1941, showing promotion of Lewis van Moppes to be Lieutenant, Auxiliary Units. Lewis and later his brother Edmund would become Group Commanders for Worcestershire Auxiliary Units. (Courtesy of the former Army Medal Office)

SHEET ONE

7TH WORC.(MALVERN) BN. HOME GUARD

PART TWO ORDERS NO. 32 D/E.5.41.

8.9

No.	NAME	COY.	PARTICULARS OF CASUALTIES ETC.

(1) APPOINTMENTS

X3875 F.W. Romney to be Capt. (Liasion Officer). Wess Gard. Orders 18

X3513/1 C.A.Arnold, M.C. to be 2nd Lt. (Ombersley).
X3817/1 C.A. Cooper, to be 2nd Lt. (Crowle).
X3550/2. E. Van Moppes, to be Lt. (Ombersley)
X3527/2. L.E. Van Moppes, to be Lt.(") Aux.Patrol.

7TH WORCESTER (MALVERN) BN. HOME GUARD.

Part Two Orders: No. 35. dated 22nd October, 1941.

No.	NAME	Coy.	Particulars of Casualty

1) Aux. Patrol (attached 7th Worcs. (Malvern) Bn. Home Guard Hqrs:1.10.41.

3527/2	Lt. L.E. Van Moppes)		
3550/2	Lt. E.M. Van Moppes)	Ombersley	
3528/2	Vol V. Poland)		
3310	R.V. Clines Sgt.	Powick	
3293	R.H. Boaz	"	
3190	W.A. Ring	"	
3274	A.V. Clines	"	
3197	P. Lester Cancelled Park Orders No 52.		
3255	Sgt. G.A. Devereux	"	
3677	Vol. R. Smith	Crowle	
3693	J. Wythes	"	
3679	J.I. Thomas	"	
2X14/1	J.D. Badger	"	
3686	M.H. Huband	"	
3685	A.J. Holt.ny.	"	
3424	A.S. Barley	Knightwick	
3416	G. Dalley	"	
3389	R.F. Mason	"	
3437	W.F. Jauncey	"	
3447	A.G. Jeynes	"	
3476	W.J. Plaskett	"	

---

3. Home Guard Part II Orders, October 1941, identifying officers and men of the Auxiliary Units patrols attached to 7th (Malvern) Battalion, Worcestershire Home Guard. (Courtesy of the former Army Medal Office)

4. Stand-Down letter and lapel badge of John Thornton, Herefordshire Auxiliary Units. (© Kate Atkin)

In view of the improved war situation, it has been decided by the War Office that the Operational Branch of Auxiliary Units stand down, and the time has now come to put to an organisation which would have been of inestimable value to this country in the event of invasion.

All ranks under your command are aware of the secret nature of their duties. For that reason it has not been possible for them to receive publicity, nor will it be possible even now. So far from considering this to be a misfortune, I should like all members of Auxiliary Units to regard it as a matter of special pride.

I have been much impressed by the devotion to duty and high standard of training shown by all ranks. The careful preparations, the hard work undertaken in their own time, and their readiness to face the inevitable dangers of their role, are all matters which reflect the greatest credit on the body of picked men

45. Tom Wintringham (1898–1949) lecturing on tank-hunting at Osterley Park Home Guard Training School, 1940. (Zoltan Glass, Picture Post, Getty Images)

46. Home Guard instruction in the use of a remote electrical detonator at Osterley Park Home Guard Training School in 1940. (Fox Photos, Hulton Archive, Getty Images)

invasion. His story is further discussed above, (see p. 71) but it is possible that Vater's cell was, unknown to him, a part of the HDS that was then absorbed into the SDB. Vater himself may have been an HDS 'Key Man' but never knew it![18]

The great weakness of the SDB in 1940 was that it had no effective mechanism for quickly delivering any intelligence that it had collected. They would have to rely on couriers creeping through enemy lines (as Grand had proposed for the HDS earlier in June). Whilst practical in a period of settled occupation, this would have been an uncertain and slow method of transmitting intelligence during what was expected to be a rapidly-moving invasion campaign. Fortunately, the War Office was increasingly able to call upon other options that seemed to by-pass the SDB and caused the latter to re-evaluate its long-term purpose.

The Phantom Unit
Reference has already been made to the recruitment of a Phantom Unit officer (John Collings) and it is useful to compare its methodology to that of the SDB. In November 1939 the No. 3 Military and Air Mission (code named 'Phantom') was created in order to provide forward intelligence to the RAF and BEF in France. Its patrols of skilled linguists, equipped with wireless and using scout cars and motorcycles, criss-crossed the front line and liaised with the forward commands of British, French and Belgian armies, as well as listening in to German wireless traffic. The unit also worked closely with SIS mobile communication units in France. Crucially, the intelligence they gathered was transmitted direct to RAF command and GHQ in France, short-circuiting the normal lines of communication. At times, theirs was the only battle intelligence reaching the GHQ of the BEF.

Within days of returning from France, the Commanding Officer of Phantom, Lieutenant Colonel Hopkinson, sent a formal proposal to the War Office on 7 June, suggesting that they consider the possibilities of employing his reconnaissance and liaison units in Britain. Their potential was stressed when Phantom officer Captain John Jackson produced a report on their activities in France to the War Office:

> It [Phantom] has continued to be not only the quickest channel, but frequently the only source of information available to the Commander-in-Chief. If this service was useful in France, it must be indispensable in the imminent battle to defend our shores.[19]

Hopkinson explained that the intention of its operation in Britain would be to provide fast and accurate information to GHQ Home Forces and the RAF regarding the points at which landings were made, their scale and their subsequent progress; it was exactly the type of information that the SDB were expected to provide, but Phantom had the great advantage of a tried and tested wireless system and a core of experienced intelligence officers operating with armed protection. The Phantom Unit was, as a consequence, reconstituted as No. 1 GHQ Reconnaissance Unit and immediately began an assessment of likely invasion beaches. By September, Hopkinson had assembled forty-eight officers and 407 other ranks, organised as an HQ Unit based in St James's Park, London, with four reconnaissance groups based in the South East, East Anglia, Yorkshire and a reserve in Gloucestershire. Each reconnaissance group, with an HQ at the regional Corps, consisted of four patrols of an officer and six men, based at divisional HQs. The patrols were equipped with a wireless-equipped scout car, a 15cwt truck and three motorcycles and were designed to be self-sufficient. Phantom had worked closely with the Communications Section of SIS on its return from France in order to improve the effective range of their wireless sets and so it is probably no coincidence that they shared their HQ in St James's Park with a mobile Special Communications Unit (SCU) of SIS. The Phantom Unit War Diary shows patrols moving up and down the coast from East Anglia to Dorset, in constant wireless contact with their HQ and day-by-day providing regular weather updates and visibility levels across the sea. In return they were fed the latest intelligence on German army and naval movements so they were ready to redeploy at a moment's notice.[20]

A review by GHQ on 24 October 1940 concluded that the difficulty in commanders receiving speedy intelligence from the battlefield had been at least partially solved by imposing 'an independent information-collecting service provided by the GHQ Reconnaissance Unit, equipped with armoured and unarmoured reconnaissance troops, liaison officers, mobile wireless sets and aircraft'.[21] It was now proposed that the assessment of the intelligence should not only be transmitted to higher commands, but would also be broadcast on a wider basis to other units via BEETLE (see above, Chapter Three). The number of units would be expanded to six:

1. West and South-west
2. Hampshire, Sussex and Kent
3. East Anglia
4. Lincolnshire, Yorkshire, Durham and Northumberland
5. Scotland
6. Ireland

On the face of it, the rapid development of the Phantom patrols over the summer of 1940 offered a proven means of supplying battlefield intelligence that would make the infant SDB superfluous. In addition, SIS were expanding a top secret wireless intelligence network (Section VII), but this was outside of GHQ control and, conceivably, beyond their knowledge (see Chapter Eleven). The existing network of Observer Corps posts spread across the country should also not be forgotten as an early warning system. If, however, SDB could use wireless communication from behind enemy lines, it could offer a complementary service by providing information (even if only briefly) on enemy supply lines and reinforcements to army commands, in areas from which Phantom or the Observer Corps had been forced to withdraw. As with the Operational Patrols, it was a cheap option as the operatives were unpaid civilians and the support staff were small in number; their loss would be a calculated sacrifice. Captain John Collings therefore made a particularly valuable recruit in being able to liaise with his former colleagues in Phantom.

The Wireless Sets

To make the new plan for the SDB work effectively they had to have a wireless network. However, unlike all existing systems, the wireless sets had to be operable by untrained civilians as the network was rapidly expanded around the coastal regions. In September, Gubbins recruited Captain John Hills, Technical Maintenance Officer at No. 1 Special Wireless Group, Harpenden (Y Service) to build a new wireless system for the SDB. Nonetheless, when Gubbins left to join SOE in November 1940, wireless communication for SDB had only reached the planning stage.[22] It was left to the new CO, Colonel Major, and to Major Petherick as the new head of SDB, to work out how to properly incorporate the HDS rebadged 'Auxiliary Units (Special Duties)' agents into the rest of the organisation, and six months after its unsteady foundation in July 1940, a major change in the organisation of the SDB via a revised War Establishment can be detected. Following Hills's success in designing the new Savage wireless, a separate War Establishment for the Auxiliary Units (Signals) was produced in February 1941, including Royal Signals technicians and operators together with ATS wireless operators, reflecting the introduction of an 'in-house' wireless system that finally provided a way forward to operational independence from SIS (Fig. 13).

Colonel 'Bill' Major (Plate 12) maintained in 1968 that he was responsible for creating the Special Duties Branch after he took command from Gubbins on 19 November 1940.[23] This was only partly true. SDB's origin was actually in Bearsted's 'Special Duties' section of the HDS and Gubbins had already made the critical appointment of John Hills in September. Major did oversee the development of SDB into what is now seen as its classic highly-structured form, but Auxiliary Units Training Officer, Major Beyts, is clear that it was the 'genius' of Major Petherick as the new CO of the SDB that established the character of the network, not just confined to the wireless network but, it will be argued, including a distinct role for the existing agents/couriers.[24] One structural model for the reorganisation may have been the pyramid system of Observer Corps posts,

Figure 13. Extract from War Establishment for Auxiliary Units (Signals), February 1941.
(BRO Museum archive)

| | | | Other Ranks | | | | | |
		Offrs	CQMS	Sgts	Cpls	L/Cpl	Sgmn	Drivers	Total O.R.s
MALE	R. Sigs	4	–	1	2	15	26		44
	RASC							6	6
	RE (attd)								
FEMALE	ATS	40							

which had so recently demonstrated its worth and efficiency during the Battle of Britain. They were organised into clusters of three to five posts, with each cluster having fixed telephone links to an individual plotter at the local Control Centre, where the information was immediately collated and forwarded to RAF Fighter Command. The RAF strenuously made the point that the primary function of the Observer Corps was to report enemy aircraft movements and that it was not an invasion reporting force; nonetheless, the nationwide observation posts were manned twenty-four hours a day and were an obvious body to report airborne attack.[25] From the spring of 1940 each post was nominally armed (one rifle and five rounds of ammunition), had flares to signal enemy landings, and carried instructions to keep reporting the enemy's position until overrun.

Most of the existing civilian agents and couriers of the HDS could transfer smoothly into the new organisation, and may have been unaware of the change in their compartmentalised existence. Not a single veteran has ever directly mentioned prior service with the HDS or SIS, even though there may have been around 1,000 of them. The stories of agents being recruited by men who gave no name, wore no visible badges of rank, did not identify their organisation (or vaguely referred to it as 'X Branch' –see below, Chapter Eleven) and carried only a copy of the Official Secrets Act as a signal of authority now seems remarkably naïve, but appears commonplace at the time.

The CO of the SDB, Major Petherick, may have created the basic structure of the re-formed SDB, but he was not a technical officer and the new system was dependent on the development of a suitable wireless system. Control of clandestine wireless systems was a touchy matter in 1940. On 15 September (just as Gubbins appointed Hills) Menzies from SIS and the new Chief Executive Officer of the SOE, Gladwyn Jebb, met formally to discuss the continuing influence of SIS. As part of major concessions by SOE to SIS over agent recruitment and the control of intelligence, Section VIII of SIS was to retain control of wireless systems used by SOE. Although drafted by Jebb on behalf of SOE, this agreement remained a major source of SOE friction with SIS until 1942. It would have provided a clear warning for Gubbins that the infant SDB of the Auxiliary Units would need to develop its own independent communication system if it was ever to come completely out of SIS control. In the event, Gubbins was only partially successful.

Captain Hills had previously designed a receiver to intercept signals from German E-Boats operating in the English Channel and appreciated the desirability of making the new sets as hard to intercept as possible. The other criteria was that SDB needed a system that avoided the need for specialist morse code training and therefore used telephony. Hills was able to draw upon a number of strands of earlier research in the mid to late 1930s. Between 1933 and 1938 a team from the Signals Experimental Unit of the OTC at Cambridge University under Professor Wilfrid Lewis and post-graduate student C.J. Milner (assisted by a number of undergraduates including Ken Ward) were developing, for the War Office, a duplex transceiver that could not easily be intercepted.[26] It was intended to provide secure short-range communications between artillery batteries and their forward observation posts. The work was taken over by the Signals Research Development Establishment at Bournemouth, which unsuccessfully tried to turn the research into production sets.[27] Similar research was continued by Dr Edward Schröter in Section D of SIS between 1938 and 1940. By July 1940, Schröter had produced a demonstration model of a short-range, VHF, duplex transceiver that used voice transmission.[28] Schröter went on to successfully oversee the development of clandestine wireless sets for SOE but there the priority was in long-range sets using morse code and work on the duplex transceiver was shelved.[29] It is quite feasible that Schröter's research was handed over to Hills as part of the transfer of the HDS, for him to develop further into what became the Savage/TRD sets, and this would partly explain why SIS claimed proprietorial rights to the TRD sets at the end of the war. In 2008, Warwicker had an un-named source who claimed that the Section D duplex transceiver was overweight, depended on foreign components and, of seven made, only one actually worked.[30] However, any failure of the prototype does not mean that the research can be too easily dismissed as a source for the TRD.

Another basic inspiration may have been the simple, short-range, WS17 super-regenerative set which had been invented by the notable radio ham Stanley Lewer in early 1939 to produce a short-range, low-power transceiver for the control of balloon barrages. The WS17 operated on the same frequency range as the later TRD wireless set, had a range of up to fifteen miles and was battery-powered in a self-contained but heavy wooden box (Plate 36). Even if the crude WS17 was not an inspiration for John Hills, it was to prove highly significant for the operations of the SDB and by the summer of 1944 it comprised nearly forty per cent of their wireless sets.

If their direct control over SDB weakened, SIS made sure they were able to keep a 'watching brief' on this alternate intelligence-gathering operation by supplying Petherick as the Commanding Officer and by keeping a financial hold on the organisation throughout the war. They provided funds that did not need to pass through any form of War Office public accounting, thus, when making arrangements for the disbandment of the SDB in 1944 it is notable that 'Tools and Components were to be returned to No. 1 SCU [SIS Communications HQ at Whaddon] if purchased from S.D. [Special Duties] funds' together with what were described as the 'special sets' – the TRDs.[31]

Hills's first product was a VHF duplex telephony unit that incorporated a quench circuit, manufactured by Savage and Parsons Ltd of Kingsbury and therefore known as the Savage set. The set was in one box with the controls on top; a second box contained the power supply. Fifty were quickly built but they proved difficult to maintain; nonetheless the set already had the quench circuitry that would make the signal *undecipherable* to anyone without the same type of receiver, but not *undetectable*. Hills used the set in November to establish a pilot network in Kent (replacing the network installed before the end of August by SIS for the XII Corps Observation Unit). There was a base-station at Maidstone and five or six out-stations. The network was then steadily expanded: from January, Hills was able to build up a small technical team at Bachelor's Hall, Hundon, Suffolk, as the core of what became the Auxiliary Units (Signals) maintenance team, including Lieutenant (later Captain) Ken Ward who had also served in the Y Intercept Service with Hills.[32] Ward was appointed Adjutant and Workshop Officer of the new Auxiliary Units (Signals) on 1 January 1941.[33] His background in Operator Training at the Y Service suggests he may have been brought in specifically because of the need to create a system that relied on minimum training. He had also been an undergraduate member of the Lewis and Milner team at Cambridge, but cheerfully described himself as merely 'one of the stooges'. It was, however, Ward who had brought this work to the attention of Hills.[34] A number of skilled former radio hams including Sergeant Ron Dabbs, Corporal Bill Bartholomew and Jack Millie were also recruited. Together the new team designed and built a replacement for the Savage set in just two weeks.[35] Jack Millie gives the breakdown of the team as follows: he and Bill Bartholomew designed the transmitter; Tom Higgins and Ron Dabbs designed the receiver; Les Parnell, Jimmy McNab and John Mackie designed the power supply.[36] Named TRD (Transmitter Ron Dabbs) in the contemporary tradition of SIS in identifying wireless sets by their team members, it was powered from a 6-volt accumulator battery and operated at 48–52MHz (similar to that of the WS17 but because of the quench circuit and differing power output they were not interoperable). Built into a single metal box $15.5'' \times 9.75'' \times 9.25''$, to simplify operations the controls were minimal and the transmitter was set for a fixed frequency (Plate 35). By June 1944 the frequencies had been rationalised with IN and OUT Stations using 60 or 65MHz and the inner circle of IN Stations using 48 or 52MHz.[37] The normal range was 30–60 miles by line of sight but the signal could, on occasion, be picked up at much greater distances. Its main handicaps were that the TRD relied on fixed frequencies and a very directional aerial which could not be relocated without specialist assistance.

Initially the workshop was producing seven or eight sets per week as they gradually replaced the existing Savage sets (with which they were mutually compatible) in the wireless stations. From 1942, the Inter-Services Research Board, a cover name for SOE and now under Schröter, took over responsibility for the manufacture of new TRDs with a contract issued to Peto Scott Ltd, but with Ward as the contract manager.[38] Some assembly and repair work was also undertaken at Coleshill. The TRD continued to evolve, with a number of different versions of unknown character, called TRM and TRF, some of which were designed for loudspeaker use.[39] In 1943 it was planned to implement a major programme of replacement of the early sets.

> Several IOs have written pressing for an exchange of their old TRD sets for new ones ... The position is that TRD sets are coming through very slowly indeed from the manufacturers, but that eventually all old sets will be replaced ... No new ones are in stock here, and replacement will be made according to plans already made, starting with EASTCC [Eastern Command].[40]

It is not known what advantages the new versions of the TRD offered except probably to reduce interference. By June 1944 there were 250 TRD, 28 TRM and 36 TRF sets in use with the SDB, together with 200 WS17 sets, distributed amongst 30 IN Stations, 125 OUT Stations and 78 SUB-OUT Stations plus IO HQs.[41]

It should be noted that a significant percentage of the wireless sets used by the later SDB consisted of the standard WS17 which has implications for an understanding of the nature of the organisation (see below, Chapter Ten). The fact that the WS17 were supplied by the War Office without their standard aerial packages suggest they were intended to be used in hidden locations that required specialist set-up but no special security.[42] By the time of their widespread introduction in 1943, however, the role of the organisation did not depend entirely on secure communications. The signal from a WS17 could be received by any wireless set tuned to its frequency. It also radiated a super-regenerative noise signal that could easily be detected within a radius of a few hundred metres. Indeed it was so noisy that it interfered with low-flying aircraft and this caused problems when they were sold on to radio hams post-war.

A legend has grown that the TRD wireless was revolutionary in design and undetectable, a story not, however, supported by the accounts of those involved. Ken Ward clearly stated in a 1999 interview that the design was essentially that of Hills's Savage set, itself probably based on the 1930s Cambridge and SIS research. The impetus for change had come from the need to rebuild the Savage set so that it was easier for the operators to use and for the technicians to service and was undertaken on the initiative of Dabbs, Bartholomew and the other radio hams rather than from any instruction from higher authority.[43] Neither Ward nor Bartholomew mention any imperative to improve wireless security in the new design beyond what already existed in the Savage set. The TRD did use a modulated sub-carrier system that produced a type of 'white noise' or 'mush' on anything other than another TRD, but the signal could still be detected. Ward believed that security was based not upon any radical design, but more simply upon (a) the relatively rare use of the VHF frequencies employed, (b) the short range of the set, and (c) the fact that the aerials were very directional.[44] One improvement Bartholomew did make was to isolate the receiver from the radiation that it caused (and thereby likely to give away its position to the enemy) by the simple means of using an untuned buffer RF amplifier.[45]

By 1944 the legend of non-detectability had already been born and Sergeant Roy Russell of Auxiliary Units (Signals), instructed to produce spoof messages for the D-Day deception plan, expressed surprise to learn that the signals from the TRD might be intelligible to German intelligence. 'It was the first intimation I had that the enemy could pick up our very-high-frequency; although maybe they couldn't, we'll never know'.[46] But one operator in Kent, Adrian Monck-Mason, had already found a Royal Signals wireless operator looking for the signal from his TRD which had been picked up locally by the army.[47] Barbara Culleton recorded that early versions of the TRD were not only particularly sensitive to thunderstorms and sunspot activity, but also to interference from tank radios.

One presumes the problem was mutual. Bartholomew's simple fix to isolate the receiver had not worked! In August 1943 Major Kirkness advised in his 'Monthly Notes for IOs' that, on 'freak days', signals from Kent OUT stations could be picked up at Coleshill on Strength 5, prompting fears that such signals could also be received in occupied Europe – assuming that the Germans were monitoring these little-used VHF frequencies. Whether they could actually resolve the signal without having a matching TRD is, however, a different matter.[48] In May 1944 a possible loophole was found in the wireless deception plan for D-Day involving a supposedly undetectable VHF coastal network. Does this tantalising reference refer to the SDB? Guy Liddell, head of counter-espionage in MI5, reported:

> steps had now been taken by TAR [Colonel Robertson] to get certain radio telephony circuits round the coast and in particular to the Scilly Isles, suspended. These were in VHF and it was commonly thought that they could not be picked up by the enemy. Evidence has however been produced that, in certain circumstances, they can have a range of anything up to 500 miles.[49]

Was the legend of undetectability deliberately spread during the war to reassure the operators, or was it just in the tradition of similar claims made by their inventors for earlier SIS clandestine sets, also designed by Schröter? Guy Liddell refers in April 1940 to the sets sent by SIS to Norway:

> These have all been supplied by SIS since other apparatus of the kind seems singularly out of date. The sets, I gather, are designed by [XXXXXXX] and SIS have them operating from German territory and from all over the continent. Stewart [Menzies] believes that they are extremely difficult to pick up and doubts very much whether any monitoring system however widespread will be effective against them.[50]

Menzies was over-optimistic. Experience was to show that agents could not use any wireless sets for more than fifteen minutes without risking discovery by German radio detection. The destruction of the TRDs by SIS at the end of the war was remarkable only in its completeness and is not, in itself, evidence of a super-secret set. SIS destroyed large numbers of other clandestine wireless sets after the war, leaving only a handful surviving of its famous Mk III or Mk V sets.

It is useful to consider other contemporary concerns with the security of the new use of VHF. Producing a VHF transceiver was evidently not complicated: in June 1941 five youths were arrested in Nottingham after using VHF for some months – including for communicating with army units. Liddell commented: 'There is of course no proper organisation for detecting VHF or for policing army traffic'.[51] Problems in the detection of VHF transmissions remained a concern for MI5 throughout the war. Interestingly in the context of the SDB, this was caused by the disinterest of the Radio Security Service (RSS), as VHF was still not considered practical for agents to use. In June 1942 Major Morton-Evans believed that 'VHF was still in the stage where it was a matter for the radio engineers and not for Intelligence'.[52] The concern of RSS was obviously in the potential of reliable long-range transmission to and from the Continent, but their fears were aroused just a few days later. 'An expedition recently sent to the Isle of Wight obtained highly interesting results in this field, and the range was found to be something in the neighbourhood of 90 miles'.[53] By September the RSS did have vans dedicated to searching for VHF signals although they 'had to turn out on an average of once a week only'.[54]

Like any system, the TRD was subject to human error. Messages were sent by voice telephony in open speech or using simple word codes that were supposed to be regularly changed; as the modulated system was supposed to be impossible to unscramble, the fact that such codes were easy to break was not considered so important, but astonishingly, in what was described at the time as an act of stupidity, one IO in 1943 openly broadcast instructions for the new 'captured drill' from his IN Station to OUT stations, thus threatening the whole network.[55]

The Wireless Network

The distribution of the SDB network (as with the Auxiliary Units Operational Patrols) was predominantly coastal in order to meet the immediate threat of coastal invasion, and was likely to provide only partial protection.[56] The defence planning of 1940 and 1941 also considered there was a real risk of parachute landings anywhere in the country 'with even less warning than in the case of seaborne landings.'[57] They would be carried out 'in very different places so as to upset us and get our troops rushing about the country'.[58] In 1940 it was accepted that the main defence against these would be warning by the Observer Corps and action by the local Home Guard, who would not only have to oppose the landings, but also ensure that information was immediately passed back to the military command. A meeting of the War Cabinet on 18 November 1941 continued to highlight the danger of large-scale parachute drops which would cut telephone communications on which the military were heavily dependent.[59] The Auxiliary Units, however, were obliged to concentrate their resources where the danger was most obvious and likely to be most concentrated.

The SDB system as it emerged in 1941 was very different to what has become known as the classic European resistance system of agents reporting via cut-outs to a wireless operator, who would, with a portable wireless, frequently move location in order to avoid detection. The SIS Section VII network in the UK changed its frequencies between odd and even every day; cautious SOE and SIS agents would never sleep in the same house for more than one night to avoid discovery or betrayal. However, as the SDB was not a resistance organisation and the task for which the wireless network was designed in 1941 was simply to provide short-term intelligence on the course of any invasion, such concerns were not considered important. In the same way that the Operational Patrols had been given a life expectancy of days then so, it seems, had the SDB wireless operators. Any arguments about security had lost out against the limitations imposed by the Savage/TRD technology.

Figure 14. Organisational responsibility for Special Duties Branch, June 1944. (TNA WO 199/1194)

	Area	Information To
Scotland	Caithness, Sutherland	North Highland District, Scottish Command
	Angus, Fife, East Lothian, Berwickshire	Scottish Command
England	Northumberland, Durham	Northumbrian District
	Yorkshire, North Riding	North Riding District
	Yorkshire, East Riding, Lincolnshire	East Riding and Lincolnshire District
	Norfolk	Norfolk and Cambridge District
	Essex, Suffolk	Essex and Suffolk District
	Kent	East Kent District, South Eastern Command
	Sussex	Sussex District, South Eastern Command
	Hampshire	Hampshire Sub-District, Southern Command
	Dorset	Dorset Sub-District, Southern Command
	Somerset, East Devon	South Western District
Wales	Pembrokeshire, Carmarthenshire Glamorgan, Monmouthshire	South Wales District

By January 1944, the SDB was organised in ten areas, each under an Intelligence Officer reporting to the army District HQ (Fig. 14).[60] Despite the overall expansion in the SDB, the number of Intelligence Officers on the War Establishment did not increase significantly after its creation in July 1940 and indeed had declined in 1943 to just nine intelligence officers (most of whom had served with SDB since 1941). There was a pyramid system of wireless stations with a number of civilian-operated OUT Stations reporting to IN Stations staffed by Royal Signals or ATS operators, generally around fifteen miles from the coast. The IN Stations might then report to an Inner Circle of stations based at Command HQs (Plate 33).[61] Later, a number of SUB-OUT Stations were established to report to the OUT Stations but it is not clear if they were using TRD or the less secure WS17 sets.

The system depended on the Auxiliary Units (Signals) which provided IN station operators and a maintenance team. The latter was small and highly qualified but was a uniformed technical body which had received no training for operating beyond enemy lines. Its history can be tracked through the detailed War Establishments (see Figs 15–18). The discrepancy between the number of male and female officers is because the ATS wireless operators were given emergency commissions so as to protect discipline. There were also no mixed stations. Until April 1942 the IN Stations were almost entirely reliant on ATS operators (Fig. 15); and there were usually three ATS subalterns for each wireless station, which made their operation more expensive than if they had used male Royal Signals other ranks as operators. As a consequence, as pressures on the overall costs of the Auxiliary Units increased, the War Establishment of April 1942 (Fig. 16) cut the number of ATS officers from 136 to just thirty-two, in favour

Figure 15. Extract from War Establishment Auxiliary Units (Signals), March 1942.
(TNA WO 199/1194)

| | | Offrs | Other Ranks | | | | | | |
			CQMS	Sgts	Cpls	Sgmn	Drivers	Total O.R.s
MALE	R. Sigs	4	1	7	24	–	–	32
	RASC						8	8
	RE (attd)							
FEMALE	ATS	136						

Figure 16. Extract from War Establishment Auxiliary Units (Signals), April 1942, after decision
to expand SDB. (TNA WO 199/1194)

| | | Offrs | Other Ranks | | | | | | |
			CQMS	Sgts	Cpls	L/Cpl	Sgmn	Drivers	Total O.R.s
MALE	R. Sigs	7	1	7	25	3	55	–	91
	RASC							12	12
	RE (attd)	4							
FEMALE	ATS	32							

Figure 17. Extract from War Establishment Auxiliary Units (Signals), February 1943.
(TNA WO 199/1194)

| | | Offrs | Other Ranks | | | | | | |
			CQMS	Sgts	Cpls	Sgmn	Drivers	Total O.R.s
MALE	R. Sigs	7	1	7	20	42	–	69
	RASC						12	12
	RE (attd)	4						
FEMALE	ATS	56						

Figure 18. Extract from War Establishment of Auxiliary Units (Signals), June 1944.
(TNA WO 199/1194)

| | | Offrs | Other Ranks | | | | | | |
			CQMS	Sgts	Cpls	Sgmn	Drivers	Total O.R.s
MALE	R. Sigs	7	1	7	20	41	–	69
	RASC						10	10
	RE (attd)	4						
FEMALE	ATS	57					3	3

of using male Royal Signals wireless operators.[62] This, at a time when the SDB was expanding in Scotland and the South-West, was admitted to be a mistake in a letter of Lord Glanusk dated 1 February 1943, and the establishment was revised back up to fifty-six ATS officers (Fig. 17).[63] The final War Establishment in June 1944 (Fig. 18) lists fifty-seven ATS officers (and three drivers). These figures do not include a small number of ATS other ranks clerks employed at the HQ of the SDB.

The network was organised on the basis of fixed IN and OUT Stations using sets with permanently installed directional aerials and a TRD that had a normal operating range of just 30–60 miles. The distance between stations could be increased by the use of unmanned relay stations (with the equipment sometimes hidden up a tree). Confusingly, Ward says that these are what were originally called SUB-OUT stations; the term was later used to identify an outer ring of manned sub-stations that from 1943 fed into the OUT Stations.[64] It was a high-maintenance system: one of the Auxiliary Units (Signals) sergeants, Roy Russell, recounted how 'Communication at the high frequency we used required accurate direction for reliable reception. High winds or even branch growth could alter the delineation and lose radio contact'.[65] IN Stations might require three or four aerials so that the dipole was at the right bearing for the various OUT Stations. Moving such stations would have been a major effort, especially during an invasion.

Early 1941 OUT Stations would be highly vulnerable after enemy occupation: some simply consisted of wireless sets buried in a large box within a woodland and could be easily tracked. One at Donnington-on-Bain, Lincolnshire, was discovered by a courting couple during a transmission and the operators were arrested as suspected spies. Subsequent stations were often more cunningly hidden underground beneath chicken coops, toilets and so on.

But the weakest link were the IN Stations, generally sited just 15 miles inland. Until early 1942 the IN Stations were based in surface Nissen huts called 'met huts' as cover, at static army HQs, and the operators were even supplied with weather forecasts every day to satisfy curious onlookers.[66] If the HQ had to move then the IN Station was either left isolated with no secure means of passing its messages to the Intelligence Officer or, if it moved with the HQ, the whole system was likely to collapse as the aerials of the OUT Stations, in territory now controlled by the enemy, might all need to be realigned. Only from early 1942 were the IN Stations provided with underground 'Zero' stations, with supplies with which to operate for up to three weeks.[67] Even then, if the military HQ had been obliged to retreat behind the GHQ stop-line then there was only a slim chance that the IN Stations would have been able to make contact with the new HQ location. The problems of maintaining this system once on a war footing are obvious and it was not a system one might recommend in the planning stage if it was seriously envisaged that the SDB would operate for any significant period during enemy occupation. As David Lampe wrote in 1968: 'The Special Duties Organisation of Auxiliary Units was beyond doubt the part of the organisation that would have collapsed most quickly after the Germans got a foothold in

Britain, for underground broadcasting from fixed stations is untenable.'[68] The wireless network was, however, planned by Petherick on the basis that all they were expected to do was to report invasion traffic in the crucial first few days of any landings, as it was during this period that GHQ was most desperate to know the details of the enemy build-up in bridgehead areas. Thereafter, reconnaissance units from the GHQ Phantom Unit could be deployed to provide specialist military intelligence on the enemy. The fact that the TRDs needed regular replacement of the batteries and adjustment of their aerials did not, therefore, matter – their task should have been completed before this was needed.

Ironically, as the SDB became fully operational with their TRD sets in early 1941, both the improving military situation and the expanding panoply of intelligence sources made their anti-invasion contribution less essential. Britain would not be so blind upon invasion as it would have been during June–August 1940. Sources of advance intelligence improved steadily through 1940 and 1941, notably through the breaking of the German signal codes at Bletchley Park. After screening, such intelligence would then be quickly passed to army commands via the mobile Special Communications Units of SIS, their wireless vehicles discretely parked behind the command HQs. The Royal Navy and RAF also jointly established their chain of 'Home Defence Units' – a series of wireless stations on the east and south coasts monitoring German wireless traffic, managed by RAF Kingsdown and feeding their information direct to Fighter Command HQ and to the Royal Navy.[69] Actual landings were likely to have been reported first by the regular troops and Home Guard patrolling the beaches, or by the anti-invasion motor boats of the naval Auxiliary Patrols. Units of the GHQ Liaison Regiment (Phantom) were dispersed across the country with an efficient high-speed communication system (supplemented by pigeons!). Their highly-trained patrols were to criss-cross the front lines, sending up-to-date information on the progress of the enemy direct to GHQ by wireless. In January 1941 the Reconnaissance Corps was also founded from infantry brigade reconnaissance units and distributed within corps areas to probe enemy lines and provide tactical information to army HQs. By now the Scout Sections of the Auxiliary Units were also in a position to be able to communicate, by wireless, from behind enemy lines.

After the initial transfer of men and women from the HDS 'Special Duties' and a burst of direct recruiting in key areas during 1940, progress in expanding the SDB slowed down until a new War Establishment was presented on 4 April 1942 that would finally allow the SDB to expand again:

> C-in-C has decided that the organisation of the Wireless Installation for the Intelligence side of Auxiliary Units should be expanded to, inclusive, MONTROSE, and should also include SOUTH WALES and NORTH SOMERSET areas.[70]

This was the high point in the expansion of the SDB, but the correspondence demonstrates that the Auxiliary Units no longer had the free hand that they had enjoyed in the desperate days of 1940. Permission now had to be sought for every expansion and, cheap as it was to run in a national context, already some in the War Office were looking towards cuts in the organisation. The SDB now came under the same pressures to reduce the War Establishment as did the Operational Branch, as seen in the promotion of David Ingrams, a civilian OUT Station wireless operator who was promoted in late 1943 to become SDB Intelligence Officer in Devon. Ingrams had originally been commissioned into the Territorial Army Royal Artillery in 1925, but had then become a local farmer. ATS commander Beatrice Temple met him in late January 1944 and was not impressed, describing him as 'very ineffectual'.[71] Nonetheless, he moved as IO to Norfolk in spring 1944.

The final key link in the information chain was the speed at which IN Station operators could transmit their information to a higher command in GHQ Home Forces. During the initial phase of development when the IN Stations were based at static District HQs this was not a problem, but later in the war, Ward pointed out that the 'Met Huts' might be at a distance from the Area, Divisional or Corps HQ or the latter might move to a location where it was difficult to establish a station. Some operators have mentioned having a secure telephone line in the Zero Station – although they did not know to where this reported. The close-down report of 28 June 1944 does, however, say that there were no line connections.[72] Ken Ward confirmed that field telephones or, from 1943, the easily-detectable WS17 wireless sets, were used to communicate from the Met Huts to the army HQ, and even bicycles were sometimes used.[73] This was hardly a secret or secure solution.

The intelligence collected during any invasion would be collated by army intelligence officers (rather than the SDB Intelligence Officers) at one of the Army District HQs local to the IN station. Major Jones listed thirteen in June 1944 (see Fig. 14). At this point any responsibility for the information therefore passed out of the hands of the Auxiliary Units, and anything of other than local significance would be passed from District to Regional Command and thence to GHQ. It was to short-circuit such a laborious system, heavily dependent on telephone links, that the Phantom reconnaissance units were created to transmit information direct to GHQ. Equally, it will be shown that agents of SIS Section VII (see Chapter Eleven) could send information direct to their communications HQ at Whaddon, where it might be combined with any ULTRA traffic and then distributed back to army commands via the Special Communications Units (SCUs). One important exception to this procedure was in the collection of intelligence on internal security which, according to Major Forbes, was processed at Coleshill, and which it will be argued, completely bypassed the SDB wireless network. (see below, Chapter Ten, pp. 129–34).

The absence of control over the collected intelligence replicates the lack of control over the actions of the Operational Patrols once they had gone to ground. One internal consequence was that there was no mechanism within the Auxiliary Units HQ by which they could re-task the Operational Patrols from information transmitted by the SDB. Oxenden records that a few joint exercises were held between the two branches of the Auxiliary Units, but he then reports that the contacts seemed to lead nowhere and were allowed to die a natural death.[74] This lack of coherence is a pointer to the rushed nature of the formation of the organisation and also to the fact that the Auxiliary Units were not intended to be an independent intelligence agency rivalling that of SIS or Military Intelligence. Its duty in this respect was to collect, not analyse, intelligence. If the SDB had only served an anti-invasion role then its significance must be considered short-term and limited – but this was not the case, as will be seen in Chapter Ten.

Chapter Ten

Auxiliary Units (Special Duties Branch) 2: D-Day Planning and Internal Security

In recent days while our own invasion forces were massing, an additional heavy burden was placed on those of you responsible for the maintenance of good security, to ensure that the enemy was denied foreknowledge of our plans and preparations. The Security Reports regularly provided by Special Duties have proved of invaluable assistance to our security staffs.[1]

General H.E. Franklyn, 1944

The now classic vision of SDB IN Station operators retreating to buried Zero stations where they could continue to secretly pass on messages from the OUT Stations, was not completed until 1942 – when it was recognised that the risk of invasion had all but disappeared. The Zero station was more sophisticated than the Operational Bases, equipped with cooking and toilet facilities as well as bunks for sleeping. There was also a generator to provide lighting and ventilation and to charge the wireless batteries (as the sets were permanently switched on). Supplies were provided for up to twenty-one days' operation underground and a degree of comfort is suggested by the fact that the Harrietsham Zero Station in Kent was discovered when a passer-by saw an ATS operator emerge from the hatch to shake out a rug.[2]

Their introduction signalled what was perceived to be an increasing risk of airborne and commando raids that particularly threatened army HQs. The SDB also took on an expanding role in internal security and became part of the D-Day deception planning. Although the importance of the Operational Branch decreased during this period of the war, it can be argued that the role of the SDB became even more significant.

Anti-Raiding Role
The fear of 'spoiling' raids accelerated greatly in the year leading up to D-Day and had a considerable impact on the development of the SDB (as well as that of the Operational Branch, see above, Chapter Eight). The new Zero stations offered the possibility of a last-ditch means of reporting an enemy attack on a nearby HQ after normal lines of communication had been broken; from them, operators could also transmit information from OUT Stations to an Inner Network at rear HQs. A new sense of urgency regarding this threat is detected in

the Intelligence Officers' *Monthly Notes* for August 1943, which announced that IN Stations were to be manned 'by night, as well as by day, in all raid areas'. The anti-raiding role appears to have been focused on the IN and OUT Stations rather than the more coastal SUB-OUT stations; there is no mention of putting OUT Stations onto 24-hour watch, which would be necessary if they were to receive immediate notice of raids from the SUB-OUT stations.[3] This in turn suggests that the main concern was for airborne attacks on the inland army HQs to which the IN stations were attached, rather than general coastal raids.

The new anti-raiding role coincides with what was surely a related concern to increase the number of WS17 wireless sets (Plate 36) across the Auxiliary Units. Speed of communication across the organisation now outweighed any concern for wireless security as the WS17 sets were considered extremely 'noisy' and easy to detect. Operational IOs had originally requested the WS17 in May 1942 for their own use in providing a wireless link from their HQ unit to their Scout Sections and to army HQs. The SDB were informed in June 1942 that the WS17 had gone out of production: now they were searching for second-hand army surplus.[4] The SDB put in a request for 170 WS17 sets in 1943.

A further 100 [WS]17 sets have now been delivered to this HQ and will be installed in accordance with recommendations already made by IOs.

Fresh sites will NOT be submitted until after the completion of the current programme, which calls for some 170 of these sets.

IOs will be asked for recommendations for further sites at a later date, and consideration will then be given to their installation in areas which at present are without them.[5]

As the above quotation shows, the WS17 was clearly considered important in specific circumstances by the IOs of the SDB who pressed for their introduction, although precise details of their deployment are lacking. Ultimately, 200 sets were ordered for the SDB during 1943; more were requested but the total number actually supplied was still only 200 in June 1944.[6]

A number of temporary and 'Scheme' SDB wireless stations were created for use in battle exercises during 1943, but unfortunately there are no details of what the SDB were rehearsing for, although it is likely the exercises were part of anti-raid scenarios. The WS17 would also be ideal for such temporary use where security was not a significant issue. In one exercise at Wendover, Buckinghamshire, during September, the station was set up in a 3-ton truck and a tent.[7] By December 1943 the SDB also had two 15cwt trucks fitted with wireless to provide a mobile capability, but which would have been difficult to link to the TRD network.[8]

A more permanent use was reported by Ken Ward, who confirmed the WS17 sets were used to communicate between the new Zero Stations and District, Brigade or Corps HQs if the latter moved away from earlier locations where they had shared a site with the IN Stations.[9] This means that whatever the claims for wireless security from OUT to IN Stations using the TRD, the final crucial link to army intelligence might not be secure and the Zero Stations, although now hidden, might be extremely vulnerable to wireless detection. By contrast, Ward was adamant that the SUB-OUT stations did not have the WS17 sets. Admittedly, their introduction was after he left the Auxiliary Units (Signals), although he was still involved in TRD procurement.[10]

By June 1944, 40 per cent of the wireless sets used by the SDB were WS17, which suggests that the network as a whole was not looking for any unusual levels of wireless security, beyond that provided by the rarity of VHF frequencies. The operational priority from 1943 was in quickly passing on warnings of raids to the 24-hour-manned IN Stations and from them to the nearest army HQ.

It was also around this time, and probably for the same reason, that the IN Stations were finally brought into the BEETLE system to allow instructions to be forwarded even if enemy raids caused an interruption to normal communications (see above, Chapter Three). In September 1943, thirty Murphy B81 (Plate 34) and B93 battery-powered wireless sets, the standard army BEETLE receivers, were requisitioned by Auxiliary Units (Signals).[11]

D-Day Deception

Another role for the SDB connected with the preparations for D-Day was as part of the wireless deception planning. General ideas for what would be known as 'Operation Fortitude' were discussed as early as February 1943, the wireless aspect being raised by MI5 from at least June 1943. The main plan involved the invention of highly detailed radio traffic to be intercepted by German intelligence in order to convince the enemy that troops were massing for the forthcoming invasion in East Anglia and Scotland – intending to invade anywhere except the Normandy beaches.

One element of the plan was periodically to fill the airwaves with bursts of intense wireless traffic, followed by periods of total radio silence across the country. This occurred from autumn 1943, but especially from February 1944, and included all wireless units in Britain, including the SDB. Periods of wireless silence/activity could be a matter of hours or a number of days: as an example, there was to be wireless silence 27–30 May and 19–29 June and intense activity 18–19 and 23–26 May. This fits with the memory of Roy Russell, who has recorded that at the end of May 1944 the SDB received orders to broadcast dummy messages in code for twenty-four hours a day.[12]

The idea was that the Germans would not be able to use periods of high or low radio traffic to predict the oncoming storm of invasion. Auxiliary Units HQ was included as part of a general order to all regional commands.[13] They were also included in instructions for Exercise PRANK in March 1944. The deception planners may not have known nor cared whether the TRDs and the new issue of WS17 sets to SDB and Intelligence Officers could be picked up by German intelligence across the Channel or by reconnaissance aircraft, but they had to ensure that no wireless system was excluded from the operation. The only exception to the blanket instructions for radio silence were those crucial CROSSBOW signals units tracking the V1 rockets into London. As part of the operation, in some areas the Auxiliary Units (Signals) devised meaningless codes to transmit; in others, operators read out poetry or discussed knitting patterns as part of 'training exercises' without knowing the real reason behind the instructions – the Fortitude planners just wanted 'noise'. Roy Russell described how 'We made up hundreds of meaningless five-letter-coded group messages and transmitted them to our OUT stations for their "dummy traffic" responses; round the clock'.[14] The transmission of dummy messages was a gamble as the main element of Operation Fortitude was to provide the detailed construct of a fake army moving around the country; these messages had to be consistent as otherwise it would become clear they were part of a deception. Swamping the radio waves with gibberish messages would eventually be recognised as a deception device; identifying gibberish from genuine code would, however, tie up the efforts of the limited number of German wireless interceptors. As German intelligence were undoubtedly looking for some form of deception exercise, perhaps it was thought best to offer up the transmission of gibberish messages as a double bluff and thereby make the main Fortitude deception exercise even more believable.

Internal Security Role
The inherited HDS structure of agents and couriers, designed for a non-wireless system, was a complication in its invasion monitoring role for GHQ. The reporting process could be a ponderous affair with observers depositing messages in dead-letter drops, passed on by 'cut-outs' to OUT Stations, then transmitted to IN Stations and finally to an intelligence officer by telephone or bicycle. Of course, this was only tested in training exercises and never in anger. In reality, by the time that the information 'column of tanks seen heading east from xxxx' reached an intelligence officer and a response was initiated, the information was probably out of date. In practice, the SDB would have had to rely almost entirely on the wireless operators to collect and then transmit the intelligence as it is unlikely that the couriers would have sufficient freedom of movement to operate in the manner intended.[15]

With hindsight, the idea of teenage couriers such as Jill Monk (née Holman) in Aylsham, Norfolk, being able to collect intelligence on German troop movements and to pass on messages to the wireless station, whilst casually pony-trekking through the middle of the German invasion forces sounds a somewhat romantic and naïve notion: 'He [Captain Collings] thought a brat on a horse was unlikely to be suspected of anything. So I was to ride out and spot any choice targets, in terms of troops or supply dumps', but this was in 1942 when German invasion was becoming more unlikely.[16] Instead, Norfolk now faced the 'friendly invasion' of the US 8th Army Air Force! Jill's father, Dr Holman, was an OUT station operator in Aylsham and Intelligence Officer Collings had become a frequent visitor. One wonders if Jill (aged 16) was simply recruited in order to keep an overly-curious teenager occupied.

Why bother to keep this complicated structure? A body of discreet citizens who had demonstrated their commitment and had all signed the Official Secrets

Act might be useful in the future – and the agent/courier network cost virtually nothing to maintain. And there is another possibility. Historians have focussed on the details of the wireless network as the most tangible aspect of the SDB. Virtually all of the recorded reminiscences have been from the IN and OUT station wireless operators or members of the Auxiliary Units (Signals). These were but a small percentage of the total number of volunteers in the SDB. In all, there may have been as few as 250 civilian wireless operators, but 3,000 other agents or couriers. The evidence suggests there was a role that made better use of the observers and couriers and also kept the SDB Intelligence Officers in what might be considered more gainful employment beyond simply arranging the regular transmission of test messages and calling up the maintenance teams of the Auxiliary Units (Signals) when required – a role of which perhaps not even the wireless operators were aware. One surprising aspect of the SDB is that in some areas the operators are said to have been the 'key men' in charge of a network.[17] Were they being misled by their Intelligence Officers? They were the agents most at risk from detection and capture and it would have been sensible to isolate them. A more 'hidden' function for the rest of the cell may well be the context for the vague stories of agents spying on their neighbours and keeping an ear open for loose talk, and explains why Colonel Major was chosen as the replacement commanding officer when Gubbins left the Auxiliary Units for SOE in November 1940 (Plate 38).

Colonel Major may have been thinking of extending the short-term anti-invasion role of the SDB when he and Petherick began to reorganise it in late 1940. The Auxiliary Units had already had to fight off one attempt at disbandment in September and as the threat of invasion diminished over the winter, they needed to find a new purpose for the network of civilian agents and couriers. Colonel Major is often criticised for the changes he made to the Operational Patrols. He was a Whitehall staff officer from the Directorate of Military Intelligence (DMI) with no background in any form of irregular warfare. On the basis of the surviving evidence, his main focus was on developing the spy network of the SDB and his appointment may be seen as a sign that DMI were wanting to properly assume responsibility for the SDB from SIS and to better integrate it into their other intelligence systems. This concern to prevent the SDB from acting in isolation can be seen later in 1942 when Lord Glanusk sought to expand the SDB. He was told by Gregson-Ellis at the War Office to make sure that this fitted in with the overall intelligence-gathering strategy.[18] Although surviving sources have skewed the balance of Auxiliary Units history towards the Operational Patrols, with the decrease in the invasion threat the internal security role of the SDB can be seen as *the* critical element of the Auxiliary Units organisation. From the appointment of Colonel Major, the character of the Operational Patrols begins to drift; but whilst Oxenden suggests that Operational IOs began to avoid visiting army HQs from 1943 in order not to draw attention to their continued existence, he implies that the SDB IOs did not withdraw in this way, suggesting that they felt themselves to be in a stronger position.[19]

Military Intelligence had been given an enhanced status at the outbreak of the Second World War as a separate Directorate (DMI). There was rapid expansion thereafter, including in May 1940 the creation of a section shared with MI5 that was responsible for military and munitions security operations, and MI14 responsible for invasion intelligence and intelligence from 'special sources'. The creation of the Intelligence Corps on 19 July 1940, finally allowed military intelligence to move away from the previously *ad hoc* operational system within DMI. The relationship of the new Corps to the existing intelligence agencies, MI5 and SIS, caused confusion within the War Office at the time, and remains so in the new history of the Corps.[20] This was not least because both agencies used the cap badge of the Intelligence Corps, literally as a badge of convenience. Thus the DMI War Diary is inwardly focussed and states that MI6 was created at the start of the war out of an expansion of MI1(c) with Colonel Menzies appointed as commanding officer and only in charge of three officers. It does, however, cryptically acknowledge that 'MI6 have other personnel in their employ not charged against DMI establishment'.[21] Even within DMI the true nature of SIS (MI6) and its funding by the Foreign Office could not be openly acknowledged.

Over the summer of 1940, DMI had made repeated attempts to take over the running of Grand's Section D (including the HDS) but had been out-manoeuvred by Hugh Dalton in his creation of SOE. Although under the War Office and GHQ, the Auxiliary Units lay outside the remit of DMI and the SDB was therefore regarded as another anomaly, although the product of its intelligence-gathering would feed into the DMI through the army HQ Intelligence Officers. There were also links with the work of the Operational Patrols; their activities in testing the security of divisional HQs, airfields etc., have since been well reported. Sometimes they would even demonstrate their skills by exploding small charges in the garden of a general who may, or may not, have been amused. Less well-known is that the expanded Field Security Section (FSS) of the new Intelligence Corps also carried out similar undercover tests of security in vital points and military bases nationwide, including planting fake explosives. Another relevant duty of the FSS was to go undercover to quietly spy on off-duty troops in order to establish any 'loose talk' or deliberate espionage. It would therefore have been logical to try to coordinate these activities.

Given his background in DMI, Colonel Major may have seen the FSS as a point of reference in his plans to reorganise the SDB as a military intelligence network beyond that of a short-term anti-invasion coast-watching service, one which could supplement the covert intelligence-gathering of the FSS in the vulnerable coastal areas by using local civilian agents; SDB Intelligence Officers would act as liaison officers. It would also provide the military with an independent ability to gather intelligence on possible fifth columnists that MI5 was so reluctant to share with army commanders (see above, Chapter Seven, p. 83). There is only one official mention of such an internal security role, but this clearly emphasises its importance: in the Stand-Down letter from the C-in-C, Home Forces, General Franklyn, he chose to emphasise its security reports in what would otherwise have been a largely unknown function of SDB (see the quote at the opening of this chapter).[22]

Major Peter Forbes, the officer in charge of the SDB in 1944, has expanded on this duty. He wrote 'at the end of '43 the out-stations were given an important new role; that of reporting rumours circulating from East Anglia and all along the South Coast. The War Office wanted to know what was being picked up about concentrations for the D-Day invasion'. Interestingly, Forbes says the reports were collated by himself and then passed on to Colonel Douglas for onward transmission; this is the only mention of Auxiliary Units HQ having any co-ordination role in intelligence work. Forbes believed 'it was probably the most important SD work'.[23] The coastal distribution of SDB was as well-fitted to this task as it was for looking for possible enemy agents in 1940. From 1943 onwards it was able to cover the assembly and embarkation zones of the invasion army and identify any loose-tongued soldiers.

Such an internal security role partly explains the situation in Herefordshire and Worcestershire, where the existence of the SDB is confirmed by a surviving memo of 26 October 1943:

Major Johnson will cease to be an Operational IO but will continue as IO SD in Glamorgan. Additionally he will take over from Captain Bucknall the duties of IO SD Herefordshire and Worcestershire.

These changes-over will take effect as from midday on 12 November 1943.[24]

Nonetheless, no wireless network is shown as existing in these areas on the SDB network map of June 1944 (Plate 33), which is explained if the SDB did not rely entirely on the wireless network, and the courier/agent network fulfilled a quite distinct role on its own account. Dansey and Grand of SIS had established a principle of intelligence organisations, and even parts of organisations, working in isolation from each other in order to increase security. It appears that fellow SIS officer Maurice Petherick continued the tradition in the SDB. (Petherick left the SDB in March 1942 and was replaced by his second-in-command, Captain Charles E. Randell.)

In 1940 Worcestershire was at the heart of a highly important strategic area intended for the relocation of the Royal Family, government and War Office in the event of invasion. The shadow BBC transmission HQ was at Wood Norton, just outside Evesham, and from 1942 the Telecommunications Research Establishment (TRE) was based at Malvern. There is evidence for one SDB-type intelligence cell at Upton on Severn, based around a local coal merchant, with a series of dead-letter drops; a telephone hidden in the basement of a building at Severn Stoke was said to be linked to the county Auxiliary Units HQ at Wolverton Hall. As usual, veterans have only spoken about training to identify German uniforms and units. An anti-invasion reporting role along the Severn Valley would undoubtedly have been important. The location of the Auxiliary Units Operational Bases in Herefordshire and Worcestershire highlights a perceived threat to

Birmingham coming from the south and in 1941 SIS explained to their agents in the Midlands that there was a risk of invasion coming up the Bristol Channel, aiming to establish an HQ at Bridgnorth (see Chapter Eleven, p. 148). The Upton cell, however, also lay between the TRE base at Malvern and its secret research airfield at Defford, well placed to listen in to indiscreet conversations in local public houses. Senior Commander of the ATS within the Auxiliary Units, Beatrice Temple, visited Worcestershire a number of times with SDB operators but the accounts are inconclusive. John Todd is documented as being Intelligence Officer for the SDB in Worcestershire in 1940/1, succeeded by Captain Henry Bucknall (ex-Royal Artillery) and then Major K. Johnson; with such a specific internal security role and in an area identified by SIS as a high risk area for invasion, is it a coincidence that both Todd and Johnson are believed to have been officers of SIS? Was the intelligence operation here maintained as a joint SIS/ SDB enterprise?

No OUT or IN Station wireless operator has ever mentioned receiving such internal security messages, and they may never have been aware of what was clearly regarded by GHQ as a most important task. It seems possible that this task bypassed the wireless network, with the agents/couriers not just feeding information to the wireless operators, but instead acting as a distinct sub-branch of the SDB. Such a mechanism would enable the Intelligence Officers to pass on information using annotated photographs, as reported by Emma, an agent from Sussex, in a way impossible using wireless. Emma was recruited by an officer dressed as a private but wearing concealed badges of rank: 'My job was to try and get them to tell me things they shouldn't have'.[25] She worked from photos of the men supplied to her, presumably by the FSS (as being one organisation that could easily acquire photographs of troops); these were placed in a dead-letter drop with either a tick or a cross, and those men with a cross against their name were quickly moved away. Emma never knew the name of the organisation for which she worked, and although she used a dead-letter drop she never knew what happened to the message thereafter. There is no other information that might identify the organisation for which she worked, but that she was part of some form of joint SDB/FSS operation is at least a possibility.

Was this internal security role the most important, and certainly the most secret, part of the Auxiliary Units activities (as their CO Major Forbes believed)? Only a handful of SDB agents and couriers have ever told their story; most sadly passed away before it was felt acceptable to recount their experiences. Perhaps not surprisingly, the few veterans who have spoken about their service (mainly the wireless operators), have chosen to mention only being trained to pass on intelligence on German troop movements following an invasion. The idea of spying on one's neighbours, even acting as 'honey-traps', can appear very 'un-British' – especially if they still lived in the area. This was, however, just one part of the government's strategy to control all aspects of life in a total war.

By June 1944 the SDB had a formal War Establishment of just fourteen officers and sixteen other ranks, not much larger than the original, if notional, establishment of 1940. The Auxiliary Units (Signals) had sixty-eight officers and seventy-nine other ranks engaged on signals maintenance, watch-keeping at IN Stations and training, including fifty-seven officers and three other ranks from ATS engaged in watch-keeping at IN Stations and training, plus four Royal Engineer subalterns and thirteen drivers; twenty-one of the other ranks from the HQ establishment were carpenters and bricklayers engaged full-time on maintaining hides. This small establishment supported an unpaid civilian network of 3,250 agents, couriers and wireless operators. We may never know the full extent of the work of the SDB, whose task it was to watch, listen and report during an invasion and also to protect the security of Allied forces.

Chapter Eleven

SIS Resistance Organisation: Section VII (1940–43)

The last thing these English know is how to practice fair play. They're very bad at accepting their defeats.[1]

Adolph Hitler, 9 February 1942

In the summer of 1940 the XII Corps Observation Unit and Auxiliary Units were created to fight a military guerrilla war during any invasion and the idea of arming civilians had seemingly been abandoned along with the SIS Home Defence Scheme (HDS). A contingency plan if Britain was partially, or fully, occupied by the enemy still, however, existed in the depths of SIS. This was the most secret and elusive of Britain's plans for resistance, known as 'Section VII' or 'DB's organisation', and probably incorporating the shadowy sabotage wing known as 'X Branch'.

If the invasion had occurred during the summer of 1940 and the GHQ defence plan had failed then it can be assumed that most of the Home Guard in the combat areas would have been destroyed in the first days of invasion. Their orders were to stand and fight to the last round and man, and they had already been declared *francs-tireurs* or, in modern parlance, terrorists, by Hitler, meaning they were unlikely to be taken as prisoners of war. The hidden Auxiliary Units would have continued to disrupt the enemy supply lines for a few days more. On the intelligence-gathering side, the Section D Home Defence Scheme (HDS) had only a rudimentary system of intelligence-gathering and even in 1941 the reborn Special Duties Branch (SDB) would have been rendered impotent once the area army command had been obliged to retreat or its surface IN Stations ('met huts') had been destroyed by bombing. Some elements of the HDS sabotage teams and *ad hoc* groups of Home Guard guerrillas could possibly have continued to provide an increasingly futile resistance to delay surrender, but such efforts would have had little coordination or strategic direction.

If defeated militarily, someone in authority would have been obliged to negotiate a formal surrender. This would have included all army formations, including the Auxiliary Units as part of the Home Guard. Lord Ismay pointed out in his autobiography the distinction in service tradition between a naval commander who was expected to go down with his ship and an army commander whose final duty was to avoid fruitless sacrifice of his men by capitulation.[2] It may be presumed that the Royal Family had been spirited out of the country to avoid them becoming a figurehead, and that Churchill had gone down fighting. Would a surviving member of the Cabinet step up to negotiate surrender terms on the grounds of preventing loss of life? Lord Halifax and David Lloyd George were known to favour a negotiated settlement. Sir Alexander Cadogan, Permanent Under-Secretary at the Foreign Office, had voiced his suspicions about Sir Samuel Hoare (cabinet minister under Chamberlain), but Churchill sent Hoare out of the country to become Ambassador in Spain. Cadogan wrote in his diary: 'He'll be the Quisling of England when Germany conquers us and I'm dead.'[3] Nonetheless, there was no obvious Quisling on the Nazi 'White List' and even the leader of the British Union of Fascists (BUF), Oswald Mosely, was adamant that he would have fought against any invader. If no quisling government emerged that could command some degree of support, the Nazis may have been obliged to install a military government and rule the country directly.

The Nazis may have been considering the possibility of occupied and unoccupied zones in the UK, similar to what was agreed in France, at least as a temporary measure, which would have the advantages of limiting the resources required to occupy the whole country and therefore allowing attention to return more quickly to Hitler's primary long-term objective of destroying the Soviet Union.[4] Thus the initial invasion plan of Operation Sealion looked no further than the campaign in southern England, hoping that this would be enough to ensure British surrender. The occupation of the British Isles would, however, not necessarily mark the end of British resistance. The empire was still intact and there were plans to establish a government in exile in Canada or the West Indies, supported by a Free Royal Navy. The hope was that if the struggle could be continued in some form, then either the Nazi state would implode from internal dissent, or the USA would eventually be drawn into a war against Nazi Germany and Britain could be liberated. An internal intelligence network capable of communication with a government in exile and able to sow the seeds of a future armed revolt was a necessary element in such long-term planning. This 'unthinkable' possibility was the context for the establishment of a last-ditch, and ultra-secret, resistance organisation created in the deepest recesses of SIS and born out of the traditional structures of SIS rather than from Section D.

Section VII

By August 1940, the concept of a civilian resistance organisation and the direct participation of SIS in the country's anti-invasion plans appeared to have been completely abandoned in favour of a more short-term military option controlled by GHQ. Lawrence Grand, the *bête noir* of both the Chiefs of Staff Committee and SIS, had been neutralised and, with a sigh of relief from all concerned, was banished to India. But did some people still whisper, out of earshot of GHQ, that there still might be a need for a resistance organisation that could operate in occupied territory? And was that organisation already in existence? SIS did indeed have another weapon hidden deep in the shadows. Even after occupation its mysterious Section VII would be able to communicate with unoccupied areas of the country and, albeit with some difficulty, to bases abroad. It would therefore be able to pass on intelligence to a government in exile and coordinate acts of strategic sabotage and disruption, until the time was ripe for outright revolt.

The traditional role of SIS had always been that of quiet intelligence-gathering rather than organising sabotage and as a consequence the noisy Section D was mistrusted as much within SIS as beyond its secretive walls. It should be no surprise, therefore, that early in 1940 a forward-thinking HQ of SIS had already begun to consider this intelligence-gathering role in relation to any invasion of Britain and under more restrained hands than the impetuous Grand was likely to manage. The evidence for the initial establishment of what was known by MI5 as 'DB's organisation' and which was identified in the official history of SIS as Section VII was mentioned by Jeffery in only a single paragraph (and he was unable to cite the source).[5] Section VII is normally associated with SIS finance and accounting, but its wartime operations have long been considered as a mystery by historians, described as a 'persistent puzzle' and vaguely responsible for 'economic intelligence'.[6] Jeffery identified the Section VII network as being initially organised by a high-level triumvirate consisting of Valentine Vivian (head of Section V, Counter-Espionage), Richard Gambier-Parry (head of Section VIII, Communications) and David Boyle (head of Section N, interception of diplomatic mail and the personal assistant to CSS). This has remained the most secret (and therefore almost by definition the most successful) of the plans for a resistance organisation. It was so secret that contemporaries avoided referring to it by name, if indeed it was ever given a formal name. Certainly the one surviving wireless operator who has recounted his story (Peter Attwater in Derbyshire) was never told for whom he was working.

Vivian was particularly well-qualified to help establish the new intelligence network in Britain. In the late 1920s, he had been responsible for overseeing the SIS agent network of 'Casuals' in Britain (see above, Chapter 2). In August 1932 he founded an SIS spy network in Eire; he had instructions to report only to the Chief of the Secret Service (then Admiral Sinclair) and not to mention the matter to anyone else inside or outside SIS, unless they were directly involved.[7] As with the later Section VII organisation, most documents connected with the Irish intelligence operation were destroyed; the scale of the Irish network would have remained even more shrouded in mystery had it not been penetrated by Eire Intelligence, some of whose reports survive. Initially the work consisted of collecting information on public opinion in Ireland using a loose network of sympathetic local contacts. On 27 November 1939, however, there was a meeting to discuss a proposal by the Director of Naval Intelligence (DNI) that SIS should expand their operation in Eire by establishing a clandestine coast-watching service. Neither SIS nor MI5 were happy with the proposal – not least because it might interfere with their existing good relations with the Irish Intelligence Service (G-2), with whom they had formally cooperated since the Anglo-Irish Agreement of 1938. Vivian expressed concern that the new plan would require wireless communications and over 1,000 agents, with great risks of being detected in a not entirely sympathetic environment. Clandestine radio networks were still at an early stage; the technology was primitive and many agents were deeply suspicious of wireless, fearing that it limited mobility and made them more vulnerable to capture. Despite the enthusiasm of the DNI, the Royal Navy were unable to guarantee the provision of a fast naval response should any German ship or submarine be spotted, and without this, the effort would have been pointless.

A compromise was reached to the effect that Vivian would 'extend his existing organisation in a very small way'.[8] In December 1939 he established three or four 'head agents' who then built up a loose network of agents strung out along the Irish coast.[9] They reported to the staff of Captain Charles Collinson in Dublin, who used the traditional, if unenterprising, cover of the passport control officer. A hidden wireless set was also installed in the house of the Air Attaché in Dublin and operated by SIS. The brief of the agents was expanded from watching for signs of German naval activity along the coast to monitoring anyone thought to be acting against the British war effort. Here were the twin functions of spying on direct enemy activity and spying on local populations that were to be at the core of the SIS-inspired SDB (see Chapter Ten). By November 1941, SIS had agents in every county of the Republic and had infiltrated the police service and government. Some wireless sets were eventually provided: in late 1940, G-2 (who had, as Vivian had feared, extensively penetrated the organisation) was reported to have been passed one of the British wireless sets by an informant within the coast watchers, which added nicely to their existing collection of German wireless sets.[10] In this friendliest of relationships between spies and counter-spies, SIS then began supplying wireless sets to the official Eire Coast-watching Service. With such experience behind him, Vivian was an obvious choice to become one of the initial triumvirate that created the pilot mobilisation of the Section VII resistance network in England.[11]

Richard Gambier-Parry, formerly of Philco, was recruited to SIS in 1938 (at the same time as Lawrence Grand) to develop their wireless communications system and to oversee the innovative idea of clandestine wireless. He was the mastermind of SIS communications strategy during the Second World War and was involved in what was probably the most extreme plan ever conceived for a 'stay-behind' unit. In 1941 he was wireless consultant for an extraordinary plan devised by Naval Intelligence on Gibraltar. The idea of Operation Tracer was, as the island was being over-run by the enemy, to seal a team inside an observation post hidden deep within 'The Rock', and for them to continue broadcasting information on enemy shipping movements back to the Admiralty in London. The men expected to be sealed in for about a year, although plans had been made for a stay as long as seven years. The plan for the hide even included an area of loose soil where bodies could be interred after embalming by the team doctor. The wireless equipment used the standard SIS combination of Mk III transmitter and an HRO receiver. Trials began in January 1942, during which the wireless communications remained undetected by the Radio Security Service. By August the Operation Tracer team was in position and plans were being drawn up to extend the scheme to Malta and elsewhere, but the plan was cancelled in the following year.[12]

David Boyle (Plate 16) was a lifelong intelligence agent, implicated in kidnapping, operations against the IRA with the notorious Auxiliary Division and trusted with the last-minute attempt to contact sympathetic German generals. He had demonstrated both ruthlessness and an ability for delicate missions, together with an unshakeable regard for secrecy. He was now the personal assistant to the CSS and therefore provided a direct conduit to the highest authority in SIS. In early 1941 he was the man chosen to act as minder and guide to William J. Donovan (the future head of OSS), who had been sent by Roosevelt as an unofficial emissary to gauge the determination of Britain to resist invasion. If Gambier-Parry was the wireless expert and Vivian brought his expertise in creating agent networks, then Boyle was probably the hard-bitten manager of the agents.

Exactly when Vivian, Gambier-Parry and Boyle began to establish their ultra-secret wireless network in the UK is unclear. Many details of Section VII have had to be reconstructed from fragments of evidence and calculated guesswork, and it is hoped that these can be either confirmed or disproved if further documentation is ever released to the public domain. The account of the establishment of a cell at the Star Brewery, Eastbourne, Sussex, put the date of its formation as March 1940. The cell was based around a number of senior brewery staff who made weekly transmissions from a wireless transceiver, contained within a 'briefcase' and hidden in a secret compartment at the top of the brewery water tower (Plate 39).[13] In their initial phase of operation they were equipped for sabotage operations as well as intelligence-gathering, but were later confined to intelligence work. Nonetheless, the cell was not included in the 1944 map of the SDB network.[14] There is certainly a logic in suggesting that Vivian began to consider a British coast-watching service immediately after expanding his network in Eire during that February. There is also a tantalising reference in Guy Liddell's diary to a security leak, involving, on 8 March, the discovery of a Foreign Office code book labelled Plan Y. Was this connected? If so, then there was also a wireless station in Berkshire at this time.

> A Mr BURGOYNE, when visiting the Manor Club, Bracknell, Berks, saw an F.O. cypher and de-cypher book on a shelf under the bar. It had a message on the fly-sheet 'open on receipt of Y plan' and contained a loose sheet of F.O. paper showing issue of cypher 147 on 19.3.39. The book is now in the possession of the manager.[15]

In late May/early June, an intelligence cell was formed in Matlock, Derbyshire, which was, in 1941, in contact with other cells formed in Manchester, Nottingham and Birmingham. Together with the other wireless stations identified by Jeffery as part of a trial in Norfolk, Suffolk, Sussex, Somerset, Cornwall and Devon, it indicates that the organisation operated nationally and on a different basis to the coastal SDB. The only date given by Jeffery is that the Plan 333 trial of the network occurred sometime in, or before, July 1940. The network was then extended to twenty-eight 'head agents' equipped with wireless sets. Recruitment of 'stay-behind' agents was restricted to 'people who, by nature of their occupation, could remain in enemy-controlled territory and continue their normal occupations without arousing undue suspicion' and included 'doctors, dentists, chemists, and small shopkeepers'. Such people would have a reasonable excuse to 'either to move around in the course of their professional duties or to receive many visits from other people'.[16] Another advantage of using such volunteers was that, in the main, they were likely to be middle-aged and not liable for call-up, which would have put the network at risk. Teenage recruit Peter Attwater in Matlock was advised by his controller to go into hiding if invasion occurred, to avoid him being commandeered by the British army. Older recruits were also less likely to be deported to Germany by the Nazis – a very real risk for anyone of military age. Grand and Bearsted would attempt to recruit similar people for the HDS, which has added to the confusion as to the relationship between the two organisations.

Lawrence Grand makes no mention of this network, possibly because he could not claim any credit for it, but also because it was wrapped in the tightest secrecy at SIS HQ. With Claude Dansey seething at what he perceived to be Grand's incompetence, this ultra-secret intelligence network, created at the highest levels of SIS, bears all the hallmarks of Dansey, the master spy, although his name is never mentioned in connection with the operation. The trial (Plan 333) of the Section VII network is said to have worked with 'mobile signal units', almost certainly a reference to the newly-created Special Communications Units (SCUs) of SIS. During the campaign in France, SIS had deployed two mobile wireless units to transmit ULTRA intelligence received from Bletchley Park and other intelligence from secret agents to the BEF HQ via their main communications centre at Whaddon. After Dunkirk, Gambier-Parry planned to deploy similar mobile wireless units across military commands in Britain. The organisation consisted of two highly compartmentalised elements: a Special Communications Unit (SCU) would handle the wireless traffic and deliver it to the adjacent Special Liaison Unit (SLU), where the message would be decoded and passed by the CO of the unit to a designated intelligence officer in the military command. The SCU/SLU would have minimal contact with the neighbouring army organisation. The operation was initially on a small scale, with mobile units ready to deploy from Whaddon and from St James's Park in London (conveniently adjacent to the HQ of the Phantom regiment). The SCUs/SLUs were formally created on 5 June 1940 and expanded rapidly thereafter with a growing fleet of Packard saloon cars fitted with wireless, wireless trucks and even a bus (Plate 41). They were then based at each regional army command, the Admiralty, Fighter Command and in St James's Park and subsequently deployed across all theatres of operation abroad. Each SCU used the standard SIS Mk III transmitter/HRO receiver combination, with a Mk V or later the Mk VII (Paraset) suitcase set as back-up (Plate 37).[17] They also had cypher machines, a mobile telephone exchange and a number of regular army No. 19 and No. 24 wireless sets. Eventually each SCU/SLU developed into a substantial self-contained unit of up to thirty-five men, with the wireless trucks protected by a fleet of jeeps armed with 20mm cannon and twin Vickers K machine guns.[18]

Although their core role was in transmitting the most secret intelligence, the basic ability of the SCUs to provide mobile nationwide communications that would not be subject to enemy interruption of telephone lines had begun to attract other interest. The Chiefs of Staff Committee had already raised, on 27 May, the need to have an emergency communications system in case an enemy invasion disrupted the telephone system. The SCUs would provide a ready-made answer but SIS were not about to relinquish control to the army. In discussions of 31 May 1940 between Stewart Menzies (Chief of SIS) and Anthony Eden (Minister for War), refereed by Lord Hankey, the latter asked Eden to emphasise to the War Office that the SIS system was 'apparatus of a very special character' using specialist personnel and 'specialist material' (i.e. ULTRA). In other words, the message to the army was 'hands off'! However, in order to encourage cooperation from the protective SIS, Hankey told Menzies that the payback would be that Gambier-Parry 'will be able to get what he wants' and that he would be given as free a hand as possible in the organisation.[19] To avoid any dispute over the matter, Eden and Hankey agreed that there was no need to refer the raising of the SCUs to the Chiefs of Staff Committee; no doubt only increasing the paranoia of the chiefs of staff towards the ambitions of SIS (in 1941 the Director of Signals at the War Office, Major General Rawson, was to describe the SCUs as the 'private army' of SIS).[20]

Gambier-Parry took full advantage of this agreement and the formal establishment of the SCU/SLU which followed on 5 June led to an immediate increase in resources and a formal allocation of frequencies to the organisation.[21] Gambier-Parry realised that the SCUs also offered an efficient means of receiving and disseminating the intelligence from the Section VII network; together they provided an integrated, and flexible, mechanism for the transmission of battlefield intelligence that the SDB was never able to achieve. A Section VII agent could transmit directly to the SIS communications centre at Whaddon, which would filter the information to hide its source (as with ULTRA) and send it on directly to Regional Command via an SCU. The SDB had a more laborious system of agents, couriers, OUT Station, and IN Station before the intelligence was finally passed to an Intelligence Officer at an area command.

If the Auxiliary Units SDB was not as efficient an intelligence-gathering body as the Section VII/SCU combination, in the machiavellian world of Boyle and Dansey's SIS, the existence of a body such as the SDB, which was likely to be quickly discovered by German intelligence upon invasion, would conveniently divert attention from a more covert resistance organisation, deeply buried by SIS. A precedent for such a coldly calculating strategy was the creation of Dansey's Z Organisation in Europe in anticipation that the traditional network of agents posing as 'passport control officers' was likely to be quickly broken. The 'public' summary dismissal of Lawrence Grand – the figurehead of the HDS and a name already known to German Intelligence – also helped in this process by implying that SIS had ceased any responsibility for a secret intelligence network within Britain.

Having been attacked in the late 1920s to the early 1930s for establishing a spy network in Britain outside its official charter and with antagonism from the War Office as a result of Lawrence Grand's HDS, SIS felt it wise to create a secret mechanism that would give Section VII a more official status, clearly distinct from the HDS. The answer came with a form of understanding with MI5 that provided a new legal basis for SIS operations within the UK. SIS already had an urgent need to 'legitimise' the work of recruiting agents to work abroad through its trawling of incoming refugees at reception centres, and this was extended to include the work of Section VII.[22] The negotiations were undertaken by Valentine Vivian, whose Section V had the prime responsibility for liaising with MI5. On 2 July – the very day that the War Office circulated the War Establishment of the Auxiliary Units – he wrote to Guy Liddell, the head of Section B of MI5, to explain his objectives, including (original lettering retained):

(d) Provision for the collection of military information in areas in this country, or Ireland, which may be occupied by the enemy;
(e) The provision of internal communications to be placed at the disposal of the military and other authorities in the event of invasion of this country and the breakdown of regular communications;
(f) The recruitment of agents for certain special activities (of which you are aware), both in this country and abroad;

The methodology for achieving such objectives was to be:

(e) The employment of British subjects of some standing (their identity will, of course, be known to your Regional Officers) as 'agents places' in areas in this country likely to be invaded by the enemy;
(f) The establishment of concealed wireless stations in various parts of the country;
(g) The recruitment and placing of agents for the special tasks of which you are aware.[23]

The provision of 'internal communications' in the above brief was probably a notional responsibility as it hardly fits with the functions of a secret agent network. It might, however, have been thought politic to at least theoretically include a function for which the army was desperate and had already agreed to give Gambier-Parry a free hand in organising, at a time when SIS were officially supposed to be handing over their interests in the UK to the Auxiliary Units. Vivian therefore borrowed the phraseology used by Hankey in regard to the emergency communications capability of the SCUs in order to help provide legitimacy for Section VII. The link to the SCUs was, however, real enough as Plan 333 demonstrated, with the SCUs providing the mechanism by which the Section VII intelligence would be distributed to the military commands. In August 1940 the SCUs held an exercise with the army which successfully demonstrated their ability to continue to deliver intelligence even if the Regional Commands were obliged to relocate frequently. It seems likely that this would also have been used to test Section VII again, although there is no documentary evidence for this. This was a flexibility that was far beyond the capabilities of the SDB.

The proposal to formally recognise the agent network was discussed on 18 July 1940 when Vivian met with his counterpart in MI5, Guy Liddell, and the Director of MI5, Jasper Harker: 'They [SIS] are also engaged in operations here in the event of a German landing'.[24] Coming as it did *after* SIS had officially transferred responsibility for a secret 'stay-behind' organisation to the War Office Auxiliary Units, this briefest series of references indicates the point at which MI5 and MI6 discussed the continuation of Section VII as a long-term intelligence/resistance organisation outside War Office control. The next day, on 19 July, Lord Swinton as head of the Home Defence (Security) Executive and now ministerial head of MI5, was given 'operational control' of the SIS with respect to its activities in Britain and Eire.[25]

The discussions were formalised on 1 August 1940 under the cover of improving relations between the counter-espionage functions of SIS and Section B of MI5. A new liaison section was created, to be known as B.26, and based within MI5, which would 'interlock the functions of MI5 and MI6'.[26] SIS did not officially exist and so, if necessary, a limited number of named SIS officers involved in B.26 were now able to identify themselves to the authorities as being from MI5, including the ability to 'arm ourselves with your permission with your office stationery'. This device was purely for the benefit of SIS and as a consequence there is no further mention of the arrangement in the Guy Liddell diaries, even though he was overall head of Section B, or in the official history of MI5.[27] For their part, SIS were determined to keep their operations totally secret.

On 28 April 1941 Felix Cowgill, Vivian's former deputy and now his successor as head of Section V, told Comyns Carr of MI5 that ' I do not think it necessary under present circumstances to place on record in your section or in any other MI5 section a list of agents whom we [SIS] are employing in this country. The keeping of such records is always a danger even though the most stringent rules are made for their safe custody'.[28] The contrast with what we now know as the practice of publishing the names of the members of Operational Patrols of the Auxiliary Units on Home Guard notice boards (see below, Chapter Twelve) is obvious. Cowgill had specific responsibilities under the August agreement for liaising with MI5 over the SIS 'special agents' in the UK, but was notoriously reluctant to share any information with MI5. Despite his cultivation of a cosy atmosphere within his Section, this secretive attitude over the scope of B.26 may well have extended to colleagues within SIS. Kim Philby often acted as a more amenable link between Cowgill and MI5, but he has made no mention of any knowledge of the British spy network. Is this a measure of Cowgill's recognition of the sensitivity of the network? Did Philby know of it but think it was of no interest in his story of dealings with his Soviet spy masters? Or did he worry that any suggestion that he might have passed on secrets of a homeland intelligence organisation might have been one step too far in a tale of betrayal? One pertinent feature of the agreement allowed SIS coordinating officers from B.26 to deal directly with Chief Constables over any problems with their local agents, and it is no coincidence that the identity passes for the SDB agents were signed by the local Chief Constable to avoid them being arrested as spies.

Section B.26 was the liaison body for UK operations rather than being the actual organising body for agents, which provided an important added level of security. The actual organisation of Section VII lay within the deepest shadows of SIS and may never have been given a formal name. If referred to at all, it was simply known as 'DB's organisation'. Thus, on 10 October Liddell wrote to Vivian confirming that he had arranged introductions to MI5 Regional Officers 'for DB and various members of his organisation'. This was done and Liddell recorded that DB's organisation 'is now I gather a going concern'.[29] DB is identified elsewhere in Guy Liddell's diary as being David Boyle, the former member of the triumvirate who supervised the pilot mobilisation of Section VII, and a man implicated in the purging of Lawrence Grand in September. This is the confirmation that David Boyle, operating at the highest level of SIS, was now given the task of running a small network of UK agents for the rest of the war.[30]

By a quirk of document survival, it is possible to suggest that Section VII amounted to around 200 members during the war. As a deep-cover organisation it was preferable to formally recruit only an essential core of sleeper agents until a wider establishment was needed after any occupation, but it may be presumed that other potential recruits had already been identified for this eventuality by the Head Agents. After the war one of the reasons given for the refusal to award the Defence Medal to members of SDB (here described as the Special Duties Organisation) was that:

> It is said that there was a Secret Service organisation in the United Kingdom of about 200 civilian members. They were to go to ground in case of invasion. It is not proposed to claim that these should be eligible for the Defence Medal. They seem to fall into much the same category as the Special Duties Organisation.[31]

The qualifying period for issue of the Defence Medal in the UK was just under three years, therefore, for the secret SIS organisation to be even mentioned in connection with this award suggests that their mobilisation was at least for that length of time and it could not have referred to the more temporary HDS absorbed by the Auxiliary Units. Details of the activities of Section VII remain sparse, although in general terms the report of the Honours Committee suggests it was broadly similar to that of the Auxiliary Units Special Duties Branch, but organised for a longer-term operation after invasion.

The Matlock Cell

The type of wireless used by the early Section VII can only be guessed at, but former SCU member Geoffrey Pidgeon identified Whaddon as 'providing the early wireless sets for the "Hidden Army" of trained wireless operators to be left behind in the event of the Germans invading and occupying the British Isles'.[32] The trial exercise, Plan 333, worked with a number of mobile signals units (SCUs) to produce 'good signalling and deciphered 76% messages'.[33] The set needed to use a morse system, more technically demanding than that of the SDB, that could reach unoccupied territory in the UK or, if necessary, neutral countries in Europe for passage to a government-in-exile in Canada. The level of training required to operate the morse set is an indicator that the network, small and specialised, was fundamentally different to that of the more widespread SDB. Peter Attwater's description of the first set at Matlock is that it was portable, used morse, and looked as though it was built by a radio ham. This would fit the 1939 Mk II with its exposed components; both this and the 1940 Mk III (which Peter did not use at Matlock) were based upon a traditional amateur 6V6 crystal circuit with a 6L6 Doubler circuit and an 807 amplifier output.[34] The undated description from Eastbourne is for a wireless that would fit into a 'briefcase'; the comparatively lightweight Mk VII Paraset, introduced in 1941 and a mainstay of both SIS and SOE, would fit into an attaché case or small suitcase (Plate 37). The Paraset had a normal range of around 500 miles, but considerably longer in the right atmospheric conditions; transmissions might be received by wireless receivers hidden in neutral ships (a common method), submarines or via stations in neutral countries. The Matlock station later used a standard No. 22 set, which had a range of only 35–50 miles using Morse code, so needing a local control centre, and may reflect a change in organisational structure or purpose.

The most detailed account of a Section VII agent comes from Peter Attwater, who operated with the Matlock wireless station between 1940 and 1943.[35] In late May/June 1940, aged just 14 years, he was recruited by a local journalist, Frank Ford, who was also an ARP organiser and knew the teenager from his work as an ARP Messenger as being someone with a good memory and artistic skills. It is not known when Ford himself had been recruited and therefore the date of the earliest SIS operations in Matlock. Peter was also an Air Cadet and so had some basic military understanding, including weapons handling. He was then introduced to his training officer, Captain William Lawrence, who wore the badge of the Royal Warwickshire Regiment but who had been commissioned into the Royal Artillery after long service as a senior NCO. Lawrence was attached to a mysterious military intelligence establishment at Matlock Hydro with the seemingly-innocuous role of billeting officer and quartermaster. This base predated the establishment there of the Intelligence Corps School in January 1941. Lawrence became the Adjutant and Quartermaster of the new School, but only formally transferred to the Intelligence Corps in April 1941. As a reliable ex-NCO with long experience in training and administration, it seems likely that Lawrence had been seconded to SIS to help manage the network, using his work at Matlock Hydro as a cover. In particular, his official role as billeting officer provided an excuse to regularly visit civilian homes in the area and provided cover for his intelligence activities.

Attwater was introduced to two female recruits to the cell, and signed the Official Secrets Act; all of them were warned to avoid having their photographs taken, and they were given code names (which bears a similarity to the system known to have been used in another clandestine operation in Birmingham). This meeting was recorded by an unknown second lieutenant who had just returned from Dunkirk, suggesting a date in early June. The cell operated what was called a 'Zero Station' (pre-dating the use of the term by the SDB but indicating their joint heritage) hidden at the rear of a tailor's shop on Smedley Street. This was only about a hundred yards from the Military Intelligence School at the Hydro, but Peter's resistance cell was warned that if the army had to evacuate the town this would be blown up, along with any other large building that might be useful to the enemy. They would then be on their own apart from the disembodied Morse code messages from 'Control'. The wireless was hidden in an alcove behind racks of uniforms; a revolver and grenade, with its pin stapled to the table so that it could be quickly withdrawn with one hand, was always kept beside the set. An adjacent window provided an emergency exit for operator and wireless, but the grenade might slow down pursuers or, if necessary, destroy the set. The SIS transceiver was later replaced by a standard army No. 22 set, first introduced to service in 1942; it was a low-powered, short-range, portable set with a range of 35–50 miles, which suggests that by then the wireless station was acting in similar fashion to an SDB OUT Station, reporting to an unknown control station. All the Matlock operators ever heard from this was the brief response to their test messages: 'Received, Control Out'. Initially a courier, Peter eventually became a wireless operator, sending out test messages in code nightly at 10.00pm. Each message had to include a 'safety' word and Peter remembers that one of these was 'duck'. As an additional security measure, frequencies were changed daily between odd and even frequencies.

'Lilian' and 'Agnes' (actually Miss Swann and Mrs Keyes) were the first to become wireless operators, under the 'keeper', shop-owner Joe Topliss (code name 'Harry'). Peter, code name 'Jim', was originally trained as a courier and observer, learning how to travel silently at night and to accurately identify enemy weaponry. His nocturnal activities were carried out under cover of his ARP Messenger duties, so his parents were never aware of his real responsibilities; he had to familiarise himself with the layout of the town, and be able to move through people's back gardens whilst knowing where any crunchy gravel paths or noisy dogs might be. He had to make plans on where to cross the River Derwent, including shuffling silently across a water pipe. One specific task was to identify abandoned stables where any fugitives after occupation could be hidden and passed along an escape route. On occasion he was given test exercises, although it seems possible that some were more real than Peter was led to believe at the time, including practising the accurate estimate of the numbers of people attending meetings and events. They included keeping a watch on a local pacifist meeting – exactly the sort of assistance that MI5 might have been looking for in agreeing to the formation of the B.26 liaison section with SIS. Peter visited Captain Lawrence's offices at the Hydro where he had to familiarise himself with lifesize prints of German armoured vehicles in order to be able to accurately identify them; the Winter Gardens (part of the Hydro) also had a large collection of German uniforms and equipment, including dummies of German paratroopers hanging from the ceiling.

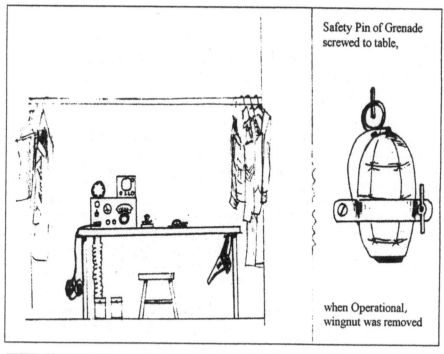

Safety Pin of Grenade
screwed to table,

when Operational,
wingnut was removed

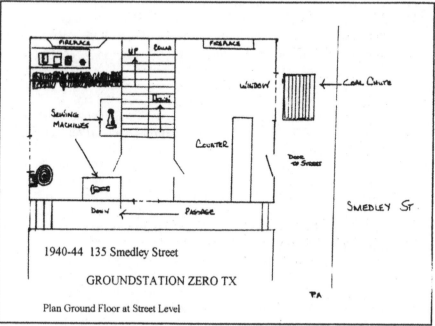

1940-44 135 Smedley Street

GROUNDSTATION ZERO TX

Plan Ground Floor at Street Level

Figure 19. Sketch of the 1943 Section VII, SIS secret wireless station at 135 Smedley Street, Matlock. Wireless set located behind rear fireplace. (Peter Attwater)

Some of Peter's training was carried out at the intelligence school at Matlock by uniformed men other than Lawrence who may, or may not, have been serving with the Intelligence Corps. They explained that they were acting under orders from the 'men in suits', a typical way of referring to SIS. Peter knew the other two wireless operators and his instructor, but no others in the network. Then, in early 1941 and still a courier, Peter went to a meeting in Birmingham attended by six other young men who came from Birmingham, Manchester and Nottingham and who would become his contacts after invasion; each was given a code to establish their identity. The meeting was managed by a huge, imposing man who, like Lawrence, seems suspiciously like an ex-NCO type; Peter described him as a strict disciplinarian and 'the most frightening man I have ever seen'. Peter was convinced, however, that the smartly-dressed civilian instructors at this meeting were those 'men in suits' from SIS, and the training included the issue of their safety phrases to prove their identity if they ever had to meet in the future. On meeting, they were to follow the traditional British habit of discussing the weather: each of the seven men had a key word they would use, which together spelt out the word BRITISH, thus **B**lizzard, **R**ain, **I**ce, **T**hunder, (more) **I**ce, **S**now, **H**ail; Peter was to introduce himself by working the words 'more ice' into conversation. The couriers were warned that the pattern of invasion might be one of initial landings on the south-east coast, but to expect a second wave with invasion coming up the Bristol Channel and the Germans establishing a general headquarters at Bridgnorth, Shropshire, before striking deeper into the Midlands, and it was clear that this scenario would then bring the Midlands spy network into the front line. Despite his huge responsibilities, Peter does not remember feeling worried or afraid about his secret activities, but rather accepted it as something that had to be done at a time when everyone was doing their bit in one way or another. Peter continued to act as a wireless operator until December 1943 when he was called up into the army. It is hardly surprising that he was posted to the Royal Signals and for a period also served with the Intelligence Corps.

Curiously, Peter remembers attending a presentation in mid-1941 at the Hydro by Colonel Gubbins (now in SOE) and Sefton Delmer (Political Warfare Executive) on the relative merits of sabotage and black propaganda. Delmer thought that sabotage would be counter-productive due to the brutal response by the Nazis. Peter remembers this well because Delmer said 'I'll spell that for you in capital letters – BRUTAL'. He also attended what was clearly an SIS briefing in which one of the 'men in suits' described the security situation in the USA and in occupied Europe. Why local cell members were invited to attend such high-powered meetings is a mystery.

Internal Security

MI5 files give other fragmentary clues to the activities of the organisation known to them simply as 'DB's organisation'. The unedited text of the Guy Liddell MI5 Diary includes two intriguing references to the operation of Boyle's network. In March 1942 Liddell records how 'The extra assistance that he [Gambier-Parry] was proposing to get to deal with the Met. problem [suspected German transmitters in Croydon and Blackpool sending meteorological reports to the enemy] would come from DB's various agents dotted about the country.'[36] Here is evidence for a specific function of the organisation. They were not merely waiting in readiness for any invasion but, in the spirit of the agreement with MI5, they were also being used on counter-espionage duties. It seems that the intention was to use the Section VII wireless sets to supplement the direction-finding vans of the RSS and possibly to use the agents for surveillance work. David Boyle was involved throughout 1941–44 in discussions with MI5 on the progress of the surveillance and infiltration of pro-Fascist groups, suggesting that this was not an isolated incident but that Section VII was playing an active part in this vital work.[37]

In April 1943 Liddell records that 'one of DB's people' (Dr Stratton) had been killed, and his house destroyed, during an air raid on the Isle of Wight and that 'Somewhere in the ruins are important papers and a wireless transmitter'. In accordance with the agreement establishing B.26, SIS asked MI5 to dispatch a local officer to investigate the scene and recover the wireless set, as well as interview another member of the cell (Dr Drummond, Yarmouth); neither are known members of the SDB cell on the Isle of Wight, which was an especially sensitive location.[38] Plans were afoot to make it the terminal for the Pluto fuel pipeline that would serve the future invasion beaches, but there had already been arrests on the island for suspected spying. SIS concern was heightened by rumours that the first person on the scene of the air raid was a suspected Nazi sympathiser, and they were clearly concerned that the network had been betrayed to the enemy.[39]

The very fact that every effort was made not to give a name to the organisation in official records is a signal of its extreme secrecy, and it seemed quite acceptable to be recruited to unnamed bodies that were only vaguely described as being part of 'military intelligence' and with no other proof being offered. Emma in Sussex and Peter Attwater in Derbyshire have been discussed; Albert Toon in Birmingham and the Grammar School boys in Worcester are mentioned below. Similarly, when Edmundson was recruiting for the early Auxiliary Units (at a time when they were heavily influenced by the HDS) he explained 'These early recruits were told nothing about being in a special unit of the Home Guard – or indeed about being in any formal organisation – and their names were never committed to paper.'[40]

Sabotage: X Branch

Section VII may not have been a purely intelligence-gathering operation. The Eastbourne cell was briefly equipped to undertake sabotage and Peter Attwater believed that the Matlock operation had an arms dump hidden in the hills surrounding the town, although it is significant that he was never given details. There are a number of accounts of recruitment for sabotage operations that do not fit either regular army or Auxiliary Units operations, but rather bear the indistinct fingerprint of the intelligence services. In many respects they answer the criticisms of Wilkinson over the direction of the Auxiliary Units and follow the suggestions of Tommy Davies from MIR (see above, p. 53). The vague reports also hark back in some degree to the original concept of Claude Dansey in 1937 for an arms-length sabotage network that would not compromise the rest of SIS.

David Boyle was certainly no stranger to such tactics, having played a leading role in the brutal secret war with the IRA in 1920–21. Whether these were formally part of a sabotage arm of Section VII or yet another body operating under the name of 'X Branch' will probably never be proved. There may not have been a unified structure to the sabotage operations. This would certainly have been a method favoured by Dansey as a means of protecting the rest of SIS operations. Nonetheless, Vivian referred in a deliberately vague fashion to 'special activities' and 'special tasks' in his agreement with MI5. Albert Toon, a Home Guard from Birmingham, was recruited by an unnamed lieutenant from a mysterious organisation called 'X Branch'. He was told to keep a low profile within his Home Guard Unit, although the various training courses that he was sent on qualified him as a weapons instructor in the Home Guard; one such course was at the isolated Western Command Altcar Training Area on Merseyside, which he attended under the cover of going on a Lewis-gun course, where he was taught how to make and use home-made explosives (so as not to be dependent on any official supply chain). Toon was also trained in Morse code (implying the use of a wireless set)[41] and in the use of the clockwork timing mechanisms that had been developed by Section D.[42] Trainees at Altcar included officers and other ranks from both the regular army and Home Guard; all were treated equally and addressed simply as students by the instructors. Given the mix of students, the likelihood is that these men were being trained to operate after both regular and Home Guard forces had collapsed and the country had been occupied, which is exactly what Tommy Davies had proposed in June 1940. The instruction for Toon upon invasion was to report to a local school where he would be given further orders and be told where his explosives dumps were hidden, at which point it is presumed that he would be given instructions on the method of his wireless communication. He was told that he would be working alone and needed to practise silent movement at night. Toon did not directly provide a date for these activities, but he did tell how he was trained to link up Type 73 'Thermos' grenades (introduced in November 1940) in order to create huge demolition charges. In another tantalising clue from the same area, an arms store was discovered at the bottom of a garden in the south-east suburb of Birmingham, including a copy of the Auxiliary Units *Countryman's Diary*, which would date the dump's existence to 1944 (see above, p. 81), but there is no evidence that the Auxiliary Units operated in this area.[43] Toon's code name was 'Charlie' and is therefore reminiscent of the series of aliases given to the SIS intelligence cell at Matlock which also connected to units in Birmingham and Nottingham.

Another story of 'X Branch' comes from south of Birmingham in Worcester. A 14-year-old pupil of Worcester Grammar School records being recruited, along with half a dozen other boys from the school OTC, by three unnamed officers from 'X Branch' and trained in guerrilla warfare by two tough, mature NCOs. The boys were given an Auxiliary-style hide on Gorse Hill, on the east side of Worcester, which although now destroyed has been independently verified. The regular appearance of two NCOs over two years suggests they had a local base, and the boys also received training at the Infantry Training Centre at Norton Barracks, Worcester – where John Todd had an office and where local Operational Patrols of the Auxiliary Units were also trained. In contrast to the local Auxiliary Units, the boys received a Vickers heavy machine-gun and later a Bren gun; they also received instruction on captured German weapons. There was a harder edge to their training that has not been reported elsewhere: they were taught to operate singly or in pairs, including acting as virtual suicide bombers. One recommended technique was to approach a German guard-post begging for bread, and having been given a chunk to tear it in half and put one part into a pocket – on the excuse that this was for 'for my brother' – and then pull out a grenade. For this task they were taught such German phrases as 'Ich habe hunger. Haben sie Früstuck?'. The presence of this additional layer of guerrilla activity in Worcestershire may explain a series of Auxiliary Units-type Operational Bases in the county which currently have no 'owner', including a mysterious arms store on the west side of Worcester in Northwick. The Gorse Hill cell was stood down in 1942 with the words from one of the 'X Branch' NCOs 'That's it lads, it's finished'. In the twenty-first century such training of boy soldiers seems abhorrent, but it was not so unusual in the 1940s, especially in resistance groups.

There are other stories of individual saboteurs and assassins. From Bristol, a Post Office communications worker revealed on his deathbed that the revolver that he had kept beside his bed throughout the war was to have been used to assassinate his supervisor following any invasion – because the supervisor knew the location of secret telephone lines. From the Black Country a man claimed he was trained how to assassinate using poison from a hidden hypodermic needle (in the manner enthusiastically proposed in the discussion over the Davies plan of June 1940, see above, p. 54).

In the Midlands, therefore, there are a number of accounts of operations run by 'X Branch' where saboteurs were told to work singly or in pairs. Linking Matlock and Birmingham there are aliases based on false personal names. The agent from the Matlock cell was instructed by a mature former NCO who became an officer and had an ambiguous relationship to Military Intelligence. He met one of the organisers in Birmingham who also showed all the signs of being at least an ex-NCO. The teenage guerrillas in Worcester were also trained by tough, mature NCOs. The evidence is circumstantial, but there are enough similarities to suggest they may have belonged to the same organisation. Did SIS recruit ex-army NCOs to organise their sabotage or 'dirty tricks' wing after the demise of Section D, in a return to the loose practice favoured by Dansey (see Chapter Two)? Comparison may be drawn with the post-war practice of SIS to recruit ex-SAS as a covert operational arm.

Here, therefore, is tantalising evidence for a small but long-term intelligence and sabotage organisation operating in the UK throughout the war by SIS. This would have been Britain's true resistance organisation. Is this what the long-term secrecy surrounding the Auxiliary Units and their covert activities was actually trying to protect? It was an effective organisation that escaped both the attention of Nazi and Soviet spies during the Second World War and later historians during the Cold War. Is it one of the last, best-kept secrets of the Second World War?

Chapter Twelve

The Role of the Home Guard (1940–44)

Part of the Home Guard's job is to carry on the struggle, if necessary, in areas temporarily overrun by the enemy. This last duty it can only carry out if it learns some of the tactics of guerrilla war.[1]

Tom Wintringham, 1941

For many years the popular view of the Home Guard was conditioned by the television series *Dad's Army*. The comedy series did not aim to be a documentary, but it failed to convey that much of the 'gallows humour' of the time was based upon the fact that members of the Home Guard did not expect to survive an invasion, knowing that their role was sacrificial. It also failed to portray the sheer exhaustion which was the overwhelming memory of veterans as they carried out their normal jobs (most were in reserved occupations) before reporting for Home Guard duty. For a more accurate sense of the times one only has to look into the eyes of the gritty Home Guardsmen painted by Eric Kennington for John Brophy's 1945 *Britain's Home Guard: a character study*. One consequence of the '*Dad's Army* effect' has been that veterans of the Auxiliary Units have played down their links to the Home Guard and, as a result, the history of the organisation has been distorted. It should also not be forgotten that the Home Guard had its own official secret duties to fulfil upon invasion, together with more unofficial plans for guerrilla warfare.

After an initial few weeks of pondering what to do with the unexpected numbers of men who had volunteered from 14 May 1940, and who vociferously demanded a fighting role rather than that of a body of observers, the Local Defence Volunteers/Home Guard was given an integral part of the defence plan.[2] In part this was due to desperation – there was no other force available to attempt to deal with the new threat of scattered parachute landings inland and by the end of June there were 1.5 million men enrolled in the Home Guard. In General Ironside's Defence Plan of 25 June 1940, they took on a responsibility for manning stop-lines and attempting to slow the advance of the enemy, by which they would be buying time for the mobile columns to mount a counter-attack. Although the chief Home Guard publicist Tom Wintringham (Plate 45 and Appendix 2) had argued the concept of 'elastic defence' against the policy of infiltration and *blitzkrieg* in his March 1940 *Deadlock War*, the official instruction was still the traditional edict that the Home Guard should hold their allotted positions to the last man and the last round. In this 'no holds barred' campaign, the life expectancy for many Home Guard in the invasion areas was likely to be much shorter than the oft-quoted two weeks of the Auxiliary Units. The invasion would not have been a 'gentlemanly' war, as General Ironside warned in his speech to the LDV on 5 June when he exhorted them to meet brutality with brutality.[3] He issued 1 million rounds of 12-bore shotgun cartridges consisting of a single large lead ball – 'lethal shot'. In the First World War the Germans had declared that the use of shotguns, as frequently used by American infantry in the trenches, was inhuman and had killed, out of hand, any soldier found with one. Now thousands of shotguns were in use by the Home Guard, using the official 'lethal shot' and also home-made versions made by binding normal lead shot with candle-wax; both types of ammunition were outside the agreed conventions of ammunition to be used in war. The Germans would have had to rely on speed to force a British surrender before their limited supplies were exhausted and are unlikely to have taken the Home Guard as prisoner; Hitler had already declared them to be *francs-tireurs* terrorists. Knowing this, and with nothing to lose, the Home Guard were advised at Wintringham's Osterley Training School to file their rifle ammunition into expanding 'dum dum' bullets (a practice also recommended to the Operational Patrols of the Auxiliary Units); the horrific wounds that these would cause would make the taking of prisoners even less likely. In dealing with paratroopers appearing to want to surrender the advice from Osterley was 'shoot first and examine later'.[4]

Home Guard and Auxiliary Units

Modern histories have tended to over-stress the separation of the Operational Patrols of Auxiliary Units from the Home Guard. Whilst recognising that the Home Guard had a formal organisational responsibility for the Operational Patrols they believed the Auxilier's uniform was merely a part of their cover story. Early researchers were perhaps too ready to accept the desire of veterans to draw a clear distinction between their work and the Home Guard at a time when TV's '*Dad's Army*' had seriously distorted the reputation of the latter. But even during the war some Auxiliers were irritated by the regular army Scout Sections referring to them dismissively as 'our Home Guards'; they knew they were special and did everything they could to keep that distinction. For example, some key sources for the work of the Auxiliary Units in Worcestershire never volunteered the information that they had been members of the LDV / Home Guard for a period of three months before being recruited into the Auxiliary Units; this only became apparent when it was possible to study their Home Guard enrolment forms. They may never have been aware that their details as members of the Operational Patrols were fully published there and on Home Guard Part II Orders pinned to company noticeboards.

Chapter Six has already explained that the initial concept of the Auxiliary Units Intelligence Officers was to act as advisory officers to the local LDVs in setting up their own sabotage cells. As early as August 1940, even as the new Operational Patrols of the Auxiliary Units were being formed, Major Peter Wilkinson was expressing concern as to the direction of the organisation and especially its relationship to the Home Guard. Given his liaison role with SIS, it is tempting to suggest that he felt the Auxiliary Units were moving too far away from the concept of the civilian Home Defence Scheme that they were in the process of absorbing.

> By the middle of August security was finally thrown to the winds...With its increased numbers the character of the organisation changed and it became virtually a guerrilla branch of the Home Guard.[5]

Wilkinson's exasperation cannot have been helped by Auxiliers travelling to Coleshill by train, ostensibly dressed as privates in the Home Guard but openly toting large American revolvers. In April 1942 Beatrice Temple, ATS Senior Commander of the Auxiliary Units, discovered that even her bank manager in Lewes knew about the Patrol Leaders' courses at Coleshill House.[6] Wilkinson left the organisation in November 1940 feeling bored and disenchanted.

Whilst GHQ had a notional *operational* responsibility for the fighting patrols, this was of limited value once they had gone into action as they were expected to act independently. It is clear, however, that the War Office regarded them as an integral part of Home Guard *organisation*. The War Cabinet on 17 June obliquely referred to their agreement of that day to create the Auxiliary Units as:

> Steps were also being taken to organise sections of Storm Troopers on a full-time basis, as part of the L.D.V.'s. Tough and determined characters would be selected. Some of these would be armed with 'Tommy' guns.[7]

The fundamental link between Auxiliary Units and LDV/Home Guard was repeatedly stressed in official documents; the progress report provided to Churchill on 8 August described the 'Auxiliary Units of the Home Guard' which were organised 'within the framework of the Home Guard organisation'.[8] Until late May 1941 local Territorial Army Associations (TAAs), who were responsible for the administration of the Home Guard within their counties, could be found holding the supplies of clothing, arms, ammunition and equipment for Auxiliary Units. Only from late May 1941 was the responsibility for holding supplies formally transferred to the local HQs of the Auxiliary Units.[9] The basic relationship was set out in a letter of 20 January 1941 from the Director General of the Home Guard to the TAAs regarding 'the control of Auxiliary Units of Home Guard known as "Scout Patrols" or "Observation Units"'. The letter stated that the men were to be formally enrolled into the Home Guard, with their enrolment form 'endorsed to show membership of Auxiliary Units'. It is ironic that this instruction was to be securely kept in a locked safe whilst the names and patrol structure could be found in Part II Orders.[10] A letter of 15 May 1944 from the CO of the Banff Home Guard in Scotland called for greater liaison at all levels between the Auxiliary Units and the Home Guard, but also refers back to a previous instruction of around May 1943 which indicated that knowledge of the scope and purpose of the Units was known within the Home Guard down to the level of Company Commander.[11]

Initially, there was a pious optimism that details of the Auxiliary Units could be kept secret, although Gubbins was not overly concerned about this as he realised that their short life-expectancy would make this irrelevant.[12] Such secrecy was maintained during arguably the most critical months of 1940 but broke down thereafter (although always firmly protected by individual patrol members). In many respects the Auxiliary Units were hiding 'in plain sight', their main defence being the tendency not to ask too many questions at a time when gossip could be regarded as a criminal offence. The volunteers were ordered to be modest, pretend that their job was dull and uninteresting, and they were never to be mysterious. If asked what they were doing they were never to say 'something secret' but to give a matter-of-fact response – fighting patrol, scout patrol, observer, runner and so on.[13] This matter-of-fact approach extended to some War Office instructions. In 1942 ACI 1724 was published in Part I Orders to remind the Home Guard to always carry their gas masks. It was addressed to 'officers, soldiers and auxiliaries'.[14]

A study of the Home Guard enrolment forms for Herefordshire and Worcestershire Auxiliers, and surviving Home Guard Part 2 Orders, revealed that movement to and from the Auxiliary patrols, together with promotions, were well-recorded at a local level from mid-1941 onwards (Plates 42 and 43).[15] As the enrolment forms included the full addresses of patrol members, it is to be hoped that these forms would have been destroyed before they could be captured by the Abwehr or Gestapo. The Worcestershire Home Guard Part 2 Orders show that administration for the patrols was initially handled at as low a level as Company HQ; their names and ranks were incorporated into general orders displayed on Company and Battalion noticeboards. Despite Warwicker's assertion that the commissions given to the Group Commanders from 1941 were not recorded on either regular Army or Home Guard lists, this is another myth.[16] The promotions of Lieutenant Edmund Van Moppes, Lieutenant Roger Smith, and Captain Lewis Van Moppes, who were the Group Commanders in Worcestershire, are recorded on both their Home Guard enrolment forms and on Part 2 Orders (Plate 42). The same may be found to be true elsewhere when the original sources become available. That the case of the Worcestershire officers was not an isolated occurrence is indicated by the fact that Auxiliary Units HQ in October 1942 was still trying to stop Auxiliary Units patrols being identified in the promotion of officers.

It was only from 18 October 1941, in an attempt to restrict access to information at lower levels of the Home Guard, that Auxiliary Units were to be shown 'for administrative purposes' on the strength of the Home Guard Battalion, rather than Company, HQ.[17] Home Guard Battalion COs had a key role to play in the administration of the Auxiliary Units, as from 30 March 1942 the War Office instructed Battalion COs to include members of Auxiliary Units on their battalion strength for the purpose of assessing capitation grants. The money would then be paid directly by the Battalion CO to the local Intelligence Officer of the Auxiliary Units.[18]

Whether the patrol members actually visited HQ to see posted Orders is, of course, a different matter. They may have been shocked to know how far their secret had been almost casually shared at a higher level. Overall, the amount of documentation on the Auxiliary Units contained in Home Guard files from 1941 suggests that once an enemy intelligence officer had made the link between the organisation name and the operation of these special forces (either by interrogation or one of them carrying his chit for petrol signed 'Intelligence Officer, Auxiliary Units) then a speedy round-up of members and their families would follow. It was not for nothing that the Group Commander gave a small .22 pistol to the wife of Ron Seymour from Samson Patrol in Worcestershire.[19]

In a belated attempt to increase security at a local level, on 15 August 1942 responsibility for the Auxiliary Units passed from the local TAAs to the regional TAA HQs. From this point, the Home Guard enrolment forms of new Auxiliers in Herefordshire and Worcestershire can be found signed and countersigned by the successive Auxiliary Units Intelligence officers, Captains Christopher Sandford and Henry Bucknall, usually including the unambiguous official stamp of 'Intelligence Officer, Auxiliary Units'. They were then forwarded directly to TAA in York without contact with the local Home Guard organisation. This is all in sharp contrast to the practice of the first Intelligence Officer, John Todd, who avoided putting his name to any document. Nonetheless, the Malvern patrols were not taken off battalion strength until November 1942.[20] TAA Regional HQs compiled a detailed national register of members of Auxiliary Units Operational Patrols, including their postal addresses and ID card numbers.[21] With members of Operational Patrols now standing out from the rest of the Home Guard by their lack of insignia, an attempt at providing a cover was made by grouping the Operational Patrols as GHQ reserve battalions of the Home Guard, according to their regional TAA. Inverness TAA managed 201 Battalion covering Scotland and Northumberland, York TAA managed 202 Battalion for Yorkshire to the Severn-Thames line and Reading TAA managed 203 Battalion for the Southern and South-East commands.[22] Their new shoulder flashes only served to make them more distinctive and members could be easily identified: from 8 October 1942 the civilian Identity Cards of Auxiliers were also to be stamped with 201, 202, 303 (GHQ Reserve) Battalion Home Guard. Drinking in the same pub as the regular Home Guard cannot have helped security. John Boaz from Samson Patrol remembered going to The Plough at Broadheath, Worcester, for a drink after one night exercise. They were plastered in mud, with blackened buttons and rubber boots, but there met the neat and tidy local Home Guard who had just returned from Sunday Church Parade. The Auxiliers had to rebuff questions as to what they were doing. The Malvern Home Guard later tried to track their local patrol to their hide and a friendly game of hide and seek ensued.[23] In order to make them less conspicuous, Auxiliers travelling to a patrol competition at Syderstone, Norfolk, were specifically ordered to travel there wearing battledress with polished brassware.[24]

The laxity of the administrative procedures outlined above clearly illustrates the problems of increasing militarisation and reliance on the Home Guard that

Wilkinson had foreseen. His response in August 1940 had been to suggest an ultra-secret 'inner core' of resistance fighters:

> With Colin Gubbins's approval I made plans to recruit an inner core of 'trustees' whose identity would, I hoped, remain secret and who would provide the nucleus of a British resistance movement.[25]

It is not known what exactly he had in mind and there is no evidence that this was put into operation before he and Gubbins left the Auxiliary Units for SOE in November 1940. Wilkinson did not believe that Gubbins's successor, the more orthodox Colonel Major, would have looked kindly on the scheme. The response of General Paget to the very suggestion that there might be permanently occupied areas also suggests that it would have not been looked upon too kindly by GHQ (see above, p. 74). In practice it would have been difficult to create any resistance organisation within the formal structure of the Auxiliary Units, as the latter was indeed so closely tied to the Home Guard. From 1943, as the Auxiliary Units were forced to contemplate ever more severe cuts in resources, it appeared that they would become even more integrated with the Home Guard. It was suggested that eleven of the nineteen Intelligence Officers could be replaced by Home Guard officers. The precedent had already been set as early as 1941. G. Woodward, aged 41, was commissioned from the Home Guard in May 1941 and appointed as an Intelligence Officer on that date; in 1943 he was an IO in Wales. Christopher Sandford was a 39-year-old book designer and publisher (founder of the Folio Society). In February 1941 he was commissioned as a lieutenant in the 1st Herefordshire (Leominster) Home Guard but, when he became Intelligence Officer for the Auxiliary Units in July, he was quietly commissioned into the Intelligence Corps as a lieutenant so as to provide authority with regular forces. He continued Todd's tradition of acting as joint IO for both Operational Patrols and SDB in Herefordshire and Worcestershire, which at first sight seems an unlikely appointment, and it is possible that he was another of Todd's existing HDS 'key men'. In the final stages of the Auxiliary Units from August 1944 Home Guard Group Commanders were increasingly taking on a general administrative role for the Auxiliary Units. It was even suggested that the Home Guard should take direct responsibility for the whole organisation.[26]

Official Home Guard Sabotage Teams

The fact that the Home Guard had their own official secret duties is often forgotten. Key among these was responsibility for sabotage in factories where they already had factory defence units. Their particular duty during the invasion campaign was to put factories out of action by disabling, not destroying, them if they were about to be overrun, which would allow production to be quickly restored in the event of a successful counter-attack. Only if this did not materialise would the HDS and 'X-Branch' attempt the actual destruction of the machinery.

This plan affected factories and engineering works both large and small. Harold Goodwin & Company Ltd, in Warley, Worcestershire, was a small garage, then working for the Ministry of Aircraft Production. When the factory

Home Guard was reorganised in 1942, the Company Secretary asked for the retention of Privates Elliott, Radburn and Leslie because these three were essential to plans already made for the immobilisation of the depot. Elliott and Leslie were to be responsible for immobilising the vehicles and battery-charging equipment; Leslie would also transport vital parts to a place of safety, while Radburn was in charge of denial of access to vital spares and tyres.[27]

In August 1941 the Air Defence Research and Development Establishment (ADRDE) at Christchurch, Dorset, carried out a review of the comprehensive plans made by their Home Guard for the immobilisation of equipment and machinery. The secrecy of the plans was stressed, as was the need to delay implementation until the last possible moment. The work would entail the destruction, or removal, of an essential mechanism to a place where retrieval by the enemy would be impossible; removal or destruction of explosives or war materials that the enemy might use; concealment of valuable records or destruction of them if copies were available elsewhere; cutting off gas and electricity supplies; immobilisation of any transport left on the premises; ensuring that any stocks of petrol or oil did not fall into enemy hands; and removal or concealment of any currency.[28]

Conscious of the ease with which the German Panzer divisions had managed to refuel from civilian petrol pumps as they tore through the Low Countries and France, special measures were taken to protect petrol supplies. Rather than destroy the fuel stocks, it was considered better to deny access to them by disabling the pumping mechanisms. Home Guard platoon commanders had a list of all petrol pumps in their area and, in a similar fashion to the Factory Unit 'Key Personnel', special 'Pump Disruption Squads' were formed to dismantle and hide the vital machinery so that only squad members would know the location.[29]

Unofficial Plans for Guerrilla Warfare – Osterley Training School

The official summary of the lectures given at the Osterley Park Training School in 1940 was published by the War Office in 1941 and openly promoted the tactics of guerrilla warfare (see the opening quotation to this chapter). By 1942 the War Office was trying to suppress any connection between the Home Guard and guerrilla warfare.

At the most basic level the Home Guard provided a reservoir of trained talent that the HDS, XII Corps Observation Unit, Auxiliary Units or 'X Branch' could draw upon. Some independently-minded members had plans of their own, which not only reflected modern experience in Spain or in Finland, but also harked back to the official role of the First World War Home Guard – the Volunteer Training Corps (VTC). In what seems a very modern concept of warfare in contrast to the static hell of Western Front trench warfare they were 'to take the form of bands of irregulars', and their duty in case of invasion was to carry on a form of guerrilla warfare (*Official History of the VTC*). They were to 'constantly harass, annoy, and tire out the enemy, and to impede his progress, till a sufficient force can be assembled to smash him' (*VTC Regulations*, 1916).[30]

In sharp contrast, the official concept of the Home Guard in 1940 was to form a static defence and buy enough time with their lives for the regular army to regroup and counter-attack. No training was considered necessary for this role as cannon fodder: all they had to do, within the traditional standing order of 'last man and last round', was sit in a hole and shoot straight! This scenario was not an appealing prospect when facing a fast-moving panzer army while armed only with a shotgun or a P17 rifle with five rounds of ammunition. Wintringham's *Deadlock War* of March 1940 challenged the convention of rigidly holding a position at all costs in favour of the principle of an 'elastic web of defence', whereby a unit would pull back or move to a flank in order to avoid a pointless annihilation and preserve the ability for counter-attack, with a network of defended points preventing any overwhelming breakthrough.[31] He also stressed the need to encourage initiative in NCOs and private soldiers, the necessity to be able to fight in small groups and the importance of infiltration as a tactic. 'And for the development of these tactics, a new spirit and discipline in the army, a release of the initiative and independent energy of the men who are our soldiers'.[32] The answer to a lack of weapons was simple – they were to make their own, based on experience in the First World War trenches, and in Spain and Finland. Similarly, John Langdon-Davies wrote encouragingly in the *Sunday Pictorial*: 'The best Home Guard section is not necessarily the one with the best shots; it is the one which has grasped the adventure, the need for using the imagination, that has had to be called into existence to destroy Nazism'.[33]

Many of the Home Guard seized enthusiastically upon the ideas of guerrilla warfare that were taught by Tom Wintringham and his former International Brigade comrades at the privately-run Osterley Home Guard Training School during the summer of 1940 or at the later Burwash Fieldcraft School, Sussex, commanded by John Langdon-Davies.[34] The Osterley Training School in Hounslow, London, had been established by a curious matching of communist, aristocrat and millionaire. There was revolutionary socialist Wintringham, the conservative publisher of *Picture Post*, Edward Hulton, and the owner of Osterley Park, Lord Jersey. Lincolnshire-born Tom Wintringham had become the public evangelist for the LDV/Home Guard. He had regular columns in the *Daily Mirror*, *Tribune*, *New Statesman* and *Picture Post*. He also frequently broadcast on the BBC. On 17 May he called out in the *Tribune* 'Now Arm The People'. On 28 May he launched his stirring slogan 'An Aroused People, An Angry People, An Armed People' in the *Daily Mirror* and was never shy of telling the Commander-in-Chief and government what they ought to be doing to strengthen defences of the country. This focussed on enlarging and fully arming the Home Guard in order to create a 'People's Army' as a means by which to defend one's home and locality. On 15 June came the first of his rousing articles in *Picture Post*, 'Against Invasion' and on 29 June 'Arm The Citizens'. He preached the need for a defence policy based on aggressive action and avoided any sense of siege mentality. On 20 June he was calling for raids on the French coast. Not for the first or last time did he seem remarkably well-informed. On 24/25 June, No. 11 Independent Company did indeed mount the first commando raid on the French coast – the unsuccessful 'Operation Collar'.

In the fraught summer of 1940 the Osterley Home Guard Training School, immediately labelled a guerrilla warfare school, offered a breath of optimism and inspiration, and also a touch of danger and rebellion in the spirit of Lawrence of Arabia. It could be an intoxicating mixture. Apart from Tom Wintringham there was the exotic Canadian 'Yank' Levy with stories of guerrilla warfare from around the world; romantic Asturian 'dynamiters'; Hugh Slater the expert tank-hunter; and Wilfrid Vernon who would show you how to make up your own explosives. Surrealist painter Roland Penrose would demonstrate the art of camouflage using a naked Lee Miller hidden beneath camouflage netting. There was always the possibility of a guest lecturer such as the charismatic, if eccentric, Orde Wingate, who had returned to England after helping train the Jewish Haganah paramilitary units and founding the notorious 'Special Night Squads'.

The 'Spanish experience' in the training at Osterley promoted new techniques of tank-hunting and street-fighting, as well as the importance of motivation and the ability to act in small units. It is notable, however, that neither Wintringham, nor the British Battalion of the International Brigade, had any experience of guerrilla warfare in Spain. This was an expertise that 'Yank' Levy brought to Osterley from his experiences in South America (his Spanish experience had ended on the second day of the battle of Jarama in February 1937 when he was captured).

Despite his prominent communist background, Wintringham had not been so completely blacklisted by the War Office as is often imagined. Immediately before war broke out, Wintringham was commissioned to write two articles for the new serial publication *Battle Training in Word and Picture*, which was officially approved by the War Office and its foreword written by the Chief of the Imperial General Staff. MI5 did block his appointment to a post in the Transport, Mechanical Section of the War Office during September 1939 on the grounds that it might give him access to confidential information, but even so, during June and early July 1940, he was engaged on a lecture tour on behalf of the War Office.[35] It also seems likely that he drafted the LDV instruction leaflet on *Tank Hunting*, later used as the basis of the regular army training pamphlet of August 1940. It was during the War Office tour that he refined the syllabus of the Osterley Training School, which opened on 10 July. The course had a 'blood and thunder' approach that the students found a welcome change from the traditional parade drill being taught in many Home Guard units. But the lectures went beyond learning techniques of camouflage, making improvised explosives and ambushing tanks – and beyond the tactics described just a month before in Wintringham's *Picture Post* articles or in his book *New Ways of War*. Even as the book was published, 'guerrilla warfare' – a term not even used in *New Ways of War* or in his 'Arm The Citizens' article in *Picture Post* of 29 June – was placed at the core of the teaching at Osterley.

Over the summer months, the term guerrilla warfare had become increasingly popular in government circles, and Wintringham seized upon it as an extension of his previous teaching on how to counter the tactics of 'infiltration' or *blitzkrieg* (recently used to devastating effect on the Continent) as described in *Deadlock War* and *New Ways Of War*. With war being carried out by pincer movements there was no longer a formal front line to face and guerrilla tactics were seen as a way of hindering the enemy advance in a more mobile campaign that struck at the flanks and rear of an advancing enemy. Like Grand before him, Wintringham stressed that the Osterley students would operate in conjunction with military forces, but he also explained that 'The Home Guard will operate under the control of the local Military commander but, as communications are so uncertain in modern wars, small bodies of the defenders must be trained to work entirely alone and under the initiative of their own leader'.

As the enemy advanced, the students at Osterley were told to pick off stragglers on the flanks of an advance including tanks, transports, dispatch riders and sentries. 'It is our job, when the enemy is on the march, or his foraging or scouting parties are out, to harass his flanks, to snipe every straggler. Hit and run. Hit and hold them up. Hit and scatter them'. They were also prepared for the task of working behind enemy lines: 'Since offence is the best form of defence, operations against such units must be carried into areas which may be overrun by the enemy'.[36] Here was a hint of them preparing to become a resistance organisation. Wintringham suggested that if being overrun, Home Guard should bury their rifles and uniforms, blend back into the community, and fight on in teams of two or three with revolvers and explosives. In 1941 Wintringham and Levy provided more advice on the methodology to be employed by suggesting that large boxes should be hidden ready to act as caches for supplies and civilian clothes.[37] Security was everything. 'The most profound secrecy should cover the actions and plans of each group. On no account should others be taken into confidence for fear of accidental betrayal'. The course included advice on how to destroy ammunition dumps and vehicle parks, and how to prepare ambushes. They were also taught how to poison the water supply in occupied areas by throwing dead dogs into wells. 'Remember that the guerrilla has to work like a ghost. He has to undermine the morale of the enemy by being always unexpected and always dangerous. If the Nazis seize an English county we must make it impossible for them to send dispatches about that county without a heavy escort of armoured cars'.[38] There were no illusions about what was to befall them: 'Above all remember the enemy is ruthless, and similar medicine must be handed to him'.[39] They were no doubt proud of the description given to them by Lord Haw Haw as the 'Osterley cut-throats'. One group that took the Osterley training on board was No. 12 Platoon of C Company (Abberley), Stourport Home Guard in Worcestershire. They made plans to go to ground in the Upper Teme valley – much against the advice of the War Office.

Official Opposition to Osterley Training School
This *ad hoc* attempt to raise a guerrilla force was not welcomed by the War Office on the grounds of maintaining disciplined control of the battle front and in case it interfered with its own official plans for the Auxiliary Units, or by MI5 for fear that the training could eventually be used to implement a socialist revolution. Osterley was tolerated in the desperate days of 1940 as a unique source of training, inspiration and good propaganda. MI5 and the War Office had to grit their

teeth against Wintringham's publicity machine. The methodology disseminated from the Osterley School provided a high-profile demonstration to both the Americans and the Nazis that Britain was preparing to stand and fight at all costs and that a *blitzkrieg* across England was unlikely to be as easy as on the Continent. The government had allowed the press to make it plain that not only would the landscape of Britain be defended crossroad by crossroad and village by village, but also that a hidden threat might lurk in every woodland or in every dark alley. The psychological impact of the unique threat posed by the Home Guard at this point of the war, however poorly armed and whether fighting openly or as guerrillas, should not be underestimated; it was an altogether more chilling image than that presented by the comfortable, bumbling, Home Guard of TV's *Dad's Army*. Wintringham was even mentioned on German radio for encouraging 'terrorist' activity. He was also producing instant instructional material that could not be ignored. With no other suitable material available, the War Office distributed 100,000 copies of his 15 June *Picture Post* article 'Against Invasion: the lessons of Spain' to the LDV and employed him on a follow-up lecture tour.[40]

Given the 'communistic tendencies' (as MI5 put it) of the instructors it is not surprising that the LDV Inspectorate asked GHQ Home Forces and MI5 to put the Osterley School under surveillance.[41] On the basis of Hugh Slater's surviving MI5 file, the LDV Inspectorate need not have doubted the attentions of MI5 as the instructors at Osterley were already under close surveillance. Sadly the six-volume MI5 file for Wintringham has been inexplicably lost or deliberately destroyed! The surviving two-volume file for Slater perhaps gives an idea of what it might have contained. MI5 was the driving force behind the opposition to Wintringham and Slater rather than the War Office. Slater's every attempt to officially join the war effort had been discreetly blocked by MI5 since the outbreak of war in 1939 and he remained under surveillance once he was commissioned, with every posting queried by MI5. Prior to becoming Chief of Operations to the International Brigades in Spain Slater had been Political Commissar for the British Battalion and was therefore considered a hard-line communist, although he became quickly disillusioned thereafter. On 18 July, Guy Liddell noted that: 'There is always the possibility that Wintringham might like to build up something in the nature of a future Red Army.' Despite such fears, he had also reported that they had found no evidence of political indoctrination.[42] This was only partly true. The course always ended with a question and answer session and someone could always be guaranteed to ask how such wars could be prevented in the future, which was the cue for a discourse on socialism. Even without clear proof of subversion, Liddell felt obliged to later warn the DMI that Wintringham was 'going round giving lectures to Western Command about guerrilla warfare' and that 'this practice is perhaps not very desirable ...'. Not desirable partly because Wintringham and some of the students such as Norman Mackenzie made it clear that they would use their new skills to fight on, even if the government tried to make peace with the Nazis. Those skills might also conceivably be used to bring about a socialist revolution in the future. It is perhaps not surprising that Wintringham complained that few of the handguns donated by American supporters actually found their way to the Home Guard to be used in his own plans for guerrilla warfare and those of Langdon-Davies.

MI5 were clearly nervous about Wintringham's relationship to his former comrades in the Communist Party and feared that any intelligence provided by the Party to Moscow might find its way to Berlin. Liddell made the interesting comment that 'We have information that Tom Wintringham's present work is regarded as highly advantageous to the C.P. and there may be danger of his picking up quite a lot of information from indiscreet officers'.[43] Wintringham did indeed have extensive contacts across the army, quite possibly including intelligence officers.

Under instruction from Stalin and despite the reservations of many members, the official position of the Communist Party in 1940 was to oppose the war as being an imperialist, rather than an anti-fascist, war. Both the Communist Party and the International Brigade Association (the veterans' organisation) told members not to support the war effort in general and were particularly contemptuous of the Home Guard. Wintringham, Slater and Levy were therefore considered renegades. Slater was finally expelled from the Communist Party in January 1941 because 'He is actively associated with the Wintringham group, and has refused to discuss his differences on Party Policy with the Party'.[44]

Wintringham was equally scathing towards his former comrades for the non-participation of the Communist Party in the war effort – until the Soviet Union entered the war in 1941 and the Party managed another *volte-face*. The real danger was not that Wintringham would directly pass on secrets, but that he may have unknowingly passed on some sensitive information to another of his colleagues at Osterley, Wilfrid Vernon, the explosives expert – who was a Soviet spy.[45] MI5 were not the only people keeping Osterley under surveillance! Eventually, on 30 September, the Osterley School was finally taken over by the War Office, closed down and reopened at Dorking on a smaller scale and with strict instructions to maintain a lower press profile.[46]

If the road to supporting the Allied war effort for the British veterans of the International Brigade was a difficult one, meeting suspicion from every quarter, the same was not true of the small number who had fought for the Nationalist rebels in Spain. Peter Kemp had fought for Franco and became an officer in the Spanish Legion, implicated in the execution of International Brigade prisoners.[47] Kemp was quickly commissioned and recruited into MIR, helped train the early commandos in Scotland and then joined SOE. Ironically at one point he was due to go to Spain to help train former Republican guerrillas. By contrast, battle-hardened members of the International Brigade who had not only demonstrated their anti-fascist credentials, but had also defied the Communist Party and the International Brigade Association to support the British war effort, found it very difficult (although not impossible) to join the British army or even to enter the Home Guard.

After 1940 the War Office tried to reassert control over the Home Guard and repeatedly stressed in the summer and autumn of 1942 that their role was not one of mobile guerrilla warfare. In April 1942 Major G.E. Walk, of GHQ Home

Forces, wrote a report reiterating that the primary role of the Home Guard was to defend their towns and villages and interrupt enemy road movements, but he was aware that some members of the Home Guard also considered guerrilla warfare as being part of their role. This had received fresh attention through reports of the activities of Russian partisans and also because it was specifically mentioned in the War Office training film, *Defence of a Small Town*. Walk thought that the whole concept damaged the primary role of static defence. He concluded that the Home Guard were not, and could not be, trained for a guerrilla role, and that they would be likely to confuse the regular troops.[48] Major Walk's paper was formally adopted in June as an order from the GOC Home Forces that guerrilla fighting by the Home Guard must not be allowed.[49] Southern Command even tried to ban the word 'guerrilla':

> The word 'guerrilla' will not be used in future, as it is often misunderstood and if guerrilla activity is generally regarded as a possible secondary role for Home Guard there is a great risk that the obligation to fight to the last in defended localities will not be met.[50]

The Auxiliary Units waded into the debate at a time when they were beginning to feel threatened about their special status. In 1942 an officer from HQ Auxiliary Units, identified only as 'Bill' but almost certainly Colonel Major, wrote a personal letter to General Gregson-Ellis, the Deputy Chief of Staff, Home Forces, complaining that the Home Guard, especially in the Eastern Counties, had laid down a policy of guerrilla warfare for their troops, saying quite openly that they were going to 'take to the woods'. He concluded:

> I cannot believe that they will be of the slightest use in this role, and will *not* function at all in the face of some Bosche attack pressed home. In my humble opinion they will run like stink without firing a shot.[51]

One wonders what the Home Guard of 1940, who had resolutely stood-to, armed only with pitchforks, when the signal for invasion was mistakenly given, would have thought of such a statement. Had Major also forgotten who comprised his own Operational Patrols? The Home Guard could not, however, be so easily controlled. Following continued pressure on the subject, Home Guard Instruction 51, issued in September 1942, was obliged to compromise by saying that guerrilla activity might be permissible in sparsely populated areas where there were no nodal points and gave details of how to train Home Guards for this role.

Covert Support for Osterley School?

Wintringham's popular promotion of ruthless guerrilla warfare, which ignored military conventions, was disliked by some in the War Office and MI5 in its threat of raising a red army and in possibly drawing attention to the existence of the Auxiliary Units. The potential that the training provided could not, however, be ignored by those hard-pressed officers engaged in the more official efforts to organise guerrilla warfare and there are suspicions that the Osterley School had unofficial links with both SIS and the Auxiliary Units.

Wintringham's concept of small sabotage teams hidden within the community, rather than having disappeared dramatically into buried hides, is exactly what the HDS and the early Village Cell phase of the Auxiliary Units intended in July 1940. His ideas were followed in late 1940 by John Langdon-Davies, former journalist and social worker in Civil War Spain. Writing in the *Sunday Pictorial*, Langdon-Davies outlined plans for 'Home Guard Guides' that are remarkably similar to the discarded concept of the Auxiliary Unit Village Cells. He wanted 100,000 of the strongest, most courageous and best-trained Home Guards, drawn from men such as gamekeepers, poachers, Boy Scouts and mountaineers to provide a network of expert guides for regular troops, working in pairs. Trained to operate silently at night, they would be armed with revolver, three hand grenades, knife, knuckleduster and cosh.[52] It is almost as if he had been given a copy of Gubbins's briefing document of July 1940! Langdon-Davies opened the Burwash Fieldcraft School in March 1941 with the rank of captain in the Home Guard. He was a more acceptable face of socialism than Wintringham, having spoken out vehemently during the Spanish Civil War against the Communist Party. But the War Office had ordered that after the Osterley School was closed, no more media attention should be given to such establishments and so the work of Langdon-Davies during the war is today almost unknown.

From 10 July to 30 September 1940 the Osterley course gave direct instruction to around 5,000 potential guerrilla fighters in weapons handling, use of high explosives, camouflage and stalking. It also inspired the creation of many local training schools across the country, armed with the Osterley lecture notes brought back by its students, extending the knowledge base even further. If Britain had been invaded during July or August, at a time when the Auxiliary Units were small in number and still in the process of initial training (see above, Chapters Four and Five), then it is perhaps reasonable to consider that they and the HDS would have shared honours with the Osterley-trained guerrillas, who did not have the advantage of supplies of plastic explosive, official booby-traps or the new time pencils, but were taught to improvise and were trained in the manufacture and use of simple electrical remote-detonating systems – something never used by the Auxiliers but very useful in creating ambushes (Plate 46). In 1941, the basic methodology of guerrilla warfare as taught at Osterley was continued at Burwash, but was also shared on a wider basis through the publication of another wartime best-seller, *Guerrilla Warfare* by 'Yank' Levy, which extended the scope of *New Ways of War* beyond guerrilla fighting into what might be considered true 'resistance'. It described the use of underground leaflets and newspapers, and how to sow confusion by unarmed methods, in other words exactly what the HDS had been intending to promulgate.

The impact of the Osterley Training School certainly went far beyond the Home Guard. The innovative courses were unofficially attended by officers of the Brigade of Guards, Royal Armoured Corps and even a Naval Shore Establishment. One has to wonder if these included men of the 3rd Division Guards tank-hunting platoons that provided the first instructors to the Auxiliary Units or men from General Thorne's battle patrols. General Thorne, CO of XII Corps and creator of the prototype Auxiliary Units system, certainly sent some officers to Osterley for training. He was a long-time supporter of Wintringham's ideas on army reform (if not his politics) having met him when *How to Reform the Army* had been published in April 1939, at a high-level meeting that also included the Deputy Chief of the Imperial General Staff and the Deputy Adjutant General.[53] They kept up a correspondence throughout the war. Thorne also became an influential patron of Hugh Slater, whom he must surely have met at Osterley, promoting him as an instructor in a Scottish Command training school.

Was there something more to Wintringham's use of the term 'guerrilla' in July 1940 than simply following a new fashion? Had Wintringham been told of the report of the Commons Committee on guerrilla warfare or otherwise been given hints as to the developing policy on irregular warfare? Is it more than just coincidence that the Osterley syllabus was so close to that of the Auxiliary Units and that both Wintringham and Langdon-Davies so accurately described the organisation of the July phase of the Auxiliary Units? Some form of collusion with the official guerrilla organisations is not a completely far-fetched idea. Wintringham was a friend of General Thorne; Edward Hulton, financier of the Osterley Training School knew Lawrence Grand and early in 1940 had worked with Section D to found a fake publishing company which would distribute propaganda in the Middle East.[54] The principles of guerrilla warfare as taught at Osterley were very similar to Section D's and Gubbins's 1939 model which included the necessity of planning for raising a partisan army after smaller resistance units had sown the seeds of revolt. One cannot help but wonder if Lawrence Grand, more pragmatic than MI5, looked upon Osterley's work with some favour and unofficial encouragement. The students could have been seen as a convenient reservoir of talent for a future partisan army, already trained to make improvised explosives, ready in time to be mobilised by HDS cells. The training course at Altcar, probably run by SIS, similarly instructed students in home-made explosives so that they would not be reliant on official supplies after occupation. The Osterley course also demonstrated a Molotov cocktail using a crude delayed-action chemical ignition that was very similar to that supplied by SIS to the HDS.

Colin Gubbins was certainly aware of Tom Wintringham's views on warfare and had quizzed Kenneth Sinclair-Loutit about Wintringham's tactical abilities when they met in Paris in August 1939. Sinclair-Loutit, a friend of Wintringham, had been a leader of the British Medical Unit during the Spanish Civil War and in 1939 was Medical Officer for the Polish Relief Fund in Paris, but reporting to the Military Attaché in the British Embassy.[55] It would be surprising if Gubbins, Wilkinson or Beyts had not investigated what was being taught at Osterley. There is an uncorroborated report that Eustace Maxwell, one of the Auxiliary Units Intelligence Officers, attended an Osterley course and later told his men in Aberdeen that the course on explosives was better than that provided by the Auxiliary Units.[56] At least one future member of the Auxiliary Units did receive his initial training in guerrilla warfare at Osterley – albeit probably to carry out surveillance for MI5! Norman Mackenzie joined the Sussex Auxiliary Units shortly after attending the second Osterley training course. Mackenzie described his time with the Auxiliary Units (before he joined the RAF) as 'the most wonderful summer of my life'.[57] Mackenzie had, however, been recruited by MI5 to infiltrate the Communist Party whilst a student at the London School of Economics in 1939. He went on to work for SIS in the post-war period.[58] As a former member of ILP and now publicly at least a 'fellow traveller'of the Communist Party one would imagine he would have had difficulty passing the security vetting required for the Auxiliary Units if MI5 had not had a quiet word with the local Special Branch.

Perhaps the most intriguing story of all is that biographer Hugh Purcell maintains that Wintringham was shown an Auxiliary Units hide near Grimsby, Lincolnshire, by his brother, Colonel John Wintringham, CO of the local Home Guard battalion and therefore 'in the know'.[59] The most likely explanation of this is that it was a means by which the War Office could convince Tom that they were actually doing something in the field of irregular warfare and therefore to lay off the criticism! In 1940 the unofficial Home Guard guerrilla training school might not be so far away from the top secret HDS and Auxiliary Units as one might think.

Wintringham into Obscurity

Wintringham acquired a growing international audience for his ideas through his publications. He was invited to the USA to advise on forming their own Home Guard. In Palestine the Irgun used Wintringham's *Picture Post* articles as the basis of one of their guerrilla manuals. Even Churchill paid Wintringham a back-handed compliment by later dismissing the Greek ELAS partisans as 'Tom Wintringham's'.[60] No doubt Wintringham was particularly proud of the fact that the Leningrad Home Guard were given exactly the same training in 1941, especially in anti-tank tactics, as that provided at Osterley a year earlier. The only difference, he said, was that for home-made grenades 'these proletarians use caviar tins instead of cocoa tins!'[61]

Nonetheless, in 1941 Wintringham was intensely frustrated by his inability to effect widespread change in the British Home Guard training and policy. This frustration came to a head in May 1941 when he learnt that his friend Hugh Slater had been conscripted as a gunner in an Anti-Aircraft regiment. He exploded in fury and resigned amidst much publicity, writing a bitter article in *Picture Post* about the continuing influence of 'blimps' in the Home Guard.[62] Wintringham was not to know that despite the opposition of MI5, the War Office (under the direct pressure of the Secretary of State) had just agreed that he should be commissioned as a major in the Home Guard. Unfortunately, his resignation made this impossible. Even more ironically, Slater's conscription was merely a device of the Directorate of Military Training, necessary to allow him to be commissioned and then return as an Instructor to the Denbies Training School. He did so at the end of June 1941 as a second lieutenant in the Border

Regiment. MI5 were furious with what they saw as the devious Directorate of Military Training ignoring their advice. But support for both Wintringham and Slater came from the highest level. The Secretary of State commented that Slater should 'have the opportunity of earning a Field Marshall's baton'. Slater remained under MI5 observation and to their dismay was then posted as an Instructor at the Company Commander's Training School of Scottish Command, having been specifically requested by General Thorne and promoted to captain. Imagine their final horror when he was then recommended for a transfer to the Intelligence Corps with the rank of major and the Director of Military Intelligence saw no objection! Fortunately for their blood pressure, Slater failed the interview, although one has to wonder if some influence was not brought to bear on the interview panel.[63] While showing the continued suspicion of MI5 to the veterans of the International Brigade, the cases of Wintringham and Slater are a reminder that the stereotypical view that all such men were shunned by the War Office on principle is not correct.[64] After resignation, Wintringham's lecture tours to the Home Guard actually increased, but it is a great irony that he was never given any official recognition for the contribution that he made to the development of the Home Guard and to training in guerrilla warfare in 1940.

Conclusion

> The secrecy of the British secret service starts with its official designation which nobody understands exactly. Novels, films, memoirs of agents, and articles in newspapers, often written by more or less authorised persons, produced more confusion than clarification for us.[1]
>
> Gestapo Report, 1940

Despite, or because of, their frequent sniping at each other, during 1940 SIS and the War Office managed to construct myriad layers of covert anti-invasion and resistance networks in Britain. The complexities designed to confuse the Nazis have proved equally confusing for modern historians to unravel. There are many unanswered questions and in places a necessary reliance on circumstantial evidence and considered speculation. This is especially true of those bodies controlled by SIS and the intelligence activities of the Special Duties Branch of the Auxiliary Units. The hope is that the present study will inspire future research and encourage more historical documents of the intelligence services to be released into public domain.

The plans for guerrilla warfare were controversial and it is a measure of the desperation of the summer of 1940 that the secret plans were implemented so quickly even if, as with both the Home Defence Scheme and early Auxiliary Units, the detail was made up as they went along. At the heart of the conflict within Whitehall were the struggles (a) between the concepts of intelligence and sabotage activities carried out by civilians or by the military, and (b) the relative importance to be given to intelligence-gathering versus campaigns of sabotage. These struggles were compounded by very strong personalities and competing personal ambitions.

Section D of SIS planned a form of civilian irregular warfare that many in government and the military saw as abhorrent, illegal, and un-British. They were also prepared to think the unthinkable and plan for enemy occupation. Lawrence Grand, head of Section D and founder of the Home Defence Scheme, was offered up as a sacrifice for this unorthodox thinking, but he had set a train of thought in action which would eventually result in the formation of the para-military SOE. Little did Grand's detractors realise that SIS had already created an even more secret version of the HDS, but with the great advantage of wireless communication. Grand's opposite number in MIR, the equally visionary Jo Holland, took a different path that would lead to military special forces such as the Commandos and SAS. Ultimately, Holland's approach would prove to be the most successful option for irregular warfare. To this mix of secret agencies must be added the very public dynamism of Tom Wintringham, who excited an interest in a mass guerrilla campaign with practical advice contained in lectures, books and newspaper articles. There was an underlying political agenda to Wintringham's activity, but in essence he was following the principle outlined in Gubbins's 1939 ideas of raising a mass partisan army. There are the barest, tantalising hints that the bastion of the 'people's army' at the Osterley Training School was being guided, knowingly or not, by Section D of SIS, living up to its reputation: 'no scruples, few morals and was without shame'.[2] Whether by accident or design, the various forms of secret warfare that had appeared during the summer of 1940, from Wintringham's public training of guerrillas at Osterley, through to the Operational Patrols of the Auxiliary Units in the Home Guard, the short-lived Home Defence Scheme, the Special Duties Branch and the ultra-secret Section VII and 'X Branch', had resulted in a series of layers where each acted to distract attention from the more secret layer beneath. This would give SIS the maximum chance of allowing the most secret layer of all – Section VII – to continue its quiet work of intelligence-gathering for as long as possible within an occupied Britain.

Many of the General Staff viewed this machiavellian approach to warfare with distaste. For some it seemed defeatist in suggesting that the army might lose an open battle and even in the darkest days of 1940 many generals refused to accept the concept of 'resistance', putting their faith in the Home Guard patrols of the Auxiliary Units and their Scout Sections to fight a guerrilla war alongside regular forces. But deep in the shadows of government, SIS quietly planned for any occupation and provided the foundations for a resistance army. The task of the sleeper agents of Section VII was to allow invasion to wash over them and thereafter to provide intelligence and seek to unsettle any occupation, preparing for the day when external support from the USA or a dissident German army would liberate the country. Would they have succeeded? Fortunately Britain never had to find out.

This is not a story of daring deeds conducted by fit, young, professional secret agents of popular fiction. Teenage members of Section VII and the Auxiliary Units apart, it is primarily a story of quiet determination by men and women who in the main were either too old to join the services or were in reserved occupations. In a peculiarly British way, many seem to have drifted into this secret world without asking for whom they were actually working and certainly without expecting any reward. Similarly the secrecy of the Auxiliary Units seems to have been largely maintained by local communities preferring to turn a blind eye as to what their neighbours were up to rather than asking too many questions; in wartime Britain gossiping could be regarded as a prosecutable offence.

The civilian volunteers, and even the army personnel involved, were not necessarily told the whole story of their role. This was for good operational reasons at the time, but it has caused confusion for later historians when, in the absence of official documentation, they have tried to build up a history of this secret warfare from the 'bottom up'. The most striking example of this is perhaps the single official reference to the internal security role of the Special Duties Branch (SDB), although its commanding officer, Major Forbes, later acknowledged that this was perhaps the most important task of his organisation (see above, p. 132). Similarly, there are only a small number of single-line references that identify the origin of the SDB as Viscount Bearsted's 'Special Duties' section of HDS. The problem has been compounded by the fact that most of the agents directly involved in this intelligence work passed away before the climate was such that the veterans felt able to talk about their work. It was only in 1992 that John Warwicker managed to secure written permission from the Cabinet Office for former members of the Auxiliary Units to tell their story.

The main virtue of all those involved was to appear to be 'ordinary'. The Auxiliary Units patrol members were not to boast about 'secret' work, and the agents of HDS or Section VII were expected to act out their role as local coal merchant, doctor or postman both before and after occupation. Perhaps the greatest temptation was for teenagers such as Peter Attwater, the young Matlock wireless operator, or Jill Monk, the Norfolk SDB courier, to tell their friends about their secret responsibilities. Instead, there was a quiet acceptance of their secret roles. It took enormous courage for men and women to join the Auxiliary Units (Operational and Special Duties Branches) knowing that their life expectancy might be measured in a few days or at most a few weeks after invasion; their chances of survival would have been slim. Bravery too, from the Section VII and HDS agents who were preparing to lay low during the actual occupation and then lead a double life, without any certainty of success; they faced the ever-present risk of capture, torture and death; and if they survived they could never tell their story. Almost without exception they kept their secrets to their dying day – the ultimate secret agents. In this, of course, they followed the lead of their wartime SIS controllers, whose basic principle was 'once a secret always a secret', remaining tight-lipped about their successes while accepting criticism for their failures! Most of the agents, already approaching middle age, grew old during the period of the Cold War when the intelligence services saw the protection of even old secrets as a matter of national security. Fortunately a few of the teenage members have lived into more relaxed times and now feel able to tell their story. Without them a whole chapter of Britain's history in the Second World War would have been lost.

Thankfully the land defences of Britain in 1940 were not put to the test. Fleming, Gubbins and Wilkinson were subsequently brutally honest about the contribution that their XII Corps Observation Unit or Auxiliary Units could have made, but they were looking at their own organisations in isolation. Together, the various irregular initiatives would have created a web of resistance across the country that the German *blitzkrieg* had not met before. Each 'flea-bite' (as Wilkinson put it), combined with the resolve of the Home Guard to defend every village and crossroad and not forgetting their vital task of destroying access to fuel supplies, would cumulatively have helped grind the enemy advance to a halt and allowed the meagre regular forces a chance to counter-attack. There is no doubt it would have been a brutal campaign. War crimes would have been committed on both sides and the cold analysis at the time was that few members of the various guerrilla groups or the Home Guard in the invasion areas would have survived. The organisation of the guerrilla fighters in isolated layers of activity would, however, have prolonged the overall life-span of this phase of irregular warfare. Even when these had been overcome, if parts of the country had been occupied then Section VII would continue its work of intelligence gathering and sabotage as a resistance organisation, and slowly build up a new partisan army.

This was a remarkable strategy born in a time of extreme crisis. There was, therefore, one particular reason for continuing to keep details of the British plans for resistance a secret: the basic idea was considered so successful that it might be needed again.

> Some little while ago I know that it was considered desirable that the whole of the organisation, its functions, role and methods should remain SECRET and pigeon-holed in the War Office just in case.[3]

There were attempts to reactivate the Auxiliary Units on a European scale during the Cold War. Small anti-communist 'stay-behind' units were created in a number of countries; the new 21 and 23 SAS (Reserve) regiments were specifically tasked to go to ground in North Germany, using underground hides on the same basic principle as those of the Auxiliary Units. Menzies from SIS is credited with promoting this old idea in a new era. Because of their earlier expertise in this field, a number of the continental units (collectively later known as 'Gladios') were trained by British intelligence officers in the UK. This, in itself, was reason enough for the security services to wish not to give too much publicity to the organisation of such forces in the Second World War. Unfortunately, some units in Italy and Belgium went 'rogue' and started a terrorism campaign to heighten the political tension and so justify a more repressive anti-communist regime. Once the story became public there was an obvious embarrassment factor in any British connection. Old secrets therefore became intertwined with new secrets. Were there plans to revive the British Auxiliary Units during this period? One Worcestershire man who had served in the Home Guard during the Second World War and was an officer in the reformed 1950s Home Guard was discretely approached to see if he was interested in joining such a body. He politely declined – he had already 'done his bit'. There is no evidence that the Auxiliary Units were actually reformed in the age of nuclear threat and if the SAS were planning stay-behind units abroad then it is probable that they had similar plans for operations within the UK. But in such a world of secrets who can be certain?

The British army tended not to look too kindly on its pioneers of irregular warfare, tolerated in times of desperate need but put to one side as quickly as possible in favour of orthodox tradition. As General Slim remarked, somewhat sniffily, in regard to Wingate's Chindits:

> We are always inclined in the British Army to devise private armies and scratch forces for jobs which our ordinary formations with proper training could do and do better.[4]

Grand and Holland were quickly moved out of intelligence work, although subsequently both had successful military careers and retired as major-generals.

General Thorne of XII Corps was rather surprisingly quickly side-lined out of south-east England to Scottish Command. Gubbins's military career was cut short by the blight of having commanded the paramilitary SOE. Although he had reached the rank of temporary major-general he was retired on the pension of his substantive rank of colonel. Tom Wintringham was virtually written out of history and his sudden death in 1949 passed almost without comment. The later *Dad's Army* TV series presented a much more acceptable, comfortably middle-class vision of the Home Guard than that which Wintringham and his International Brigade comrades fiercely promoted in 1940–41. The main characters from SIS kept their secrets to their dying day and beyond. Immediately after his death, the widow of Claude Dansey loyally burnt, in their garden, what must surely have been illuminating private papers relating to his intelligence work. Most magnificently of all, David Boyle – the man who led the British resistance organisation – managed to write a 323-page autobiography without once mentioning that he had spent most of his working life in the service of British intelligence.[5]

Directive 16

The Führer and Supreme Commander of the Armed Forces
Führer Headquarters
16th July 1940

Directive No. 16
On preparations for a landing operation against England

Since England, despite its hopeless military situation, still gives no sign of any readiness to come to terms, I have decided to prepare for invasion of that country and, if necessary, to carry it through.

The aim of this operation will be to eliminate England as a base for carrying on the war against Germany and, if necessary, completely to occupy it.

For this purpose I am issuing the following orders :-

1. The landing will be in the form of a surprise crossing on a wide front from about Ramsgate to the area west of the Isle of Wight. Some Air Force units will act as artillery, and some Naval units will act as engineers. Exercises will be carried out on the part of all units of the armed forces to ascertain whether it would be practicable before the general operation to undertake small-scale actions, such as the occupation of the Isle of Wight or Cornwall, and the results will be reported to me. The final decision I reserve for myself. Preparations for the entire operation must be completed by the middle of August.

2. These preparations include the creation of those conditions which can make invasion possible;

   a. The English Air Force must be beaten physically and morally to a point that they cannot put up any show of significant attack against the German crossing.

   b. Mine-free channels must be cleared.

   c. The Straits of Dover must be closely sealed off with minefields on both flanks; also the Western entrance to the Channel on the line from about Alderney to Portland.

   d. Strong forces of coastal artillery must command and protect the forward coastal area.

   e. It is desirable that the English Navy be tied down shortly before the crossing, both in the North Sea and in the Mediterranean (by the

Italians) and an attempt will be made to cripple naval forces based in England by air and torpedo attacks.

3. Command organisation and preparations.

Commanders-in-Chiefs will direct the forces concerned under my order and according to my general directions.

From 1 August 1940 Command HQ's (Army, Navy and Air Force) will be within a radius of 50 kilometres (at the outside) from my Headquarters (Ziegenberg).

I think it would be an advantage to have the command HQ (Army and Navy) jointly stationed in Giessen.

Commander-in-Chief Army will detail one Army Group to carry out the invasion.

The invasion will be called 'Sealion'.

In preparing and carrying out the operation, units of the armed forces will have the following tasks:-

a. Army:

Will draw up a plan for the operation and will tabulate a ferry plan for the transport of the first wave.

AA guns detailed for the first wave will be under the command of the Army (the individual ferry groups) until they can take their share of the tasks of support and cover for the ground troops, for disembarkation harbours and for occupied air bases.

The Army will further distribute ferrying craft to the individual ferry groups and in agreement with the Navy will determine places of embarkation and landing.

b. Navy:

Will ensure transport craft and sail them according to the wishes of the Army, as far as they conform with the naval point of view to the individual embarkation areas. As far as possible shipping of conquered enemy states will be seized.

For every crossing point, the Navy will create the necessary HQ with escort ships and covering forces.

Besides the Air Forces employed in providing cover, the Navy will protect both flanks of the whole Channel crossing.

Orders will follow regarding the organisation of command during the crossing.

Another Naval task will be the disposition of coastal artillery, that is the unit grouping of all batteries, army and Navy, for sea targets and the organisation of the general control of fire.

The largest possible number of heavy artillery pieces will be deployed at the earliest moment to ensure the crossing and to screen the flanks from the enemy naval action.

In additional, railway artillery supplemented by all available captured guns, except those batteries (K5 and K12) intended for long-range shelling of targets in England will be brought forward and set up, using railway turntables.

Apart from this, all the available heavy coastal batteries will be built in under concrete in order to withstand the heaviest air attacks and thus, in all circumstances, command the Straits for as long as they can remain effective.

The Todt organisation will be responsible for the technical work.

c. The Task of the Air Force will be:

To prevent counter-attack by the enemy air forces, to neutralise coastal fortifications which could be brought into effect against the landing positions, to eliminate initial enemy resistance on the part of ground forces, and to destroy any reserves on the march. The closest cooperation between individual Air force groups and Army transport groups is essential for this task.

Further tasks will be :-

To destroy important roads used for bringing up enemy reserves and to attack approaching enemy naval formations in areas far removed from the crossing positions.

I am requesting schemes for the employment of parachute and airborne troops. It is a question to be examined in liaison with the Army, whether it would be advantageous to keep them for the present as a reserve which could be quickly put in in case of emergency.

4. Necessary preparations for signals communication from France to England is the province of the Chief of Armed Forces Signals. The construction of the remaining eighty kilometres of the East Prussian Cable will be undertaken with the cooperation of the Navy.

5. I am requesting the Commanders-in-Chief to submit to me at the earliest moment :-

a. the plans of the Navy and Air Force to establish the necessary conditions for crossing the Channel (see paragraph 2),

b. the dispositions of coastal batteries in detail (Navy),

c. a survey of the shipping tonnage to be employed and methods of getting in readiness and fitting out. Participation of civil authorities Navy),

d. the organisation of air cover for assembly areas of invasion troops and transport (Air Force),

e. the operational and transport plans for the Army, organisation and equipment of the first wave,

f. the organisation of the Navy and Air Force and the measures taken for carrying out the crossing itself, providing cover and support for the landing,

g. proposals for employment of parachute and airborne troops as well as for the deployment and control of anti-aircraft guns after sufficient ground has been gained on English soil (Air Force),

h. proposal location of Army and Navy Command HQs,

i. an appreciation from Army, Navy and Air Force as to whether and which minor operations would be considered advantageous,

j. proposals from the Army and Navy for the chain of command during the crossing.

[signed] ADOLF HITLER

Appendix 2

Key Personalities

Bearsted (Walter Samuel), 2nd Viscount (1882–1948) (Plate 4)
Educated at Eton College and New College Oxford. Bearsted served during
the First World War in the Queen's Own West Kent Yeomanry, reaching the
rank of captain and being awarded the MC as well as being twice mentioned in
dispatches. In 1921 he succeeded his father as Chairman of Royal Dutch Shell
and became a Director of Lloyds Bank. Bearsted was also a notable art collector
and philanthropist, campaigning during the 1930s for the emigration of Jews
from Nazi Germany and funding a number of Jewish charities. In 1938 he was
recruited by SIS as one of a number of wealthy international businessmen, who
could provide both important contacts and act as a conduit for secret funding.
Co-opted by Section D, he was initially expected to undertake work in China, but
was later involved in the development of resistance networks in Scandinavia,
using his contacts in Shell. In June 1940 he was named as the main contact for the
Section D Home Defence Scheme and then took charge of the transfer of the
intelligence branch of the HDS into the GHQ Auxiliary Units as Auxiliary Units
(Special Duties).

David Boyle (1883–1970) (Plate 16)
Educated at Wellington School and New College Oxford. Following a pre-war
career as a Customs Officer in Peking, a tea planter in Ceylon and a timber
merchant in Bombay, during the First World War he joined the intelligence
service, initially as a 'Political Officer' in Ashanti. In March 1919 he was commissioned as a reserve second lieutenant in the Argyll and Sutherland Highlanders,
which provided a cover for his later activities. He then served as Deputy Head of
Station for SIS in New York, ostensibly whilst working for the Ministry of
Pensions. While in New York, he was implicated in the failed attempt to kidnap
De Valera and was obliged to leave the country. He was then posted by SIS to
Ireland, where in August he became an officer of the notorious Auxiliary Division
of the Royal Irish Constabulary – a British intelligence and assassination unit. In
1921 he became head of Dublin District Special Branch (D Branch) which he
reorganised to more effectively counter the operations of the IRA. Later in 1921
and in 1922 he is reported as working for the Foreign Office on unspecified duties
in the Far East. From 1924–38 he was Head of Section N, covertly opening
diplomatic mail, all the while being a director of Cunard and the Anchor Line.
In 1938 he became personal assistant to the Chief of SIS (Admiral Sinclair). By
now he was operating under the cover of being a King's Messenger. In 1939
Boyle was sent on an abortive mission to Berlin to try to make contact with

dissident members of the German General Staff. From 1940 there are repeated references to his being head of the UK resistance organisation of SIS – Section VII.

In 1948 Boyle was invested as a Companion of the Order of St Michael and St George (CMG) with the citation merely saying 'attached to a department of the Foreign Office'. His 1959 autobiography is majestic in never once mentioning that he had spent much of his life in the service of British Intelligence, and he finally took his many secrets to his grave in 1970.

Mike Calvert (1913–1998)

Born in India and educated at Bradfield College and the Royal Military Academy, Woolwich. After being commissioned in the Royal Engineers he entered Cambridge University and graduated with a degree in Mechanical Engineering in 1936. He commanded a detachment of Royal Engineers during the Norway campaign in 1940 and then became Demolitions Instructor at the new commando training school at Lochailort. After service with the XII Corps Observation Unit he trained commandos in Australia, leading a number of their raids. He then joined the Chindits under Orde Wingate and commanded the 77th Chindit Brigade. After being evacuated back to England following an injury, in March 1945 he took command of the Special Air Service Brigade and post-war also commanded their successor, the Malayan Scouts. He lived up to his nickname 'Mad Mike' as a hard fighting, hard-drinking soldier who won a reputation as one of the outstanding leaders of irregular warfare during the Second World War.

Winston S. Churchill (1874–1965) (Plate 6)

One of the most charismatic politicians of all time. As a young army officer he served in India, the Sudan and the Boer War. Before the First World War he was a cabinet minister and was First Lord of the Admiralty until leaving government after the disastrous Gallipoli campaign in 1915. He then briefly served on the Western Front as CO of the 6th Royal Scots Fusiliers. He returned to government office but in the 1930s was in 'the wilderness', out of both office and favour. He led the warnings about German rearmament and appeasement and on the outbreak of the Second World War returned to government once again as First Lord of the Admiralty. He became Prime Minister on 10 May 1940 and established a new resolve in fighting the war whatever the cost. This included proposing the use of poison gas if Britain was invaded. He interfered regularly in the military conduct of the war and one of the main duties of the CIGS came to be to temper his tendency to make rash decisions. Despite having an immense personal following, his Conservative Party lost the 1945 election with one of the largest defeats in British electoral history. He became Prime Minister again in 1951 before finally retiring from politics in 1955.

Hugh Dalton (1887–1962)

A Labour Party politician who opposed appeasement. In Churchill's coalition government he became Minister of Economic Warfare from 1940–42. As part of his ministerial duties he became head of an independent Special Operations Executive. He had a reputation for being peevish and lacking administrative talent, but he was also an innovative thinker, with a nickname of 'Dr Dynamo'. He later became President of the Board of Trade in 1942 and was Chancellor of the Exchequer in the post-war Atlee government.

Claude Dansey (1876–1947) (Plate 2)
Dansey joined the Lancashire Fusiliers at the age of 20 in 1898 and in 1902, during the Boer War, was seconded as a Staff Intelligence officer. After the Boer War he joined MI5, serving in port security during the First World War until he transferred to what became SIS. He then worked both part-time and full-time for SIS until his death in 1947. This included setting up the 'shadow' Z organisation in Europe and being appointed Assistant Chief of the Secret Service. He was reputed by some to be the best intelligence agent of his generation, but at the same time he was widely hated and feared as being vindictive and short-tempered.

John Dolphin (1905–1973)
Educated at Marlborough College and Loughborough Engineering College. By 1938 he had his own engineering consultancy business, as well as being a territorial reserve officer in the Cheshire Regiment. He was recruited to Section D, SIS in 1939 (code name D/XE) and became a specialist in sabotage techniques at The Frythe, Hertfordshire (later SOE Station IX). In 1940 it was he that first proposed the idea of the Section D Home Defence Scheme to Lawrence Grand. After transferring to SOE, he became Commanding Officer of Station IX at Welwyn in 1943, where some of his most famous inventions were the folding 'Welbike', the 'Welman' one-man submarine and the 'Welfreighter' miniature submarine. In 1950 he became Chief Engineer at the UK Atomic Energy Authority and continued to be a prolific inventor. He finally retired from the Territorial Army Reserve in 1960 with the rank of lieutenant colonel.

Peter Fleming (1907–1971) (Plate 8)
Educated at Eton and Christ Church, Oxford. Before the outbreak of the Second World War he had led a varied life as a writer and explorer. He served with MIR in Norway and in late May was tasked with investigating the use of the LDV in guerrilla warfare. He then joined XII Corps Observation Unit and pioneered elements that would later be taken up by the Auxiliary Units. Fleming then joined SOE and from 1942 was head of D division, which was responsible for military deception operations in south-east Asia.

Richard Gambier-Parry (1894–1965)
Born at Highnam Court, Gloucester and educated at Eton. He served in the Royal Welsh Fusiliers during the First World War and was wounded three times (Mentioned in Dispatches twice). He was seconded to the Royal Flying Corps in 1918 but rejoined the Royal Welsh Fusiliers in 1925 as a captain. Gambier-Parry

then joined the BBC where he became interested in radio and in 1931 joined the radio manufacturer Philco, becoming General Sales Manager. In 1938 he was recruited by SIS to run its new communications section (Section VIII) and brought over a number of key engineers from Philco. In 1939 he was promoted colonel. Gambier-Parry revolutionised attitudes to radio communication within SIS and the Foreign Office. He established Station X in the tower of the SIS War Station at Bletchley Park, but then relocated it to nearby Whaddon Hall. This then became the hub of SIS wireless communications and the base from which the 'Ultra' intelligence traffic was distributed worldwide. In 1941 Gambier-Parry also took charge of the Radio Security Service, monitoring the airwaves for illicit wireless stations, and until 1942 his Section was also responsible for SOE communications. He was promoted Brigadier in 1942 and post-war he became Director of Government Communications at Hanslope Park until his retirement in 1955. Gambier-Parry was a man of great charm, regarded with great affection by his staff (to whom he was 'Pop') but distrusted by outsiders as something of a pirate in his willingness to aquire new responsibilities for his organisation. Gambier-Parry was one of the triumvirate (with David Boyle and Valentine Vivian) that established the secret SIS network in the UK during 1940 and in 1942 was also radio consultant for the Naval Intelligence plan of a stay-behind unit in Gibraltar (Operation Tracer).

Lawrence D. Grand (1898–1975) (Plate 3)
Educated at Rugby and Royal Military Academy, Woolwich. Having been commissioned in the Royal Engineers, he served pre-war in Imperial Chemical War Research and the Indian Army. He was recruited to form Section D of SIS to research techniques and strategies for irregular warfare. In the period before the outbreak of the Second World War he began active campaigns of subversion and sabotage across Europe. The D Scheme was modified in May 1940 to form a British civilian guerrilla and resistance organisation. Grand was witty, bombastic and uncontrollable, to the despair of his superiors, who preferred not to know what he was planning – but were then dismayed when they eventually found out! He did not survive the transfer of Section D to SOE and was dismissed to India in late 1940. After the war he became Director of Fortifications for the War Office and retired as major general.

Colin Gubbins (1896–1976) (Plate 11)
Educated at the Royal Military Academy Woolwich and then commissioned in 1914 into the Royal Artillery. In 1916 he was awarded the Military Cross for action during the Battle of the Somme. In 1919 he joined the staff of General Ironside in the North Russian campaign and from December 1919 to October 1922 served as an intelligence officer in Ireland during the Anglo-Irish War. Following service in Signals Intelligence and the Military Training Directorate he joined what was to become MIR in April 1939 as a brevet lieutenant colonel. From there he was the Chief of Staff to the Polish Mission and played a key role in

the smuggling of the Enigma code machine into Britain. From March to June 1940 he led the first 'Independent Companies' (Commandos) in Norway, where he was awarded the DSO. He was then appointed to found and command the Auxiliary Units, which he left in November for SOE. He became Executive Head of SOE in September 1943. Although he finished the war as an acting major general his role in SOE had not endeared him to the establishment and he was retired on his substantive rank of colonel.

Halifax (E.F.L. Wood), 1st Earl of (1881–1959)

A senior Conservative politician of the 1930s and Foreign Secretary 1938–40. Educated at Eton and Christ Church, Oxford. He served in the First World War as a major in the Queen's Own Yorkshire Dragoons and as a staff officer. He had an undistinguished career as a minister in the 1920s, clashing with Winston Churchill, but became Viceroy of India 1926–31. He was Lord President of the Council in 1937–38. Halifax supported German remilitarisation as a move towards the 'normalisation' of Germany after the restrictions of the Versailles treaty. He also supported an expansion of Germany into Poland, Austria and parts of Czechoslovakia – as long as the moves were peaceful. He became Foreign Secretary in February 1938 and as such was the minister in charge of the SIS at the time that Section D made both their plans for sabotage in Germany and neutral countries and later planned resistance operations in Britain.

Halifax took a pragmatic line on appeasement, believing it would buy time for rearmament. It was, however, Chamberlain who directed foreign policy and Halifax came to believe that the concessions made towards Germany were too great. On 31 March 1939 it was Halifax who gave a firm guarantee to Poland that Britain would come to its aid upon any German invasion and so provided the trigger for the Second World War. Halifax was the popular choice among the Conservative and Labour parties, as well as the King, to succeed Chamberlain, but Halifax believed he did not have the personality or energy to compete with Churchill. Upon the fall of France Halifax supported the idea of a negotiated peace and almost succeeded in winning support for this view, but was out-manoeuvred by Churchill. He did, however, remain as Foreign Secretary until January 1941 when he became Ambassador to the USA.

Maurice Hankey (1st Baron Hankey) (1877–1963)

Educated at Rugby School and then joined the Royal Marine Artillery. From 1902–04 he was a coastal defence analyst in the Naval Intelligence Department – experience he frequently referred to in dealing with defence matters in the Second World War. Moving to the Civil Service, in 1912 he became Secretary to the Committee of Imperial Defence, a post he held until 1938. In 1914 he was also appointed Secretary of the War Council, which led in 1919 to him becoming the first permanent Cabinet Secretary. He retired from the Civil Service in 1938 and was created Baron Hankey in 1939. Frequently called upon for advice, Chamberlain appointed him a Minister without Portfolio and a member of the War Cabinet. During this period he conducted reviews of both MI5 and SIS.

Although dropped from Churchill's War Cabinet, from May 1940 to July 1942 he was Chancellor of the Duchy of Lancaster. Throughout 1940 and beyond, he was a key security advisor and conduit between government, the services and the intelligence services, as well as fielding all manner of suggestions from individuals keen to support the war effort. He finally left the government in 1942.

John (Jo) F.C. Holland (1897–1956) (Plate 5)

Born in India. Educated at Rugby and then went to Royal Military Academy, Woolwich. He was commissioned into the Royal Engineers in 1915, serving in the Balkans for most of the rest of the war. He was then seconded to the RAF and in 1918 won the DFC. He continued to serve with the Air Ministry 1918–19. Holland was badly wounded during the Irish War of Independence 1919–21, during which period he learned to admire the guerrilla tactics of the IRA. He held a series of staff posts from 1934 and was then appointed to lead the think tank on irregular warfare, MIR. In 1943 he was appointed to become Deputy Engineer-in-Chief and was then promoted temporary major general in 1944. He retired from the army in 1951.

Hugh Miles Gladwyn Jebb (1st Baron Gladwyn) (1900–1996)

Educated at Eton and Magdalen College, Oxford. Jebb entered the diplomatic service in 1924. From 1929–31 he was Private Secretary to Hugh Dalton, then Parliamentary Under-Secretary of State for Foreign Affairs in the Labour government, which was to provide an important personal contact for his later career. Jebb later became Private Secretary to the Permanent Under-Secretary of State at the Foreign Office and as such had close dealings with Section D of SIS as the formal conduit between SIS and other government departments. In August 1940 he was appointed to the Ministry of Economic Warfare with the formal rank of Assistant Under-Secretary and 'Foreign Policy Advisor', but in reality he was the Chief Executive of SOE. He left SOE in 1942 to become Head of the Reconstruction Department. After the war he worked for the United Nations and became the UK ambassador to the UN 1950–54. He later took up party politics as a Liberal party peer.

Guy Liddell (1892–1958)

Educated at the University of Angers in France. Liddell served with the Royal Artillery in the First World War when he was awarded the Military Cross. In 1919 he joined Scotland Yard as a counter-intelligence officer. He and his section transferred to MI5 in 1931 and he became Deputy Director of the counter-espionage section, B Division. In June 1940 he became Director of B Division and established a reputation as one of the finest intelligence officers of his generation. He became Deputy Director of MI5 in 1945, but his close friendship with Guy Burgess and acquaintances with the other Soviet spies Kim Philby and Anthony Blunt cast a shadow over his later career. In 1953 he took early retirement from MI5 and became a security advisor to the Atomic Energy Authority.

During the Second World War he kept an almost daily diary, which provides a unique insight into the workings of Britain's wartime intelligence services. Although published in edited form, some of the key entries relating to the SIS intelligence network in the UK were not included. As a consequence, all references to the Diary in the present book are to the original documents in The National Archives.

Stewart Menzies (1890–1968) (Plate 1)
Educated at Eton College and then commissioned into the Grenadier Guards before transferring to the Life Guards, with whom he served in the First World War, winning the MC and DSO. After being gassed in 1915 he joined the counter-espionage section of the General Staff. After the war he joined SIS and was promoted to lieutenant colonel. By 1929 he was Deputy Director of SIS and succeeded Admiral Sinclair as Chief in 1939. He was then known as 'C'. During the Second World War he had the difficult task of building up SIS from being a small and impoverished organisation and in managing the top secret distribution of intelligence gained from 'ULTRA'. He was highly adept at political intrigue, although was thought by many to be unduly under the influence of Claude Dansey. He was outflanked by the creation of SOE in 1940 and the two organisations had a very bumpy relationship. He retired from the Service in 1952 as a major general.

Frank Nelson (1883–1966)
Educated at Bedford School and at Heidelberg. He then moved to India, making a fortune in the shipping firm of Symons, Barlow and Co. During the First World War Nelson served with the Bombay Light Horse. After the war he became both a successful businessman and politician in India, but returned to England in 1924, when he was knighted and became Conservative MP for Stroud. He resigned his seat in 1931 in order to go back into business and to work for SIS, becoming part of Claude Dansey's Z organisation, with the cover of being Vice-Consul in Basle. In 1940 he was appointed Executive Director of SOE. After retiring from SOE in 1942 due to ill health, he worked for the Air Intelligence branch, retiring with the rank of Air Commodore.

Maurice Petherick (1894–1985) (Plate 13)
Educated at Marlborough College and Trinity College, Cambridge. At the start of the First World War he served with the Royal Devon Yeomanry, but was wounded in 1915 and then served in the Foreign Office during 1916–17. This may well have been his first contact with the intelligence services. He rejoined the Royal Scots Greys in 1917. Petherick became a successful Conservative Party MP, representing Falmouth and Penryn from 1931–45. In October 1939 he was recommissioned onto the General List, probably as a member of SIS. During part of 1940 he was a liaison officer at the Paris Embassy and was on personal terms with Lawrence Grand, if not a member of Section D itself. He then became

commanding officer of the Special Duties Branch of the Auxiliary Units, supervising the final integration of the HDS with the Auxiliary Units and masterminding the new wireless network.

Duncan Sandys (1908–1987)
Educated at Eton and Magdalen College, Oxford. Served in the Foreign Office in London and Berlin, but in 1935 entered Parliament as a Conservative MP. In that year he also became the son-in-law of Winston Churchill and thereafter became a close ally. In 1937 he was commissioned into the territorial army (Royal Artillery) and when war broke out he served with the BEF in Norway. On his return he appears to have spent much of summer of 1940 as one of Churchill's inner circle of unofficial advisors, based around family members. According to John Colville, Private Secretary to the Prime Minister, he spent his time 'drinking in all the most secret information'.[1] As such, he was clearly privy to knowledge of both Section D and the new Auxiliary Units and acted as a conduit between the Prime Minister and the General Staff on their development. In August he was given a formal post in the Cabinet Office under General Ismay (which became the Offices of the Minister of Defence) and as such was responsible for producing reports on the Auxiliary Units for the Prime Minister. He then returned to active service to become CO of an anti-tank regiment in Wales, although his military career was cut short by a car accident in 1941. He then became Finance Secretary to the War Office. In 1943 Sandys became Chairman of the War Cabinet committee to investigate defence measures against the German flying bombs. He had a successful post-war political career and was given a life peerage in 1974.

Hugh Sinclair (1873–1939)
Sinclair joined the Royal Navy as a teenager, promoted to rank of lieutenant in 1894. He had a succession of staff posts but in January 1919 he was appointed head of the Naval Intelligence Division, promoted to rear admiral in 1920. He was appointed Chief of the SIS in 1923 and went onto the Naval Retired List in 1926. He was promoted to full admiral on the Retired List in 1930. Sinclair clearly foresaw the threat of Nazi Germany, clashing with contemporary government policy of appeasement. Some of his key innovations of the late 1930s were clearly aimed to bring SIS to a war footing, including the creation of the Wireless Communication Section (Section VIII), Section D (Sabotage Section) and Dansey's shadow SIS organisation – the Z Organisation. All have a direct relevance to the present study. He died on 4 November 1939, on his deathbed recommending Stewart Menzies as his successor.

Andrew Thorne (1885–1970) (Plate 9)
Educated at Eton College and Royal Military Academy, Sandhurst. He was commissioned into the Grenadier Guards in 1904, becoming CO of 3rd Battalion in 1916. In 1932 he became Military Attaché in Berlin and while in Germany got the idea of stay-behind guerrilla units. In 1938 Thorne became major general commanding London District and the Brigade of Guards. He commanded

48th (South Midland) Division as the rearguard for the Dunkirk evacuation and then was given command of XII Corps in Kent and Sussex. Here he created the XII Corps Observation Unit, which was the inspiration for the Auxiliary Units. In 1941 he was appointed commanding officer of Scottish Command where he had a key role in the D-Day deception plan, Operation Fortitude (North). At the end of the war he was put in charge of plans for the liberation of Norway.

John Stewart Ellerman Todd (1899–1980) (Plate 15)
Born in Putney. He joined the Honourable Artillery Company in 1917 and after the war became a successful London stockbroker. He was commissioned as second lieutenant on the General List on 31 May 1940 'without pay and allowances', a common identifier of an officer in SIS. Two months later he was an acting captain on 'special employment'. This marks his appointment as an Intelligence Officer for the Auxiliary Units in Monmouthshire, Herefordshire and Worcestershire. Unusually, he served as IO for both the Operational and Special Duties Branches of the Auxiliary Units, possibly while still an officer of SIS. In July 1941 he was promoted acting major. The following month he was appointed a local lieutenant colonel in the Intelligence Corps, marking his transfer to SOE where he led the East Africa Mission to organise espionage and the recapture of Madagascar. He retired from the army in May 1945 as an honorary colonel in the Intelligence Corps, but maintained contacts with the Auxiliary Units. In an act that belies his fascinating secret career in intelligence, he was knighted in 1963 for services as a Commissioner for the Public Works Loan Board. He died in 1980.

Valentine Vivian (1886–1969)
Joined the Indian police service in 1906 and in 1914 became Assistant Director of Criminal Intelligence. Having joined SIS, in 1925 Vivian became head of SIS counter-espionage section (Section V). He ran the SIS 'Casuals' agent network in Britain in the late 1920s until they were taken over by MI5. In 1932 he created the SIS intelligence network in Eire and in 1940 was one of the triumvirate (with Boyle and Gambier-Parry) who established the SIS intelligence network in the UK, negotiating its presence on the mainland with MI5. He had an uncomfortable relationship with Claude Dansey, both regarding themselves as Deputy Head of SIS during the war years.

Tom Wintringham (1898–1949)
Born in Grimsby, Lincolnshire and educated at Gresham School, Norfolk and Balliol College, Oxford. In the First World War he served as a mechanic and dispatch rider for the Royal Flying Corps. At the end of the war he was involved in a barracks mutiny and formed the British branch of the Third International. He then joined the new Communist Party of Great Britain and was imprisoned in 1925 for seditious libel. In 1930 he founded the *Daily Worker* and became the party's chief spokesperson on military matters. He was a steadfast adherent to the concept of the 'popular front' and during the Spanish Civil War was a

leading proponent of the idea of the International Brigades, for a time commanding the British Battalion. His beliefs fell out of tune with Stalinism and he was expelled from the Communist Party in October 1938. At the start of the Second World War he condemned both the Communist Party for their subservience to the Hitler-Stalin Pact and the Conservatives for their policies of appeasement. He became the main publicist for the Home Guard and founded the innovative Home Guard guerrilla Training School at Osterley Park. Wintringham returned to politics in 1942 and formed the Common Wealth Party; in 1946 he joined the Labour Party. He died in 1949, already largely forgotten.

Notes

Introduction

1. Section D Closing Report, 'Great Britain's only successful experiment in total warfare', August 1940, p. 8: TNA HS 8/214.
2. Schellenberg 2001, p. 123.
3. Warwicker 2008, p. 82.
4. Fleming 1957, p. 9.
5. Duncan Stuart, 'Of historic interest only: the origins and vicissitudes of the SOE archive', in Seaman 2006.
6. The newspaper for troops of South East Asia Command.
7. Fleming 1952; 1957.
8. Mackenzie 2000, p. 52.
9. Foot 1984, p. 17.
10. Stafford 2010, p. 122.
11. Davies 2004, p. 119.
12. Seaman 2006, p. 19.
13. Section D, Early History to September 1940: TNA HS 7/3.
14. 'SO2 have been giving a great deal of trouble. They act in a very slapshod and indiscrete manner. The result is that all their people get rounded up and some of Stewart's as well' (Diary of Guy Liddell, MI5 for 11 March 1941: TNA KV 4/182).
15. Jeffery 2010, p. 361.

Chapter 1

1. German radio broadcast upon the founding of the LDV: Graves 1943, p. 16.
2. *Official Regulations of the Volunteer Training Corps*, 1916, p. 78.
3. United Nations War Crimes Commission, *Law Reports of Trials of War Criminals*, Volume VIII, 1949.
4. On 21 November 1920 in Dublin (Bloody Sunday), the IRA assassinated twelve British under-cover army officers, a policeman and a civilian informant all believed to be associated with the 'Auxiliary Division' intelligence network that was organised by Dublin Special Branch. The future leader of the British SIS resistance organisation in 1940, David Boyle, then became the command-ing officer of the Auxiliary Division.
5. Langdon-Davies 1941, p. 54.
6. Pers comm Janet Hollington, with thanks.
7. House of Commons debate for 13 November 1941, *Hansard*, vol. 376, c. 109.
8. House of Commons debate for 7 May 1940, *Hansard*, vol. 360, c. 1120.
9. House of Lords debate for 30 July 1940, *Hansard*, vol. 117, cc. 26–27.
10. *Sunday Dispatch*, 16 May 1943.
11. Graves 1943, p. 16.
12. Wintringham archive at LHCMA, quoted by Purcell with Smith 2004, p. 190.
13. TNA WO 199/3237.
14. Graves 1943, p. 15.
15. Draft Notes and Lessons, section 19: TNA HS 7/5.
16. Macleod and Kelly 1962, p. 368.
17. Wilkinson 2002, p. 103.

18. Danchev and Todman 2001, p. 173.
19. TNA CAB 67/7/27.
20. War Cabinet Minutes for 23 August 1940: TNA CAB 65/8/45.
21. George Orwell 1938, *Homage to Catalonia*, chapter 3.

Chapter 2

1. TNA HS 7/5, handwritten notes by Grand.
2. Report by Lawrence Grand, 10 June 1940: TNA HS 8/255. Grand had borrowed the term from Chamberlain who had used it to describe the importance of financing the war effort in 1939; the Merchant Navy also had good claim to the title.
3. Hugh Dalton, *The Fourth Arm*, 19 August 1940: TNA HS 8/258.
4. Brown 1988, p. 229.
5. TNA HS 7/5, handwritten notes by Grand.
6. Section D, Draft Notes and Lessons, p. 1 and p. 34: TNA HS 7/5.
7. Memo from an officer of SIS, 11 May 1942: TNA FO 1093/155.
8. Quoted in Foot 2004, from MIR files: TNA HS 8/256–61.
9. The time pencil was not brought back from Poland by Colonel Gubbins as is sometimes alleged; Section D: Early History to September 1940: TNA HS 7/3.
10. TNA HS 8/214.
11. Philby 2002, p. 9.
12. Warwicker 2008, p. 30.
13. Sweet-Escott 1965, p. 24.
14. Philby 2002, p. 15; in one of Section D's most successful missions, in May 1940 the 48-year-old Chidson was responsible for the smuggling of industrial diamonds out of Amsterdam – a mission that formed the basis of the film *Operation Amsterdam* (1959). He was later Head of D Section's German Section.
15. Andrew 2009, p. 129.
16. Jeffery 2010, pp. 226–35.
17. Jeffery 2010, p. 352.
18. Bennett 2009, p. 213.
19. TNA HS 7/4.
20. Turner 2011, p. 33. When SOE took over Aston House, Langley transferred to SIS Section XIII at Whaddon.
21. Section D: Early History to September 1940: TNA HS 7/3.
22. Pimlott 1986, p. 85.
23. Jebb to Cadogan, 13 June 1940: TNA FO 1093/193.
24. Jebb 1972, p. 103.
25. Section D: Early History to September 1940: TNA HS 7/3, p. 9.
26. TNA CAB 63/192, p. 71.
27. TNA CAB 63/192, ff. 83–4.
28. TNA CAB 63/192, f.87.
29. TNA FO 1093/137.
30. TNA CAB 63/192, f.92.
31. TNA HS 8/255.
32. TNA HS 8/255.
33. Section D, Draft Notes and Lessons, p. 2; TNA HS 7/5.
34. Mackenzie 2000, p. 37.
35. Meeting of 23 March 1939, quoted in Foot 2004, p. 5.
36. TNA HS 8/256.
37. TNA HS 8/256.
38. Section D, Draft Notes and Lessons: TNA HS 7/5.
39. Section D, Draft Notes and Lessons, p. 9: TNA HS 7/5.
40. Memo from an officer of SIS, 11 May 1942: TNA FO 1093/155.
41. Section D: Early History to September 1940, p. 4: TNA HS 7/3.

42. Jeffery 2010, p. 352.
43. Read and Fisher 1984, p. 12.
44. Jeffery 2010, pp. 352–3.
45. Philby 2002 (first published 1968). Philby joined SIS, Section D on 17 July only a few weeks before it officially transferred to SOE.
46. West and Tsarev 2009.
47. Liddell Diary, 4 December 1944: TNA KV 4/195, f. 307.
48. Read and Fisher 1984, pp. 271–2.
49. Read and Fisher 1984, p. 206.
50. Canaris was a complex character who, whilst head of the Abwehr, organised the escape of a number of German Jews, maintained contact with British intelligence and was implicated in the plot against Hitler. He was executed in Flossenbürg concentration camp on 9 April 1945.
51. Grand Diary mss: TNA HS 7/5.
52. In October 1940 the Independent Companies and Commandos were formed into a Special Service Brigade of five Special Service Battalions. Each battalion was subsequently reorganised into an HQ and two commandos and in 1941 the battalion structure was finally dropped so that the Special Service Brigade comprised eleven Commandos.
53. TNA HS 8/256.
54. Notes on MIR history: TNA HS 8/263.
55. Section D, Draft Notes and Lessons, section 15: TNA HS 7/5.
56. *Scheme D*, 20 March 1939: TNA HS 8/256.
57. Astley 2007, p. 20.
58. TNA HS 7/4.
59. On their substantive ranks, Holland and Grand were promoted Major on 18/1/33 and 28/9/37 respectively. Holland was then promoted to Brevet Lieutenant Colonel on 1/1/38 whilst Grand was only appointed an Acting Lieutenant Colonel on 3/9/39.
60. Mackenzie 2000, p. 10.
61. TNA CAB 63/192, f.66.
62. TNA CAB 127/376; West and Tsarev 2009, p. 201.
63. Astley 2007, pp. 20–1.
64. Functions and Organisation of MIR, 20 December 1939: TNA HS 8/256.
65. MIR Technical Reports: TNA HS 8/262.

Chapter 3

1. Winston S. Churchill, speech to the House of Commons, 4 June 1940: Hansard, vol, 361 cc. 787–98.
2. Chiefs of Staff report to War Cabinet, *Urgent measures to meet attack*, 19 June 1940: TNA CAB 66/8/43.
3. Chiefs of Staff report to War Cabinet, *British strategy in a certain eventuality*, 25 May 1940: TNA CAB 66/7.
4. Chiefs of Staff report to War Cabinet, *Urgent measures to meet attack*, 19 June 1940: TNA CAB 66/8/43.
5. Wilkinson and Astley 1993, p. 69.
6. *Seaborne and airborne attack on the United Kingdom*, War Cabinet Chiefs of Staff Committee, 10 May 1940: TNA CAB 63/167.
7. Liddell Diary for 5 September 1939: TNA KV 4/185, f. 27.
8. Fifth Column Activities in the United Kingdom, War Cabinet, Chiefs of Staff Committee, 2 May 1940: TNA CAB 63/167.
9. TNA CAB 63/167, f. 93.
10. TNA CAB 63/167, f. 96.
11. Ismay 1960, p. 305.
12. Royle 2010, pp. 165–7.
13. Tom Wintringham, 'Against invasion: the lessons of Spain', *Picture Post*, 15 June 1940, p. 10.
14. Purcell with Smith 2012, p. 189.

15. TNA HS 8/259.
16. Letter of Lord Hankey to Stephen King-Hall, 9 July 1940: TNA CAB 63/92, f. 101.
17. *Intelligence Report No. 3*: TNA CAB 63/167, f. 129 .
18. Vice-Chiefs of Staff Committee, 26 June 1940: TNA CAB 63/167, f. 159.
19. Later head of SOE Station IX at Welwyn, responsible for the development of the Welman submarine and Welbike folding bicycle.
20. *Organisation of civil resistance in Belgium, France, UK and Ireland*, 23 May 1940. Document from unknown source provided by FCO SOE Adviser 1997, with thanks to Stephen Sutton for making it available to this author. Version as *Organisation of Civil Resistance in Belgium and France* at TNA CAB 21/1476.
21. *Mobilisation of National Resources, moral, physical and material, to deny to the enemy the advantages obtained by his methods of invasion*, ISPB, 27 May 1940: TNA CAB 63/167, f. 71; TNA CAB 21/1476.
22. *Mobilisation of National Resources, moral, physical and material, to deny to the enemy the advantages obtained by his methods of invasion*, ISPB, 27 May 1940: TNA CAB 63/167; TNA CAB 21/1476.
23. Minutes of ISPB meeting, 27 May 1940. Document from unknown source provided by FCO SOE Adviser 1997, with thanks to Stephen Sutton for making it available to this author; TNA CAB 21/1476.
24. *Mobilisation of National Resources, moral, physical and material, to deny to the enemy the advantages obtained by his methods of invasion*, ISPB, 27 May 1940: TNA CAB 63/167, f. 72.
25. Memo of Major General Rawson, 14 July 1941: TNA WO 208/4697.
26. Minutes of ISPB Meeting, 27 May 1940: TNA HS 8/193
27. TNA CAB 63/167.
28. TNA CAB 63/167.

Chapter 4

1. Section D Closing Report: Great Britain's only successful experiment in total warfare, 27 August 1940, p. 8: TNA HS 8/214. According to Mackenzie, the final document contained adverse comments from CSS. These are not present in the version deposited with TNA.
2. TNA HS 7/4; Gerald Holdsworth later ran the 'Helston Flotilla' for SOE, running agents in and out of Brittany, and had a distinguished career with them.
3. D/XE, *Pessimism*, 22 May 1940. Document provided by FCO SOE Adviser 1997, with thanks to Stephen Sutton for making it available to this author.
4. Minutes of ISPB Meeting, 27 May 1940: TNA HS 8/193.
5. *D Organisation for Home Defence*, 1 June 1940. Document provided by FCO SOE Adviser 1997, with thanks to Stephen Sutton for making it available to this author.
6. *Notes on Regional D Scheme*, 2 June 1940 and *Preliminary Notes on the Regional D Scheme*, 4 June 1940: TNA HS 8/255.
7. Jeffery 2010, pp. 352–3.
8. Mackenzie 2000, p. 52, quoting SOE Archives File 1/470/7.1.
9. Wilkinson and Astley 1993, p. 72.
10. Section D, Draft Notes and Lessons, section 19: TNA HS 7/5.
11. Note on First Meeting of the Secret Service Committee, 3 June 1940: TNA FO 1093/193.
12. Section D, Early History to September 1940, p. 14: TNA HS 7/3.
13. Section D, Draft Notes and Lessons, section 19: TNA HS 7/5.
14. TNA HS 8/214.
15. *D Organisation for Home Defence*, 1 June 1940. Document provided by FCO SOE Adviser 1997, with thanks to Stephen Sutton for making it available to this author.
16. TNA CAB 63/89, f. 43.
17. Section D Closing Report: Great Britain's only successful experiment in total warfare, 27 August 1940, p. 8: TNA HS 8/214. According to Mackenzie, the final document contained adverse comments from CSS. These are not present in the version deposited with TNA.
18. Oxenden 2012 (typescript 1944), p. 2.
19. TNA HS 8/255.

20. Section D Closing Report: Great Britain's only successful experiment in total warfare, 27 August 1940: TNA HS 8/214.
21. Warwicker 2008, p. 178.
22. Williamson 2004, p. 13.
23. Lampe 1968, p. 105.
24. Sweet-Escott 1965, p. 38.
25. Wilkinson 2002, p. 100.
26. Pidgeon 2003, p. 125; TNA WO 208/4697.
27. Section D: Early History to September 1940, p. 8: TNA HS 7/3.
28. *Preliminary Notes on the Regional D Scheme*, 4 June 1940: TNA HS 8/255.
29. Section D had used Bearsted as a facilitator for a number of their operations. He had been part of Section D's operations in Scandinavia, supplying their agent there, Gerald Holdsworth, with information on contacts in Shell, and also instructing Shell to provide any funds that Holdsworth might need. He took part in Section D's convoluted plans to distribute black propaganda into Germany. Bearsted obtained the loan of the addressograph facilities at Shell, together with two trained operators. He also persuaded Shell to purchase three American stencil cutting machines. After Section D had compiled a mailing list, this equipment was used in London to send propaganda material into Germany, but apparently emanating from the USA. Eventually this scheme had to be dropped as the risk that the Americans would discover the ruse was considered too great during their election year.
30. Section D, Early History to September 1940: TNA HS 7/3.
31. Preliminary Notes on the Regional D Scheme, 4 June 1940: TNA HS 8/255.
32. Section D Closing Report: Great Britain's only successful experiment in total warfare, 27 August 1940, p. 8: TNA HS 8/214.
33. TNA HS 8/255.
34. Letter of A. Gordon MacLeod to the Prime Minister, 3 July 1940: TNA CAB 120/241.
35. Letter of General Paget to Captain Sandys, 30 July 1940: TNA CAB 120/241.
36. TNA HS 8/258.
37. TNA CAB 63/192, f. 108.
38. Wilkinson and Astley 1993, p. 35.
39. Mss letter of Gladwyn Jebb to Lord Cadogan, 13 June 1940: TNA FO 1093/193.
40. Meeting of 1 July 1940 to discuss the direction of sabotage: TNA FO 1093/193; MIR, *An aide-memoire on the co-ordination of subversive activities in the conquered territories*, 6 July 1940: TNA HS 8/259.
41. TNA HS 8/258; MIR, *An aide-memoire on the co-ordination of subversive activities in the conquered territories*, 6 July 1940: TNA HS 8/259.
42. Report VIII on the activities of D Section during July 1940, p. 1: TNA HS 8/214.
43. MIR War Diary for 22 July 1940: TNA HS 8/263.
44. Mackenzie 2000, p. 52, quoting SOE Archives File 1/470/7.1.
45. Lampe 1968, p. 68.
46. Oxenden 2012 (typescript 1944), p. 2.
47. Report VIII on the activities of D Section during July 1940, p. 23: TNA HS 8/214.
48. Turner 2011, p. 96.
49. Turner 2011, pp. 22–3.
50. Turner 2011, pp. 94–5; TNA HS 7/27; Turner 2011, pp. 200–1.
51. Section D, Draft Notes and Lessons, section 19: TNA HS 7/5.
52. Section D, Draft Notes and Lessons, section 19: TNA HS 7/5.
53. Annex II, minutes of a meeting between C and D, 15 September 1940 in memo of H.M. Gladwyn Jebb (CEO of SOE), 5 October 1940: TNA FO 1093/155. This meeting between C and Jebb (the new D) has often been mistakenly interpreted to suggest that the meeting was between C and Grand and was one of the reasons for the final dismissal of Grand: TNA HS 3/174, quoted in Bennett 2009, p. 262).
54. Seaman 2006, pp. 18–19; Dalton to Grand 18 September 1940 (Dalton papers LSE/DALTON/7/3, quoted in Bennett 2009, p. 262).

55. Philby 2002, p. 20.
56. Captain T. Davies, *Need for organisation of civil resistance*, 18 June 1940: TNA CAB 21/1476.
57. Letter of Hollis to Ismay, 20 June 1940: TNA CAB 21/1476.
58. Letter of Cavendish-Bentinck to Ismay, 21 June 1940: TNA CAB 21/1476.
59. Letter of H to Hollis, 22 June 1940: TNA CAB 21/1476.
60. Letter of Ismay to Pownall, 23 June 1940: TNA CAB 21/1476.
61. Letter of Pownall to Ismay, 25 June 1940; letter of Findlater-Stewart to Ismay, 26 June 1940: TNA CAB 21/1476.
62. Memo of Hollis to Ismay, 27 June 1940: TNA CAB 21/1476.

Chapter 5
1. MIR War Diary: TNA HS 8/263.
2. Wintringham, *Deadlock War*, 1940, p. 279.
3. Lindsay 1987, p. 109.
4. MIR War Diary: TNA HS 8/263.
5. Lovat Scouts War Diary for 19 June 1940: TNA WO 176/337.
6. XII Corps War Diary: TNA WO 166/344.
7. Lovat Scouts War Diary for 11 November 1940: TNA WO 176/337.
8. Warwicker 2008, pp. 68–9.
9. Arnold 1962, p. 53.
10. Pidgeon 2003, p. 189.
11. Calvert 1996, p. 47.
12. Calvert 1996, pp. 48–9.
13. Memories quoted on www.kentauxiliaryunits.org.uk.
14. Hart-Davis 1987, p. 234.
15. Fleming 1952, p. 13.
16. Hart-Davis 1987, pp. 236–7.
17. Lindsay 1987, p. 142.
18. Fleming 1952, p. 13.

Chapter 6
1. Section D, Early History to September 1940, pp. 17–18: TNA HS 7/3.
2. Interview of Peter Wilkinson by Mark Seaman, 1993: IWM Audio Interview, Cat. No. 13289 reel 5.
3. Minutes of War Cabinet, 17 June 1940: TNA CAB 65/7/65.
4. TNA CAB 79/5/79.
5. TNA HS 8/256.
6. Quoted in Wilkinson and Astley 1993, p. 69.
7. Liddell Diary, 3 May 1941: TNA KV 4/197.
8. Astley 2007, p. 31.
9. Gubbins, circular letter to LDV Commanders, 5 July 1940: TNA CAB 21/120.
10. TNA WO 260/9.
11. Lowry and Wilks 2002, p. 75.
12. Report of Colonel Gubbins, 26 July 1940: TNA WO 199/738.
13. TNA CAB 120/241.
14. Interview by Mick Wilks, 26 May 2000.
15. Report in Croft Papers, courtesy of Julia Korner (daughter) and with thanks to Will Ward.
16. TNA CAB 120/241.
17. TNA CAB 120/241.
18. Letter of Gubbins to Colonel Hall, GSO1 HQ Southern Command, 20 September 1940: TNA WO 199/2151.
19. TNA CAB 120/241.
20. 'Directive to Intelligence Officers as to policy for organisation of their areas', 17 June 1940: TNA CAB 120/241.

21. TNA HS 7/4.
22. Interview with Geoffrey Morgan-Jones, 26 May 1999, by Bernard Lowry; Lowry and Wilks 2002, pp. 53–4.
23. Lampe 1968, pp. 88–9.
24. Lowry and Wilks 2002, p. 84.
25. Gubbins 1939b, *Art of Guerrilla Warfare*, paragraphs 47 and 62; Gubbins 1939a, *Partisan Leader's Handbook*, paragraph 11.
26. 'Progress report of Auxiliary Units', Duncan Sandys for General Ismay to Churchill, 8 August 1940: TNA CAB 120/241.
27. Precis of the lecture on Intercommunication, Messages and Orders, 25 October 1941: BRO Museum Archive.
28. Interview of Peter Wilkinson by Mark Seaman, 1993: IWM Audio Interview, Cat. No. 13289 reel 5.
29. *Gubbins Private Papers*, quoted in Wilkinson and Astley 1993, p. 74.
30. Pryce-Jones 1975, p. 184.
31. Wilkinson 2002, p. 104.
32. S. Sutton, 'Farmers or Fighters. Dissertation on the existence and function of Britain's 'secret army'. Auxiliary Units in southern England during 1940–44'. Unpublished BA dissertation 1995, Canterbury Christchurch College.
33. Duncan Sandys to Churchill, 8 August 1940: TNA CAB 120/121.
34. Letter of General Paget to Captain Sandys, 30 July 1940: TNA CAB 120/241.
35. *German Occupied Great Britain: Ordinances of the Military Authorities*, 1941.
36. Stuart Edmundson, quoted in Warwicker 2004, p. 93.
37. Progress of Auxiliary Units to 1 September 1940, p. 4: TNA CAB 120/241.
38. Lowry and Wilks 2002, p. 79.
39. Instructions to Intelligence Officers, 27 July 1940: TNA CAB 120/241.
40. Letter of 9 April 1941 from War Office to TAAs: TNA WO 199/3251.

Chapter 7
1. TNA WO 199/1517; TNA WO 166/8110.
2. Mark Seaman interview with Wilkinson in 1993: IWM Interview Cat. No. 13289, reel 5.
3. Letter of Brigadier Richie, HQ Southern Command to Major General Gammell, 3rd Division, 1 August 1940: TNA WO 199/2151.
4. Record of a meeting between Colonel Hall, HQ Southern Command, and Major Beyts, Auxiliary Units, 9 August 1940: TNA WO 199/2151.
5. Thanks to Richard Thorpe for passing on this information.
6. Auxiliary Units, Progress report for period ending 1 September 1940: TNA CAB 120/241.
7. Letter from War Office to Eric Seal, Principal Private Secretary to Winston Churchill, 1 November 1940: TNA PREM 3/223/5.
8. *Target for Tonight* lecture notes 1941: BRO Museum Archive.
9. TNA WO 215/2; Warner 2005, p. 137.
10. *Target for Tonight* lecture notes 1941: BRO Museum Archive.
11. Auxiliary Units, *Calendar 1937*, 1940, p. 12.
12. Auxiliary Units, *Calendar 1938*, 1941, pp. 14 and 47.
13. *Calendar 1937* – Amendments, 4 April 1941; *Calendar 1938* – Amendments, 31 January 1944: BRO Museum Archive.
14. Lowry and Wilks 2002, p. 85.
15. Lowry and Wilks 2002, p. 55.
16. Calvert 1996, pp. 48–9.
17. Liddell Diary for 9 June 1940: TNA KV 4/186, f. 494.
18. Liddell Diary for 20 June 1940: TNA KV 4/186, f. 505.
19. Liddell Diary for 24 June 1940: TNA KV 4/186, f.510.
20. Warwicker 2002, pp. 97 and 100.
21. Mick Wilks, Home Guard interview archive.

22. Lowry and Wilks 2002, p. 65.
23. *Scheme D*, 20 March 1939: TNA HS8/256.
24. Calvert in a post-war radio broadcast, recounted in Warwicker 2008, p. 68.
25. War Cabinet, 30 May 1940: 'The Prime Minister thought that we should not hesitate to contaminate our beaches with gas if this course would be to our advantage. We had the right to do what we liked with our own territory.': TNA CAB 65/7/43.
26. Précis of lecture of Intercommunication, Messages, Orders, 25 October 1941, BRO Museum Archive.
27. Progress report on Auxiliary Units to 1 September 1940, p. 2: TNA CAB 120/241.
28. Mark Seaman interview with Wilkinson in 1993: IWM Interview Cat. No. 13289, reel 6.
29. Oxenden 2012 (typescript 1944), p. 7.
30. Ismay 1960, p. 131.
31. Hart-Davis 1987, p. 237.
32. S. Sutton, 'Farmers or Fighters. Dissertation on the existence and function of Britain's 'secret army'. Auxiliary Units in southern England during 1940–44'. Unpublished BA dissertation 1995, Canterbury Christchurch College.
33. Mark Seaman interview with Wilkinson in 1993: IWM Interview Cat. No. 13289, reel 5.
34. S. Sutton, 'Farmers or Fighters. Dissertation on the existence and function of Britain's 'secret army'. Auxiliary Units in southern England during 1940–44'. Unpublished BA dissertation 1995, Canterbury Christchurch College.
35. *Gubbins Private Papers*, quoted in Wilkinson and Astley 1993, p. 74.

Chapter 8
1. Lindsay 1987, pp. 141–2.
2. Hamilton-Hill 1975, p. 17.
3. Report of Colonel Gubbins, 26 July 1940: TNA WO 199/738.
4. *Auxiliary Units, Home Forces*, p. 5, attached to letter of 30 July by General Paget: TNA CAB 120/241.
5. Oxenden 2012 (typescript 1944), p. 7.
6. War Establishment report of 26 July 1940, quoted in Warwicker 2004, pp. 67–8.
7. Angell 1996, p. 15.
8. Oxenden 2012 (typescript 1944), p. 7.
9. Grigson-Ellis to Glanusk, 10 September 1942: TNA WO 199/738.
10. Cyril Ralph 'Bill' Major had served in the ranks for nearly three years in Mesopotamia during the First World War before being commissioned into the Dorset Regiment in 1918. Most of his subsequent career was as a staff officer at the War Office, apart from ten months spent with the Shanghai Defence Force in 1927.
11. Oxenden 2012 (typescript 1944), p. 2.
12. The British branch of the Van Moppes family was involved with SIS in acquiring industrial diamonds from South America and from Europe via their office in Switzerland. The family were not, however, involved in Major Chidson's famous removal of diamonds from Amsterdam that was immortalized in the film *Operation Amsterdam*.
13. Quoted in S. Sutton, 'Farmers or Fighters. Dissertation on the existence and function of Britain's secret army. Auxiliary Units in southern England during 1940–44'. Unpublished BA dissertation 1995, Canterbury Christchurch College.
14. Danchev and Todman 2001, p. 166.
15. Joint Intelligence Sub-committee, *German Invasion of the British Isles*, 31 January 1941: TNA CAB 121/209.
16. Danchev and Todman 2001, p. 220.
17. Letter of 4 April 1942, referring to agreement of 13 August 1941: TNA WO 199/738.
18. TNA WO 260/9; TNA WO 199/1194.
19. Letter of Forbes to Warwicker, January 2002: BRO Museum Archive.
20. Quayle 1990, p. 230.
21. TNA WO 199/3251.

22. Oxenden 2012 (typescript 1944), p. 13.
23. Colonel Douglas, 'Economy in Manpower', June 1944: TNA WO 199/738.
24. Warwicker 2004, pp. 107–8.
25. Letter of 22 May 1942: TNA WO 199/738.
26. TNA WO 199/738.
27. Oxenden 2012 (typescript 1944), pp. 14–15.
28. TNA KV 4/194, f. 16.
29. Extract from circular memo to Home Guard Battalion Commanders, 10 June 1944: TNA WO 199/ 2892.
30. TNA WO 200/738.
31. Colonel Douglas, 'Economy in Manpower' June 1944: TNA WO 199/738.
32. Memo of 14 January 1943: TNA WO 199/738.
33. War Office, January 1943, quoted in Warwicker 2004, p. 43.
34. TNA WO 199/3251.
35. Memo of Director of Staff Duties, 16 August 1943: TNA WO 199/738.
36. Letter of Colonel Douglas to General Franklyn, 15 July 1944: TNA WO 199/738.
37. Letter of General Franklyn to Under-Secretary of State, War Office, 16 August 1943: TNA WO 199/738.
38. Oxenden 2012 (typescript 1944), pp. 17–18.
39. TNA WO 199/936.
40. TNA WO 199/936.
41. TNA WO 199/936.
42. TNA WO 199/936.
43. War Office to Major General Callander, GHQ Home Forces, 25 April 1944: TNA WO 199/738.
44. Memo of War Office to Colonel Douglas, 17 May 1944: TNA WO 199/738.
45. TNA WO 199/738.
46. TNA WO 199/738.
47. TNA W0 199/937.
48. Auxiliary Units War Diary: TNA WO 166/16349.

Chapter 9
1. TNA WO 199 / 1194 for June 1944.
2. Hinsley *et al.* 1979, pp. 167–75.
3. TNA WO 260/9.
4. Sandys/Ismay progress report to Churchill, 8 August 1940: TNA CAB 120/241.
5. TNA CAB 120/241.
6. Letter of Major Petherick to Lawrence Grand, 15 July 1940, quoted in Warwicker 2008, p. 190.
7. Wilkinson 2002, p. 100.
8. Report VIII on the activities of D Section during July 1940, p. 4: TNA HS 8/214.
9. Section D: Early History to September 1940, pp. 17–18: TNA HS 7/3.
10. Lampe 1968, p. 127.
11. Application for the award of Defence Medal to the Auxiliary Units, 1948: WO 32/21918
12. Letter of War Office to Sir Robert Knox, 23 October 1947: WO 32/21918
13. Oxenden 2012 (typescript 1944), p. 2.
14. Section D, Draft Notes and Lessons: TNA HS 8/5.
15. TNA WO 260/9; thanks to Will Ward for information on the early IOs.
16. Diary of fellow Phantom officer, Lieutenant Christopher Cadogan, quoted in Warner 2005, pp. 144–5. Cadogan joined SOE but was killed in 1941.
17. BBC interview in 1998, quoted in Simak and Pye 2014, pp. 7–8.
18. Correspondence of George Vater with Mick Wilks in 2000.
19. Letter of Hopkinson to DDMO, 7 June 1940; Jackson, J., *Short History of Phantom from June 1940 to March 1941*: TNA WO 215/10.
20. TNA WO 215/9.
21. 'The collection and transmission of information in battle', 24 October 1940: TNA 215/10.

22. Warwicker 2004, p. 182.
23. Lampe 1968, p. 122; Gubbins was released from the Auxiliary Units on 18 November: Mackenzie 2000, p. 810.
24. Beyts 1983, p. 21.
25. Wood 1976, pp. 67–71.
26. Wilfrid Lewis (1908–87) was a Cambridge academic who in 1933 was also CO of the University OTC Signals. From 1939–1946 he was Senior Military Scientist at the Telecommunications Research Establishment (TRE), Malvern. He later became head of Canada's nuclear power programme. C.J. 'Kit' Milner (1912–98) worked with Lewis whilst a PhD student of Lord Rutherford. He gained his PhD in 1936 and worked on radar-jamming devices in the UK and then the Manhattan Project in the USA during the Second World War. After the war he became Chair of Applied Physics and later Dean of Science at the University of New South Wales. The work was published as Lewis and Milner 1936.
27. Video interview with Ken Ward by John Warwicker *et al.* in 1999: IWM recording Cat. 29472, reel 1.
28. Section D, Draft Notes and Lessons, 1945, paragraph 6: TNA HS 7/5; Closing Report, August 1940, paragaph 5: TNA HS 8/214.
29. Turner 2011, p. 136; Boyce and Everett 2003, p. 206.
30. Warwicker 2008, p. 213.
31. TNA WO 199/1194.
32. Video interview with Ken Ward by John Warwicker *et al.* in 1999: IWM recording 29472, reel 1.
33. Ken Ward (1915–2011) enlisted with the Royal Signals aged 18. With the aid of an army scholarship, he entered Pembroke College, Cambridge, in 1933 to study Mechanical Sciences with telecommunications as an additional subject, and graduated in 1936 aged 21. As an RCS entrant, he was attached to the Signals Research Section of the Cambridge University Officers' Training Corps under Professor Milner and assisted on the duplex transceiver receiver project. He then embarked on a two-year apprenticeship with English Electric and was also commissioned into the Royal Signals Reserve. After service as an operator training instructor to the Y Service, in January 1941 he joined the Auxiliary Units (Signals) as a lieutenant and was promoted to temporary captain in June 1941. Following posting to SOE in early 1942 he reverted to his substantive rank of lieutenant on '*special employment*'. In SOE, Ward was a procurement and contracts officer, working with John Brown who invented many of their wireless sets. He does not, however, appear to have been employed as a technical officer working directly in their development.
34. Video interview with Ken Ward by John Warwicker *et al.* in 1999: IWM recording 29472, reel 1.
35. TNA WO 199/1199.
36. Letter of Jack Millie to Arthur Gabbitas, 9 January 1996: BRO Museum Archive.
37. Map by Major Jones: TNA WO 199/1194.
38. Notes by Ken Ward: BRO Museum Archive.
39. TNA WO 199/1194.
40. Monthly Notes to IOs, No. 5, July 1943: BRO Museum Archive.
41. Report of Major Jones, 28 June 1944: TNA WO 199/1194.
42. TNA WO 199/936.
43. Letter of Ken Ward to John Warwicker, 24 April 1999: BRO Museum Archive.
44. Video interview with Ken Ward by John Warwicker *et al.* in 1999: IWM recording 29472, reel 1.
45. Letter of Bill Bartholomew to Arthur Gabbitas, 28 June 1997: BRO Museum Archive.
46. Adventures of Roy Russell during World War II: BRO Museum Archive.
47. Lampe 1968, pp. 125–6.
48. Monthly Notes for IOs, August 1943: BRO Museum Archive.
49. Liddell Diary for 11 May 1944: TNA KV 4/194, f. 394; Colonel T.A. Robertson (TAR) was a key officer in the deception plans for D-Day, being head of MI5's Section B1(a) and in charge of running the Double Cross agents.
50. Liddell Diary for 24 April 1940 in West 2009, p. 78.
51. Liddell Diary for 2 June 1941: TNA KV 4/199 f. 926.
52. Liddell Diary for 11 June 1942: TNA KV 4/190 f. 642.

53. Liddell Diary for 18 June 1942: TNA KV 4/190, f. 648.

54. Liddell Diary for 29 September 1942: TNA KV 4/290, f. 811.

55. Monthly Notes for IOs, No. 6, August 1943: BRO Museum Archive.

56. At Matlock, Derbyshire, the site of a secret wireless station that was hidden in a house on Smedley Street has been signposted by the local Civic Association as a 'Ground Zero Station' of the Auxiliary Units. The wireless station operated from June 1940 and is more likely to have been part of an SIS operation.

57. Ironside Diary for 29 June 1940, p. 374.

58. Ironside Diary for 13 July 1940, p. 385.

59. TNA KV 4/188.

60. Colonel Douglas, *Economy in Manpower*, June 1944: TNA WO 199/738.

61. TNA WO 199/738.

62. TNA WO 199/738.

63. Memo of Lord Glanusk to War Office, 1 February 1943: TNA WO 199/738.

64. TNA WO 199/738.

65. Adventures of Roy Russell during World War II: BRO Museum Archive.

66. Video interview with Ken Ward by John Warwicker *et al.* in 1999: IWM recording 29472, reel 5.

67. Closing Report by Major Jones, 28 June 1944: TNA WO 199/1194.

68. Lampe 1968, p. 135.

69. Hinsley *et al.* 1979, p. 180.

70. Referred to in a letter of Beyts to GHQ, 4 April 1942: TNA WO 199/738, and War Establishment of 4 April 1942: TNA WO 199/738; Memo of Gregson-Ellis, 30 March 1942: TNA WO 199/738.

71. Diary of Beatrice Temple, 30 January 1944: BRO Museum Archive.

72. TNA WO 199/1194.

73. Video interview with Ken Ward by John Warwicker *et al.* in 1999: IWM recording 29472, reel 2. It is, however, odd that no IN Station operators have mentioned using a WS17.

74. Oxenden 2012 (typescript 1944), p. 10.

Chapter 10

1. Letter of C-in-C Home Forces, General H.E. Franklyn to SDS on Stand Down, 4 July 1944, quoted in Angell 1996, p. 83.

2. Edwina Burton interview by Mick Wilks, April 2000.

3. Monthly Notes for IOs, No. 6, August 1943: BRO Museum Archive.

4. Memo of War Office to Beyts, 3 June 1942: TNA WO 199/738.

5. Monthly Notes for IOs, No. 6, August 1943: BRO Museum Archive.

6. Monthly Notes for IOs, August 1943: BRO Museum Archive; Report by Major Jones, 28 June 1944: TNA WO 199/1194.

7. Unpublished Beatrice Temple Diary: BRO Museum Archive.

8. TNA WO 199/738.

9. Video interview with Ken Ward by John Warwicker *et al.* in 1999: IWM recording 29472, reel 2.

10. Video interview with Ken Ward by John Warwicker *et al.* in 1999: IWM recording 29472, reel 2.

11. TNA WO 199/936.

12. Adventures of Roy Russell during World War II: BRO Museum Archive.

13. TNA 199/1313.

14. Adventures of Roy Russell during World War II: BRO Museum Archive.

15. Imperial War Museum audio interview with Stanley Judson by John Warwicker: IWM 29468.

16. Quoted in Simak and Pye 2014, p. 131.

17. Simak and Pye 2014, p. 9.

18. Gregson-Ellis to Lord Glanusk, 10 September 1942: TNA WO 199/738.

19. Oxenden 2012 (typescript 1944), p. 18.

20. Van Der Bill 2013.

21. TNA WO 208/5568.

22. Letter of C-in-C Home Forces, General H.E. Franklyn to SDS on Stand Down, 4 July 1944, quoted in Angell 1996, p. 83.
23. Forbes to Warwicker, 31 January 2002: BRO Museum Archive.
24. Memo from Auxiliary Units HQ, 26 October 1943: BRO Museum Archive.
25. Ward 1997, pp. 21–2.

Chapter 11
1. Quoted in H.R. Trevor-Roper, *Hitler's Table Talk 1941–44: Secret Conversations*, 2013, p. 233.
2. Ismay 1960, p. 220.
3. Dilks 1971, p. 287.
4. *German Occupied Great Britain: Ordinances of the Military Authorities*, 1941.
5. Jeffery 2010, pp. 361–2.
6. Jeffery 2010, pp. 361–2; Davies 2004, p. 82.
7. MI5 Irish Section History: TNA KV 4/9; Jeffery 2010, p. 281.
8. Liddell Diary for 27 November 1939: TNA KV 4/185, f. 186–7.
9. McMahon 2011, p. 290.
10. O'Halpin 2010, p. 73.
11. In 1941 the plans for a British intelligence network in Eire went further with the suggestion by SOE to make preparations for setting up a sabotage network (Claribel II) if the Germans did invade the Irish Republic. SIS only agreed on the condition that sympathetic officers within G-2 would be involved. In the end the idea was dropped in favour of advising G-2. The SIS Irish network began was wound down in 1944 and was finally closed in 1945. For their part, the Irish set up a top secret intelligence network whereby G-2 and IRA elements cooperated as the 'Supplementary Intelligence Service' (ISIS) to carry out surveillance operations on British clandestine activity; it was also intended to form the core of a 'stay-behind' organisation in the event of German, or British, occupation. Unlike its British counterparts, members of ISIS were later formally recognised and were awarded the 'Emergency Medal' for their contribution to the Irish defence forces 1939–45; see O'Halpin 2010, pp. 74 and 131–4.
12. TNA ADM 223/464 f. 268.
13. Angell 1996, p. 8.
14. TNA WO 199/1194
15. Guy Liddell was head of MI5's B Division (counter-espionage); Liddell Diary for 8 March 1940: TNA KV 4/186, f. 368.
16. Jeffery 2010, pp. 361–2.
17. SCU War Establishment: TNA WO 208/4697.
18. See Geoffrey Pidgeon's *Secret Wireless War* (2003) for the most comprehensive published account of the SCU/SLU organisation.
19. TNA CAB 63/167, f. 85.
20. TNA CAB 63/167, f. 85; Memo of Director of Signals, 14 July 1941: TNA WO 208/4697.
21. Hankey to Menzies, 7 June 1940: TNA CAB 301/70.
22. *History of the Security Service 1908 – 1945, The Curry Report*: TNA KV 4/2; Jeffery 2010, p. 361.
23. Letter of Valentine Vivian to Guy Liddell, 2 July 1940: TNA KV 4/205.
24. Liddell Diary for 18 July 1940: TNA KV 4/186, f. 534.
25. Memo of the Lord President of the Council to the War Cabinet, 19 July 1940: TNA CAB 66/10/1. Swinton was the former Air Minister, appointed Chairman of the new Home Defence (Security) Executive on 28 May 1940: TNA CAB 66/8/2.
26. Director's Circular No. 150, 27 July 1940: TNA KV 4/205.
27. Vivian to Liddell, 2 July 1940: TNA KV 4/205.
28. Cowgill was the former head of Special Branch in India who joined SIS in 1939; Cowgill to Comyns Carr, 28 April 1941: TNA KV 4/205.
29. Letter of Guy Liddell to Valentine Vivian, 10 October 1940: TNA KV 4/205.
30. Liddell Diary for 21 October 1943: TNA KV 4/192, f. 309.
31. Report of Sir Robert Knox, Central Honours Committee: TNA WO 32/21918.
32. Pidgeon 2003, p. 90.

33. Jeffery 2010, p. 361.
34. Pidgeon 2003, p. 73.
35. Interviews with Peter Attwater in 2000 by Bernard Lowry, and in 2014 by the author.
36. Liddell Diary, 5 March 1942: TNA KV 4/189, f. 398.
37. TNA KV 2/3800.
38. As confirmed by Stewart Angell, with thanks.
39. Liddell Diary for 12 April 1943: TNA KV 4/191, ff. 217–18.
40. Lampe 1968, pp. 88–9.
41. Lowry and Wilks 2002, p. 113.
42. Turner 2011, Appendix A.
43. *Newsletter* no.3, 1999, British Resistance Organisation Museum, Parham, p. 2.

Chapter 12
 1. Wintringham 1941, p. 3.
 2. The name of the Local Defence Volunteers was changed to Home Guard on 22 July 1940.
 3. *Local Defence Volunteers: Notes of a meeting between the Commander-in-Chief, Home Forces, and leaders of the Local Defence Volunteers held on Wednesday 5 June 1940*, June 1940
 4. J. Piling, *Report on Osterley Park LDV Training School*, 5–6 August 1940, p. 3 and p. 15.
 5. Wilkinson 2002, p. 104.
 6. Entry for 7 April 1942, Diary of Beatrice Temple.
 7. TNA CAB 65/7/65.
 8. Duncan Sandys to Churchill, 8 August 1940: TNA CAB 120/241.
 9. Letter of 22 May 1941: TNA WO 199/3251.
10. Letter from Director General, Home Guard to county TAAs, 20 January 1941: TNA WO 199/3251.
11. TNA WO 199/2892.
12. Wilkinson 2002, p. 104.
13. *Target for Tonight* lecture notes 1941: BRO Museum Archive.
14. Part I Orders, 12th Worcestershire Battalion, Home Guard, 7 September 1943: Worcestershire Regiment Museum Archive.
15. Formerly held by the Army Medal Office, Droitwich; Worcestershire Regiment Museum Archive.
16. Warwicker 2008, p. 109.
17. TNA WO 199/3251.
18. TNA WO 199/3251.
19. Lowry and Wilks 2002, p. 82.
20. Worcestershire Home Guard Part I and II Orders, formerly held by the Army Medal Office, Droitwich, until its closure in 2005; Worcestershire Regiment Museum Archive.
21. TNA WO 199/3389.
22. TNA WO 199/3251.
23. Lowry and Wilks 2002, p. 83.
24. Simak and Pye 2014, p. 194.
25. Wilkinson 2002, p. 104.
26. Memo of the War Office to Colonel Douglas, 17 May 1944: TNA WO 199/738.
27. Wilks 2014, p. 40: correspondence between the Harold Goodwin Company Secretary and the Warley Battalion Home Guard, dated 14 September 1942: on Home Guard files formerly held by the Army Medal Office, Droitwich.
28. Wilks 2014, p. 40–1.
29. Wilks 2014, p. 86; War Office letter of 13 March 1941 to the Central Midland Area HQ, found in Part 1 Orders for the 17th Battalion, Warwickshire Home Guard.
30. *Official History of the VTC*, 1920; *VTC Regulations* 1916.
31. Wintringham 1940a, pp. 176–83.
32. Wintringham 1940b, p. 279.
33. John Langdon-Davies in *Sunday Pictorial*, 6 October 1940.

34. Wintringham had been CO of the British Battalion of the International Brigade and continued to be a leading exponent of the principle of the 'popular front' against fascism after this had been discarded by the Communist Party. He and former comrades from the Spanish Civil War such as Hugh Slater and Yank Levy defied both the Communist Party and the International Brigade Association to set up the Home Guard Training School in Hounslow on 10 July 1940. John Langdon-Davies was a left-wing journalist who had been a social worker in Civil War Spain.

35. Liddell Diary for 5 September 1939: TNA KV 4/185, f. 21.

36. Levy 1941, p. 74.

37. Levy 1941, p. 36.

38. Wintringham 1941, pp. 27–8.

39. J. Piling, *Report on Osterley Park LDV Training School*, 5–6 August, 1940, pp. 1 and 4: Wintringham Papers.

40. Minutes of Home Guard Inspectorate 2 July 1940: TNA WO 199/62.

41. Letters of Inspectorate of LDV to MI5, July 1940: TNA WO 165/92.

42. Hugh Slater MI5 file: KV 2/2325-6; Liddell Diary for 18 July 1940: TNA KV 4/186, f. 532.

43. Liddell Diary for 31 July 1940: TNA KV 4/186, f. 545.

44. Circular letter of Communist Party of Great Britain, 7 January 1941, and intercepted by MI5: TNA KV 2/2325.

45. Vernon had been a pre-war engineer at the Royal Aeronautical Establishment at Farnborough before the war and made no secret of the fact that he was at least a 'fellow traveller' of the Communist Party. He was dismissed in 1937 for failing to take proper care of classified information (which he had taken home). In 1945 he became a Labour MP but was then unmasked by MI5 as a long-time Soviet spy. He was never prosecuted.

46. Tom Wintringham, 'The truth about guerrilla war', *The Tribune*, 19 September 1941, pp. 8–9.

47. Peter Kemp served in the Spanish Civil War during 1936–38 on the side of the Nationalist rebels as an officer, first in the Carlist forces and then in the elite Spanish Legion. During this time he was involved in the execution of captured members of the International Brigade. After recovering from wounds received in Spain, Kemp was recruited to MIR by his university friend Peter Wilkinson and, in January 1940, was commissioned onto the General List as a second lieutenant. He served from May as Assistant to Lord Lovat, the Senior Fieldwork Instructor at the new Irregular Warfare Training Centre at Lochailort in Scotland. He later served with MIR in Norway and in June 1940 he was promoted to acting captain within the new Intelligence Corps. By December 1941 he was on 'special employment' with SOE, and served in Albania, Poland and the Far East.

48. TNA WO 199/363.

49. TNA WO 199/1869: GOC instructions to Corps Commanders – Operational Role of the Home Guard June 1942.

50. Southern Command order quoted in Hylton 2004, p. 52.

51. Letter of Bill xxxxx to Major General PGS Gregson-Ellis, 10th xxxxx: TNA WO 199/364. Although filed with papers of autumn 1942, the letter is most likely to have been written in early 1942 by Colonel Bill Major. He had formerly been a staff intelligence officer for Eastern Command.

52. Langdon-Davies 1941, pp. 179–82.

53. Purcell with Smith 2012, p. 181–2

54. Section D: Early History to September 1940: TNA HS 7/3.

55. In Paris, Sinclair-Loutit would have met not only Gubbins but also Maurice Petherick. When he returned to London to become Medical Officer for Civil Defence in Finsbury he became one of Wintringham's circle of friends but relations became strained after he began an affair with Hugh Slater's wife Janetta. In 1944 he was commissioned as a Lieutenant Colonel on the General List, posted to the Allied Military Mission for the Balkans, later becoming Director of the United Nations Relief and Rehabilitation Administration (UNRRA) in Belgrade.

56. Pers. comm. Richard Thorpe, with thanks.

57. Purcell with Smith 2012, p. 195; Mackenzie is not identified as a member of any of the Sussex patrols in Angell 1996, although the information is not complete.

58. The machinations of 1930s left-wing politics was complicated! Mackenzie had been a member of the the Trotskyite ILP which detested the Stalinist Communist Party for, in their view, betraying the socialist revolution in Spain. It was therefore possible to retain his ideas of a pure socialist revolution whilst spying for MI5. The ILP also opposed the British participation in the Second World War as furthering imperialist interests. Many members, however, like Mackenzie (and indeed members of the Communist Party) refused to draw a distinction between fighting the Nazis in Spain or in the Second World War and so were equally appalled by the Hitler-Stalin Pact.
59. Purcell with Smith 2012, p. 205.
60. David Stafford, *Churchill and the Secret Service*, 2000, p. 311.
61. Tom Wintringham, 'The truth about guerrilla war', *The Tribune*, 19 September 1941, pp. 8–9.
62. Tom Wintringham, 'Train the Home Guard for war, *Picture Post*, 17 May 1941, pp. 24–8.
63. MI5 file on Hugh Slater: KV 2/2325-6.
64. Even Alan Gilchrist, former commissar of the British Battalion of the International Brigade, who as Secretary of the International Brigade Association in 1940, argued against support for the Home Guard ended up as a captain in the Royal Artillery. Bill Alexander, another CO of the British Battalion, became a captain in the Reconnaissance Corps.

Conclusion
1. Schneider, H., von Ostrymiecz, A., *et al.* (eds), *Beiträge zur Geschichte und Praxis des Englischen Geheimdienstes*, 1940
2. Brigadier Shearer, Deputy Director of Military Intelligence: TNA HS 7/4.
3. Colonel Douglas 'Economy in Manpower', June 1944: TNA WO 199/738.
4. Royle 2010, p. 323.
5. Boyle 1959.

Appendix 2: Key Personalities
1. John Colville, *The Fringes of Power: Downing Street Diaries 1939–55* (1985), Hodder and Stoughton, p.156.

Bibliography

The National Archives (TNA)
ADM 223/464 Operation Tracer.
CAB 21/120 Auxiliary Units.
CAB 21/1476 ISPB Minutes.
CAB 63/167 Minutes of Chiefs of Staff meetings; ISPB Minutes.
CAB 63/89 Miscellaneous papers of War Cabinet.
CAB 63/192 Hankey report on SIS, March 1940 and correspondence.
CAB 63/193 Section D.
CAB 65/7 Minutes of War Cabinet.
CAB 65/8 Minutes of War Cabinet.
CAB 65/10 Minutes of War Cabinet.
CAB 66/7 Chiefs of Staff Report to War Cabinet.
CAB 66/8 Chiefs of Staff Report to War Cabinet.
CAB 66/10 Lord President of Council to War Cabinet.
CAB 67/7 War Cabinet Minutes.
CAB 79/5 Minutes of Chiefs of Staff Committee.
CAB 120/241 Auxiliary Units.
CAB 127/376 Hankey report into SIS.
FO 1093/137 Section D.
FO 1093/155 Memo from an officer of SIS.
FO 1093/193 Minutes of Secret Service Committee.
HS 3/174 Section D.
HS 7/3 Section D.
HS 7/4 Section D.
HS 7/5 Section D.
HS 7/27 Section D.
HS 8/193 Minutes of ISPB.
HS 8/214 Section D.
HS 8/255 Section D.
HS 8/256 Section D.
HS 8/258 MIR Functions and organisation.
HS 8/259 MIR Strategy.
HS 8/262 MIR Technical Reports.
HS 8/263 MIR War Diary; Notes on MIR.
KV 2/2325-6 MI5 file on Hugh Slater.
KV 2/3800 MI5 use of agent provocateurs.
KV 4/9 MI5 Irish Section History.
KV 4/182–290 MI5 Guy Liddell Diary.
KV 4/205 MI5 correspondence.
PREM 3/223/2 Auxiliary Units.
WO 32/21918 Report of Honours Committee.
WO 166/337 Lovat Scouts War Diary.
WO 166/344 XII Corps War Diary.
WO 166/8110 Auxiliary Units.

WO 199/62 Home Guard Inspectorate.
WO 199/16349 Auxiliary Units.
WO 199/337 Auxiliary Units.
WO 199/363 Home Guard Organisation.
WO 199/364 Auxiliary Units.
WO 199/738 Auxiliary Units.
WO 199/936 Auxiliary Units: Stores and Supplies.
WO 199/937 Auxiliary Units: Stores and Supplies.
WO 199/1869 Operational Role of Home Guard.
WO 199/1194 Auxiliary Units and SDB, including network map.
WO 199/1313 Auxiliary Units.
WO 199/1517 Auxiliary Units.
WO 199/1869 GOC Instructions to Home Guard.
WO 199/2151 Auxiliary Units.
WO 199/2892 Auxiliary Units.
WO 199/3237 Home Guard Diary.
WO 199/3251 Auxiliary Units.
WO 199/3389 Auxiliary Units.
WO 199/3892 Auxiliary Units.
WO 208/5568 Directorate of Military Intelligence War Diary.
WO 215/2 Auxiliary Units.
WO 260/9 Auxiliary Units 1940.

Published works
Andrew, Christopher (2009), *The Defence of the Realm: The Authorized History of MI5*, Allen Lane.
Angell, Stewart (1996), *The Secret Sussex Resistance*, Middleton Press, Midhurst.
Arnold, Ralph, (1962), *A Very Quiet War*, Rupert Hart-Davis, London.
Astley, Joan Bright (2007), *The Inner Circle: A View of War at the Top*, The Memoir Club, Stanhope (first publ. 1971).
Bennett, Gill (2009), *Churchill's Man of Mystery: Desmond Morton and the World of Intelligence*, Routledge.
Beyts, Geoffrey (1983), *The King's Salt*.
Boyce, Fredric and Douglas Everett (2003), *SOE: The Scientific Secrets*, Sutton Publishing, Stroud.
Boyle, David (1959), *With Ardours Manifold*, Hutchinson, London.
Brown, Anthony Cave (1988), *The Secret Servant: The Life of Sir Stewart Menzies, Churchill's Spymaster*, Michael Joseph, London.
Calvert, Mike (1996), *Fighting Mad: One man's guerrilla war*, Airlife, Shrewsbury (2nd edn; first publ. 1964).
Danchev, Alex and Daniel Todman (eds) (2001), *War Diaries 1939–1945: Field Marshall Lord Alanbrooke*, Weidenfeld and Nicolson, London.
Davies, Philip H.J. (2004), *MI6 and the Machinery of Spying*, Cass, Abingdon.
Dilks, David (1971), *The Diaries of Sir Alexander Cadogan, OM, 1938–45*, Cassell, London.
Fleming, Peter (1952), 'Bows and arrows', *The Spectator*, 4 April 1952, p. 13.
Fleming, Peter (1957), *Invasion 1940*, Rupert Hart-Davis, London.
Foot, M.R.D. (1984), *SOE: An Outline History of the Special Operations Executive 1940–46*, BBC.
Foot, M.R.D. (2004), *SOE in France*, Cass, Abingdon (revised edn; first publ. 1966).
Graves, Charles (1943), *The Home Guard of Britain*, Hutchinson, London.
Gubbins, Colin (1939a), *Partisan Leader's Handbook: Principles of Guerrilla Warfare and Sabotage* [War Office].
Gubbins, Colin (1939b), *The Art of Guerrilla Warfare* [War Office].
Hamilton-Hill, Donald (1975), *SOE Assignment*, New English Library, London (first publ. 1973).
Hart-Davis, Duff (1987), *Peter Fleming: A Biography (Oxford Lives)*, (first publ. 1974).
Hinsley, F.H. *et al.* (1979), *British Intelligence in the Second World War*, Vol. 1, HMSO, London.

Hinsley, F.H. and C.A.G. Simkins (1990), *British Intelligence in the Second World War, Vol. 4*, HMSO, London.

Hylton, Stuart (2004), *Kent and Sussex 1940: Britain's Front Line*, Pen & Sword Military, Barnsley.

Ismay, Lord (1960), *The Memoirs of General The Lord Ismay*, Heinemann, London.

Jebb, Gladwyn (1972), *The Memoirs of Lord Gladwyn*, Weidenfeld and Nicolson, London.

Jeffery, Keith (2010), *MI6: The History of the Secret Intelligence Service 1909–1949*, Bloomsbury, London.

Lampe, David (1968), *The Last Ditch*, Cassell, London.

Langdon-Davies, John (1941), *Home Guard Warfare*, Routledge, London.

Levy, 'Yank' (1941), *Guerrilla Warfare*, Penguin Books.

Lewer, Stanley (1996), 'On the back of an envelope ... how the Wireless Set No. 17 was born', *Radio Bygones*, no. 41, June/July 1996, pp. 4–8.

Lewis, Wilfrid B. and C.J. Milner (1936), 'A portable Duplex Radio-Telephone', *The Wireless Engineer*, September 1936, pp. 475–82.

Lindsay, Donald (1987), *Forgotten General: A Life of Andrew Thorne*, Michael Russell (Publishing), Salisbury.

Lowry, Bernard, and Mick Wilks (2002), *Mercian Maquis*, Logaston Press.

Mackenzie, William (2000), *The Secret History of SOE*, St Ermin's Press.

Macleod, Roderick and Denis Kelly (eds) (1962), *The Ironside Diaries 1937–40*, Constable, London.

McMahon, Paul (2011), *British Spies and Irish Rebels: British Intelligence and Ireland, 1916–1945*, Boydell Press, Woodbridge (first publ. 2008).

O'Halpin, Eunan (2010), *Spying on Ireland: British Intelligence and Irish Neutrality during the Second World War*, Oxford University Press (first publ. 2008).

Oxenden, Nigel (2012 reprint), *Auxiliary Units: History and Achievement 1940–1944* (typescript 1944; first publ. 1998), BRO Museum, Parham.

Philby, Kim (2002), *My Silent War*, Modern Library, New York (first publ. 1968).

Pimlott, Ben (ed) (1986), *The Second World War Diary of Hugh Dalton 1940–45*, Jonathan Cape, London.

Pidgeon, Geoffrey (2003), *Secret Wireless War*, UPSO, East Sussex.

Pryce-Jones, David (1975), 'Britain's Secret Resistance Movement', in Richard Cox (1975), *Operation Sealion*, Thornton Cox Ltd, pp. 177–86.

Purcell, Hugh, with Phyll Smith (2012), *The Last English Revolutionary: Tom Wintringham, 1898–1949*, Sussex Academic Press (enlarged, revised and updated; first publ. 2004).

Quayle, Anthony (1990), *A Time To Speak*, Barrie & Jenkins, London.

Read, Anthony and David Fisher (1984), *Colonel Z: The Life and Times of a Master of Spies*, Hodder and Stoughton, London.

Royle, Trevor (2010), *Orde Wingate: A Man of Genius, 1903–1944*, Frontline Books, London (first publ. 1995).

Schellenberg, Walter (2001), *Invasion 1940: The Nazi Invasion Plan for Britain*, St Ermin's Press, in association with Little, Brown and Company (first publ. 2000).

Seaman, Mark (ed) (2006), *Special Operations Executive: A New Instrument of War*, Routledge, London.

Simak, Evelyn and Adrian Pye (2013), *Churchill's Secret Auxiliary Units in Norfolk and Suffolk*, self-published.

Simak, Evelyn and Adrian Pye (2014), *Churchill's 'Most Secret' Special Duties Branch*, self-published.

Stafford, David (2010), 'Secret Operations versus Secret Intelligence in World War', in T. Travers and C. Archer (eds) *Men at War: Politics, Technology and Innovation in the Twentieth Century* (reprint; first publ. 1982), pp. 119–36.

Sweet-Escott, Bickham (1965), *Baker Street Irregular*, Methuen, London.

Turner, Des (2011), *SOE's Secret Weapons Centre: Station 12*, The History Press, Stroud (first publ. 2006).

Van der Bijl, Nick (2013), *Sharing the Secret: A History of the Intelligence Corps 1940–2010*, Pen & Sword Military, Barnsley.

Ward, Arthur (1997), *Resisting the Nazi Invader*, Constable, London.

Warner, Philip (2005), *Phantom*, Pen & Sword Military, Barnsley (first publ. 1982).

Warwicker, John (ed) (2004), *With Britain in Mortal Danger: Britain's Most Secret Army of WWII*, Cerberus, Bristol (first publ. 2002).

Warwicker, John (2008), *Churchill's Underground Army: A History of the Auxiliary Units in World War II*, Frontline Books, London.

West, Nigel (1983), *MI6: British Secret Intelligence Service Operations 1909–45*, Weidenfeld and Nicolson, London.

West, Nigel (1992), *Secret War: The Story of SOE, Britain's Wartime Sabotage Organisation*, Hodder and Stoughton, London.

West, Nigel (ed) (2009), *The Guy Liddell Diaries, Vol.I: 1939–1942*, Routledge (first publ. 2005).

West, Nigel and Oleg Tsarev (eds) (2009), *Triplex: Secrets from the Cambridge Spies*, Yale University Press.

Wilkinson, Peter (2002), *Foreign Fields*, I.B.Tauris Publishers, London (first publ. 1997).

Wilkinson, Peter and Joan Bright Astley (1993), *Gubbins and SOE*, Pen & Sword, London.

Wilks, Mick (2007), *The Defence of Worcestershire and the Southern Approaches to Birmingham in World War II*, Logaston Press.

Wilks, Mick (2014), *Chronicles of the Home Guard*, Logaston Press.

Williamson, Alan (2004), *East Ridings Secret Resistance*, Middleton Press, Midhurst.

Wintringham, Tom (1940a), *Deadlock War*, Faber and Faber, London.

Wintringham, Tom (1940b), *New Ways Of War*, Penguin.

Wintringham, Tom (1941), *The Home Guard Can Fight*.

Wood, Derek (1976), *Attack Warning Red: The Royal Observer Corps and the Defence of Britain 1925 to 1975*, Macdonald and Jane's, London.

Index